Fictional Minds

FRONTIERS OF NARRATIVE

Series Editor
David Herman,
North Carolina State University

Fictional Minds

Alan Palmer

University of
Nebraska Press
Lincoln and
London

Parts of this volume previously
appeared in "The Construction
of Fictional Minds," *Narrative*
10 (1):28–46.

Library of Congress Cataloging-in-
Publication Data
Palmer, Alan, 1950–
Fictional minds / Alan Palmer.
p. cm.—(Frontiers of narrative)
Includes bibliographical references
and index.
ISBN 0-8032-3743-x (cl.: alk. paper)
ISBN 978-0-8032-1835-2 (pa.: alk. paper)
1. Fiction—Technique.   2. Charac-
ters and characteristics in literature.
3. Intellect in literature.
I. Title.   II. Series.
PN3383.C4P35 2004
809.3'927–DC22
2003019700

Contents

Acknowledgments

I would like to thank the following: my mother; Brian and Sheila Barford; Kenneth Parker; Susannah Radstone; Linda Rozmovits; Molly Andrews and Corinne Squire of the Centre for Narrative Research at the University of East London; James Phelan; Lisa Zunshine; Couze Venn, for his thoughtful guidance and encouragement; Marie-Laure Ryan, for telling me about the theory-theory/simulation debate; Uri Margolin, for some stimulating and very helpful email discussions; Brian King for his rigorous and sensitive copyediting; and the editors of the University of Nebraska Press for their invaluable assistance.

There are three people to whom I owe a particularly large debt of gratitude. Robert Chase and David Herman have been extremely conscientious and amazingly enthusiastic and supportive mentors. Both have been unfailingly generous with their time, advice, assistance, and support. The pure, disinterested scholarship of Bob and David has been an inspiration. Finally, I would like to dedicate this book to my partner, Sue: *sine qua non*.

Fictional Minds

Introduction

"We never know them well, do we?"

"Who?"

"Real people."

"What do you mean, 'real people'?"

"As opposed to people in books," Paola explained. "They're the only ones we ever really know well, or know truly. . . . Maybe that's because they're the only ones about whom we get reliable information. . . . Narrators never lie." – Donna Leon, *A Sea of Troubles*

so, right away, seems like characters – people

1. Background

Fictional Minds is about "people in books." In particular, it is about the amount, range, variety, and reliability of the information on the fictional minds of people in books that we are able to obtain from those books.

A little personal history may be helpful here in order to explain the purpose of this book. I began studying fictional minds in 1995. I did this by looking at the Box Hill chapter in Jane Austen's *Emma* and the Waterloo ball chapter in William Makepeace Thackeray's *Vanity Fair* to see how the minds of the characters in those chapters were constructed. I chose those two texts because I thought that it would be interesting to examine the consciousnesses of characters interacting in groups. At that time, I am ashamed to say now, I was not even aware of the existence of narrative theory, or narratology, although as it happened this direct approach to primary texts turned out to be an absolutely inspired idea. Then once I had discovered that there was such a thing as narrative theory, I thought that it would be interesting to find out what it said about my chosen area of study. After all what could be more central to the theoretical analysis of fiction than the workings of characters' minds? My first encounter with narrative theory was with what I will call the *speech category approach*, and I was immediately struck by the fact that it did not provide a convincing explanation or even description of how the whole minds of characters in action were constructed. It seemed to me that there was a good deal that was going on in the Austen and Thackeray chapters that had not been captured by classification of the specific examples of direct access to fictional minds into the various speech categories. I felt as though I had stumbled into a large, fascinating field that I very much wanted to explore further. A small corner of it had been tended and retended with, perhaps, obsessive care, while the rest of it appeared to me at that time to be neglected.

I read more widely within narrative theory and soon discovered the concept of *focalization* or what used to be called *point of view*. So another small corner of the field had been cultivated. Focalization was informative, but it was still only a small part of the story. The third corner turned out to be *story analysis*—the structuralist study of the basic elements of plot structures. Next I came across *characterization* and, in particular, how the reader brings to the text preexisting cultural and literary stereotypes in order to construct satisfying patterns of behavior and convincing fictional personalities. Finally, and inexcusably late in the day, I encountered *possible-worlds theory*. This has proved very helpful indeed, although I soon found out that in certain ways it is not that well suited to the study of fictional minds. (You may have noticed that there are five corners—it is an irregularly shaped field.)

So, the corners of the field are well tended, but in the middle there remains a very large and apparently unexplored patch of land that still looks just as interesting to me today as it did at the beginning. But the oddest thing of all, as I continued my search within narrative theory for a comprehensive treatment of the whole of my area of interest, was that I found very little recognition of the fact that there *was* an area of interest at all. The various corners adjoin other fields and appear to be viewed primarily as adjuncts to those other fields: the analysis of spoken speech in the case of the speech categories; various aspects of discourse analysis in the case of focalization; intertextuality in the case of characterization; classical structuralism in the case of story analysis; and modal logic in the case of possible-worlds theory. This seemed strange to me then, and it still does now. In fact, it is this continued sense of strangeness that drives this book. Even now, I still think, Why don't other people ask themselves what aspect of literary theory could be more important than fictional minds? This study is an attempt to mark out the boundaries of the field as a well-defined subject area in its own right by linking together the previously well-trodden parts of it and by tending a few new patches of my own. I decided on the title *Fictional Minds*, instead of other possibilities such as *The Presentation of Consciousness in the Novel*, because it sounds to me as much the name of a new subject area within narrative theory as it does the title of a single study.

I will describe my exploration of the field with the use, I am afraid, of another and final agricultural metaphor. Somewhere (I have been unable to find the exact reference) the philosopher Ludwig Wittgenstein suggests that there are two ways of exploring a piece of land such as a hill. One way is to attempt to define it by establishing its boundaries with precision. In this way once you have drawn an exact line around the land in question, you can say with confidence that the hill consists of all the land within the border created by the line and whatever lies outside the boundary is something else. The other way to do it is to explore the hill by criss-crossing it from various directions. That way you get to know it intimately, and you have a fairly clear idea about what is the hill and what is not, even though you do not ever draw a precise line around it. Each method has its own kind of value, and of course they are not mutually exclusive. Perhaps he had in mind a comparison between the early working method of the *Tractatus Logico-Philosophicus* and the later, very different approach of the *Philosophical Investigations*. I would say that the modus operandi of *Fictional Minds* is the criss-crossing of the field, rather than the strict delineation of its exact borders, although I hope that it will become clear that the boundaries of the fictional mind in discourse extend much further than have previously been recognized.

During my studies, I discovered reader response theory, which proved to be of great value. I will pick out one specific issue here: the sheer scale of the input required from readers in constructing minds from novels. Have you ever, while rereading a novel containing a scene or a character that had a profound effect on you when you first read it, been surprised at how little there actually was to that scene or character and how few words were used to describe them? You think, Does that scene really last for only a page? Or, Does that character really only appear in only those scenes? (A particularly good example of this phenomenon is Orson Welles's Harry Lime character in the film *The Third Man*. Lime does not appear until after the best part of an hour and says almost nothing apart from the famous cuckoo-clock scene.) On rereading a scene of this sort, you find yourself surprised that your imagination, as it then was, contributed so much to flesh out the words in the text, and it can sometimes happen that your current imaginative state does not do the same. It is almost as though the text is simply the scaffolding on which you build the vivid psychological processes that stay with you for so long afterward. I recently felt this sort of disappointment while rereading Umberto Eco's novel *The Name of the Rose*, which is ironic since he is a leading reader response theorist! It can also happen with historical narrative, as it did for me with Emmanuel Le Roy Ladurie's *Montaillou*. I find that the same sensation can also occur when someone recommends that I read an episode in a novel or see a scene in a film. I think, I am not really sure that there is enough here for me to feel that it justified the build-up that it got. There is a good deal that has been brought to this scene by the other person, and I am not sure what it is. All this is an illustration of what the narratologist Monika Fludernik refers to in the vivid phrase the "human urge to create significance" (1993, 457). What I am describing is one of those rare occasions when you are acutely aware of the creative nature of the reading process in general and the strangeness of character construction in particular. Any theory that attempts to explain this process, or a part of it, has to recognize the intense power of reader response to fictional minds.

I decided at an early stage that it would be rewarding to illuminate the study of fictional minds by making use of the insights of some of the disciplines relating to real minds. For example, I noticed right at the beginning that during my analyses of the *Emma* and *Vanity Fair* passages I was finding it difficult in a number of cases to separate out presentations of consciousness from descriptions of action, and I was aware that an illuminating perspective on this issue could be derived from the philosophy of action. (By the way, this point is a perfect illustration of the benefits of theorizing about novels before reading literary theory: the theory that I read later appeared to assume that dividing the two was entirely unproblematical, while the naïve reader that I then was could spot immediately that this was not the case.) In addition to philosophy such as the philosophy of mind as well as the philosophy of action, this book also makes use of other real-mind disciplines such as cognitive science, psychology, and psycholinguistics. I hope that the result is a rich, flexible, sensitive, and inclusive paradigm of the fictional mind that is well suited to capturing as much information as possible from fictional texts. *Fictional Minds* is an interdisciplinary project that is in a sense designed to be a source book for non-specialists of some of the ideas about the mind that are current in the various real-mind discourses. However, it is worth pointing out right from the start that a good deal of humility is required when theorizing about the mind. The relationship between knowledge and its representation in the brain was characterized by the psychologist William James (brother of the novelist Henry James) in 1890 as "the most mysterious thing in the world" (1981, 216). And for every mystery that has been dispelled since James's time, three more seem to arise to take its place.

Handwritten annotations:

① thesis: narrative fiction = presentation of fictional mental functioning (I really like this idea!)

One particular aspect of my approach is worth emphasizing here. The entry by Colwyn Trevarthen in *The Massachusetts Institute of Technology Encyclopedia of the Cognitive Sciences* (1999) (from now on referred to as MITECS) on the topic of intersubjectivity describes two different perspectives on the mind: the *subjective first* and the *intersubjective first*.

> The Western philosophical tradition (as exemplified by René Descartes and Immanuel Kant) generally assumes that human minds are inherently separate in their purposes and experiences, seeking rational clarity, autonomous skills, and self-betterment. . . . [People] construct an awareness of the self in society but remain single subjectivities. . . . We will call this view of intelligent and civilized cooperation as an artificial acquisition the . . . "subjective first" position. . . .
>
> A different conception of human consciousness . . . perceives interpersonal awareness, cooperative action in society, and cultural learning as manifestations of innate motives for sympathy in purposes, interests, and feelings—that is, that a human mind is equipped with needs for dialogue [and] intermental engagement with other similar minds. . . . We will call this view of how human cooperation arises the . . . "intersubjective first" position. (1999, 417)

Handwritten margin note: subjective first vs. intersubjective first

Mine is very much an intersubjective first approach to fictional minds, but not because I deny the importance of the subjective first approach. It is important to stress that both perspectives are equally valid, informative, and, indeed, necessary. The reason why this study favors the intersubjective first approach is that the subjective first position has become the dominant paradigm for the study of consciousness within narrative theory, and the bias contained in this book is intended to redress the balance a little. For a contrasting and very subjective first approach to the relationship between the novel, narrative theory, and cognitive science, see *Consciousness and the Novel* (2002) by the narrative theorist and novelist David Lodge.

It is probably the case that anyone working in the field of narrative theory has a working definition of narrative that they may make explicit or that may remain implicit. To make things easier for you, I will now make mine explicit. My thesis is a fundamental one: narrative fiction is, in essence, the presentation of fictional mental functioning. I state my thesis here in this bald, stark manner for purposes of clarity. The full implications of it will emerge later on. If I am right, then it follows that the study of the novel is the study of fictional mental functioning and also that the task of theorists is to make explicit the various means by which this phenomenon is studied and analyzed. This is another way

Handwritten margin note: hmm... v. int. to follow this logic through

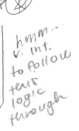

of making the point made earlier that the study of fictional minds should be established as a clearly defined and discrete subject area within literary theory.

I do not know how many narrative theorists will agree or disagree with my claim regarding the centrality of fictional minds to any informative definition of fictionality, although I refer to some potential skepticism in the next section. I hope that it will strike some as obviously true, even though I am aware that the world is full of people who have advanced theories that they thought were obviously true but then found to their astonishment that they were bitterly contested. But, true or not, and obvious or not, I am not aware that it has been explicitly formulated before, with the possible exception of Monika Fludernik's emphasis on her notion of *experientiality* in *Towards a "Natural" Narratology* (1996). My thesis has always been implicit in discussions of fictionality, and should be made explicit. As the narratologist Dorrit Cohn points out, in narratology, "as elsewhere, norms have a way of remaining uninteresting, often even invisible, until and unless we find that they have been broken—or want to show that they have not been broken" (1999, 43). The description of fictional mental functioning has been regarded as an uninteresting and even invisible norm within narratology, and it would be of benefit to the discipline if it were given the central place within the conceptual framework of the subject that it deserves.

Some scholars in other disciplines tend to regard literary theory as arid, willfully obscure, solipsistic, dreary, stultifying, and literature-hating. The list is discouragingly long. Whether or not this view is true of literary theory generally, as a picture specifically of narrative theory, it is completely misguided. It takes no account of the very large body of thorough, illuminating, and exciting work that is simply the result of systematic and rigorous analyses of narrative texts. However, all literary theorists, including narrative theorists, have a responsibility to reach out to the rest of the academic world by making literary theory as reader-friendly as possible. Literary theory should speak to, and be shared with, other scholars. Although this study is aimed primarily at specialists in literary theory in general and narrative theory in particular, it also tries to be genuinely helpful to scholars in other fields, for example, researchers into and teachers and students of English and other literatures. I believe that the interdisciplinary reconceptualization that is explored here will be of real value not only to research in fields that involve the practical criticism of fictional texts but also to the teaching of practical criticism. Such criticism depends on the ability to use the available evidence to pronounce with confidence on characters' thought processes. My work is concerned with examining precisely how this ability is

concern: social mind in action

made possible. The sort of questioning that I have in mind could occur not only in courses on literary theory but also within sessions of practical criticism. In this way, I suggest, theory and practice could genuinely interpenetrate and synergistically enrich one another. I am aware that this approach does not appear to fit easily within current literary-studies approaches, but is it such a bad thing for a discipline to question some of the foundations on which it is based? Surely literature studies would gain new insights from a perspective that is both radically innovative and also directly relevant to all other perspectives on the novel.

In 1981, when reviewing Dorrit Cohn's brilliant work on thought representation *Transparent Minds* (1978), the narratologist Brian McHale commented that the "history of our poetics of prose is essentially a history of successive differentiations of types of discourse from the undifferentiated 'block' of narrative prose." He then added that "there is still a sizeable block of undifferentiated prose left" (1981, 185). In my view, no one has yet responded to McHale's challenge, and a good deal more work is required before the "sizeable block of undifferentiated prose" that is related to characters' minds is reduced any further. As far as I know, Cohn's is still the only full-length study devoted solely to this topic. All the other full-length studies of which I am aware refer to speech as well as thought or are concerned with narratology generally. It is now a long time since Cohn wrote her pioneering work and since McHale wrote his wholly justified praise of it, and yet there has been no successor in the sense that there has been no other book wholly devoted to her subject. Given the obvious importance of this issue for any formal study of the novel, this seems extraordinary. The purpose of *Fictional Minds* is to begin the attempt to theorize a part of the block of prose that remains undifferentiated: the aspect of narrative fiction that is concerned with the whole of the social mind in action.

This enterprise is intended to fit comfortably within the perspective on narrative that is offered by the Frontiers of Narrative series. The editor of the series, the narrative theorist David Herman, in advocating an approach that he calls *postclassical narratology*, contends that we have recently witnessed "a small but unmistakable explosion of activity in the field of narrative studies; signs of this minor narratological renaissance include the publication of a spate of articles, special issues, and books that rethink and recontextualize classical models for narratological research" (1999a, 1). He also remarks that postclassical narratology is "marked by a profusion of new methodologies and research hypotheses; the result is a host of new perspectives on the forms and functions of narrative itself" (1999a, 2–3). The narratologist Gerald Prince agrees with Herman that "the very domain of narratology is (and has been) in flux" and "the discipline keeps on changing as its boundaries are (re)drawn" (1996, 160). Herman also makes the heady claim that recent work in narrative theory has "displaced and transformed the assumptions, methods, and goals of structuralist narratology" (1999a, 2) and that this research has "highlighted aspects of narrative discourse that classical narratology either failed or chose not to explore" (1999a, 2). This is precisely what *Fictional Minds* attempts to do. It does so by using concepts and ideas drawn from a variety of different disciplines because, as Herman says, postclassical narratology is an "inherently interdisciplinary project" (1999a, 20).

My argument lays great stress on the need to examine how fictional minds work within the contexts of the storyworlds to which they belong. Postclassical narratology's attempt to break free from the structuralist purity of classical narratology is also concerned with the question of context. For example, Gerald Prince, in considering the role of gender in narratology, maintains that narrative poetics "ought to be more sensitive to the role of context . . . in the production of narrative meaning" (1996, 163). Prince has in mind the various real-world, sociocultural contexts in which narratives are produced. However, I will use the notion of context in a more narrow sense to focus on both the context of the whole fictional mind during the analysis of a particular part of that mind and also on the social and physical context of the storyworld within which that mind functions.

The following passage illustrates the kind of fictional mental functioning that I am interested in. In it a policeman is confronting a suspect:

> Brunetti watched as Murino absorbed this information, then waited as the other man began to consider what his visible response should be. All of this took only seconds, but Brunetti had been observing the process for decades and was familiar with it. The people to whom he presented himself had a drawer of responses which they thought appropriate, and part of his job was to watch them as they sifted through them one at a time, seeking the right fit. Surprise? Fear? Innocence? Curiosity? He watched Murino flip through them, studied his face as he considered, then discarded various possibilities. He decided, apparently, on the last.
>
> "Yes? And what would you like to know, Commissario?" (Leon 1996, 199)

At this point, I will simply say that, for the reasons set out in chapters 2 and 3, current narratological approaches do not do a great deal to bring out the full significance of this passage. I will refer to it again at the end of chapter 7, by which time I hope that, when you read it there in the light of chapters 4 to 7, much more of its significance will have been revealed. Of course, there is nothing to stop you going straight there now except possibly the feeling that you might have missed some interesting stuff along the way!

2. Summary

This summary of the argument of the book is placed here to assist readers who wish to read the rest of the book and who will find it helpful to see from the beginning the purpose of the theoretical groundwork that is laid in later chapters, readers who are not yet sure whether or not they wish to read the rest of the book and may find a summary of the argument helpful in deciding, and readers who are sure that they will not read the rest of the book but who will want to know what they are missing.

What do we mean when we talk about the presentation of consciousness in fiction? It is clear what Dorrit Cohn has in mind when she refers to her "predilection for novels with thoughtful characters and scenes of self-communion" (1978, v) and her interest in "moments of lonely self-communion minutely tracing spiritual and emotional conflicts" (1999, 84). And, as I will suggest in chapter 3, her liking for private and heavily introspective thinking is shared by other narrative theorists. Self-communings lend themselves to the highly verbalized, self-conscious form of thought that is known as *inner speech*, and the theoretical predilection for fictional introspection is accompanied by a decided preference for this form of thought. As the eminent narratologist Gerard Genette has argued in *Narrative Discourse* (1980), the "novelistic convention, perhaps truthful in this case, is that thoughts and feelings are no different from speech, except when the narrator undertakes to condense them into events and to relate them as such" (1980, 171). Examples of self-communing characters who are popular with narrative theorists include Dorothea Brooke in George Eliot's *Middlemarch*; Isobel Archer in Henry James's *Portrait of a Lady*; Stephen Dedalus, Leopold Bloom, and Molly Bloom in James Joyce's *Ulysses*; and Mrs. Ramsay in Virginia Woolf's *To the Lighthouse*.

This emphasis on the privacy of thought explains why it is customary in studies of this sort to refer to the basic reality of our lives that we do not have direct access to the thoughts of others. R. D. Laing put the point memorably: "*your experience of me is invisible to me and my experience of you is invisible to you. I cannot experience your experience. You cannot experience my experience. We are both invisible men. All men are invisible to one another*" (1967, 16, quoted in Iser 1978, 165). In contrast, the vast majority of novels present directly to readers their main characters' thoughts, and we have learned to accept this as perfectly natural. One of the pleasures of reading novels is the enjoyment of being told what a variety of fictional people are thinking. As Paola explains in the epigraph for this chapter, we get "reliable information." This is a relief from the business of real life, much of which requires the ability to decode accurately the behavior of others. It is worth dwelling on the strangeness of this activity for a moment. In one sense to read "she felt happy" is the most natural thing in the world: we know what it is to feel happy. In another sense, it is the oddest: we do not know and can never know what it is to experience directly how another person can feel happy. The literary critic Georges Poulet captures the peculiar quality of reading about the thoughts of others in this way: "Because of the strange invasion of my person by the thoughts of another, I am a self who is granted the experience of thinking thoughts foreign to him. I am the subject of thoughts other than my own. My consciousness behaves as though it were the consciousness of another" (1969, 56).

But how does this intensely private, individualistic view of the mind account for the following scene in the sit-com *Friends*? One friend, Phoebe, lets slip to another, Rachel, that all the other friends think that she, Rachel, is still in love with Ross. Rachel protests that this is not true and that she is over him, but then eventually agrees that yes, all right, she *is* still in love with him. "But why didn't you tell me?" Rachel demands to know. "Because we thought you knew!" exclaims Phoebe. What this exchange appears to show is that Rachel's feelings about Ross were more accessible to the other friends than they were to her. They all knew that she was still in love with Ross even though she herself did not know. On the other hand, we should not go too far in this direction because the conversation also shows that the knowledge that people have of the inner states of others can be patchy. Rachel did not know that the other friends knew, and the others did not know that Rachel did not know! In a sense, the humor in this scene is a new take on the familiar, clichéd old joke about the two psychiatrists (or the two behaviorists, depending on your prejudice) who say to each other when meeting, "You're fine, how am I?" However, the *Friends* scene is more interesting, it seems to me, for two reasons: it acknowledges that all of us, not just specialists in the study of the mind, have some sort of access to the thinking of others; and it also acknowledges that thought can be private and inaccessible as well as public and shared.

So, what would happen to the narratological study of private and introspective fictional minds if we applied to it some of the various discourses on real minds? Well, the philosopher Gilbert Ryle suggests that to "talk of a person's mind is . . . to talk of the person's abilities, liabilities, and inclinations to do and undergo certain sorts of things, and of the doing and undergoing of these things in the ordinary world" (1963, 190). This is an alternative picture that consists of the social mind in action while engaged in purposive mental functioning in a physical context. Other disciplines share this view of the mind. Within anthropology, Clifford Geertz argues that "thought is consummately social: social in its origins, social in its functions, social in its forms, social in its applications. At base, thinking is a public activity—its natural habitat is the houseyard, the marketplace, and the town square" (1993, 360). Another anthropologist, Gregory Bateson, discusses the extent of the individual mind in these vivid terms: "Suppose I am a blind man, and I use a stick. I go tap, tap, tap. Where do *I* start? Is my mental system bounded at the handle of the stick? Is it bounded by my skin? Does it start halfway up the stick? Does it start at the tip of the stick? But these are nonsense questions. The stick is a pathway along which transforms of difference are being transmitted. The way to delineate the system is to draw the limiting line in such a way that you do not cut any of these pathways in ways which leave things inexplicable" (1972, 465). These views lead the psycholinguist James Wertsch to remark in *Voices of the Mind* that, "to borrow from theorists such as Gregory Bateson . . . and Clifford Geertz . . . mind is viewed here as something that 'extends beyond the skin'" (1991, 14).

This social perspective on what might be termed the *mind beyond the skin* shows that the strangeness of the device of direct access should not allow us to forget that the reader's experience of the minds of characters in novels does not depend solely on that device. Just as in real life the individual constructs the minds of others from their behavior and speech, so the reader infers the workings of fictional minds and sees these minds in action from observation of characters' behavior and speech. In one sense, as Laing says, we are invisible to each other. But in another sense the workings of our minds are perfectly visible to others in our actions, and the workings of fictional minds are perfectly visible to readers from characters' actions. Most novels contain a wide variety of evidence on which readers base their conjectures, hypotheses, and opinions about fictional minds.

This study suggests that narrative theory has been concerned for too long primarily with the privacy of consciousness and that an emphasis on the social nature of thought might form an informative and suggestive perspective on fictional minds. Reduced to the very minimum, a character is simply a collection of the words that relate to a particular proper name occurring at intervals within the long series of words that makes up a narrative. The perspec I am advocating might help provide the beginning of an answer to q

ke these: How precisely do these groups of words become the recognizable
fictional minds that are clearly contained in fictional texts? Narratives are about
the minds of characters, but how are these minds constructed by the narrator
and the reader of the text? Obviously these are huge questions that a single study
of this sort cannot hope to answer. Instead, I will focus in particular on some
of the areas of fictional mental functioning that have not been explored within
narratology. In doing so, I will work within the possible-worlds framework that
is explained in chapter 2, section 2. A leading possible-worlds theorist, Lubomír
Doležel, asserts that from "the viewpoint of the reader, the fictional text can be
characterized as a set of instructions according to which the fictional world is
to be recovered and reassembled" (1988, 489). My argument is that we need to
look more closely at the sets of instructions that relate to mental functioning in
fictional texts.

Fictional Minds argues that the constructions of the minds of fictional characters by narrators and readers are central to our understanding of how novels work because, in essence, narrative is the description of fictional mental
functioning. However, narratology has neglected the whole minds of fictional
characters in action. At first sight, this may seem to be an implausible claim.
Surely characters' minds are considered within a number of the subject areas
that make up narrative theory? For example: the study of how narrators give
readers direct access to characters' thoughts (the speech category approach); the
analysis of the structure of narrative stories in which characters are considered
as units or functions within the structure; the concept of focalization or point
of view; and the issue of characterization, or how narrators and readers use the
various sorts of knowledge of character types that are gained from real life and
other novels in order to build a sense of a character's personality. My answer
is that these perspectives do not add up to a complete and coherent study of
all aspects of the minds of characters in novels. What is required is a holistic
view of the whole of the social mind in action that avoids the fragmentation
of the approaches listed earlier. It is a functional and teleological perspective
that considers the purposive nature of characters' thought in terms of their
motives, intentions, and resulting behavior and action. This will involve some
provisional and tentative typology, but as Brian McHale observes, "we should
not underestimate the usefulness of 'mere' typology. Before a phenomenon can
be explained it must first exist for those who would explain it, which means that
it must be constituted as a category with boundaries and a name" (1981, 185).
This discussion will take us a long way from analyses of lonely introspective self-
communings in terms of the speech categories. But this is just as well perhaps, as

[Handwritten margin notes:] So here's our point of diff. I care about what they reveal about our own lives vs he thinks it looks (sort of) as a formal device; at least it's phrased here

the characters in a large number of novels are not given to intense introspection, and the narrators of many novels make little use of the speech categories of free indirect thought or direct thought that are described later.

The six chapters that are sandwiched between this introductory chapter and the concluding one can be grouped into three pairs. Chapters 2 and 3 are concerned with existing narratological approaches toward fictional minds, chapters 4 and 5 consider the implications of real-mind discourses for fictional minds and lay the theoretical basis for a new approach toward this area of narrative theory, and chapters 6 and 7 explore the new approach in various specific directions.

In chapter 2, "Some Narratological Approaches," I will refer to a few of the ways in which some narratological subject areas can be brought together within a new theoretical perspective and thereby contribute toward a coherent study of fictional minds. In chapter 3, "The Speech Categories," I will consider in a little more detail the problems inherent in one particular area that I have referred to several times already: the speech category approach toward fictional consciousness. I use the term *speech category approach* because the narratological analysis of characters' thought processes is based on the assumption that the categories that are applied to fictional speech can be unproblematically applied to fictional thought. The main categories, which are explained in more detail in chapter 3, section 1, are these:

- *direct thought*: The train pulled away. He thought, "Why the hell am I still waiting for her?" (When untagged and without quotes, this is *free direct thought*.)
- *thought report*: The train pulled away. He wondered why he was still waiting for her.
- *free indirect thought*: The train pulled away. Why the hell was he still waiting for her?

This approach does not give an adequate account of the form or the function of presentations by narrators to readers of fictional characters' minds. In summary, the following problems occur: It privileges the apparently mimetic categories of direct thought and free indirect thought over the diegetic category of thought report; views characters' minds as consisting primarily of a private, passive flow of consciousness because of its overestimation of the importance of inner speech; and neglects the thought report of such states of mind as emotions, sensations, dispositions, beliefs, attitudes, intentions, motives, and reasons for action. I devote a separate chapter to these problems because the speech category approach has become the dominant theoretical discourse on fictional consciousness and, therefore, it has to be addressed before I go on to build up what I hope is a richer and more informative discourse on the whole of fictional minds; because its shortcomings form an illuminating context within which the benefits of the new perspective will become clear; and because the grip of the *verbal norm* (that is, the preoccupation with inner speech) is strong and has to be loosened before the new perspective is fully understood.

The required reconceptualization of fictional minds becomes an interdisciplinary project in chapter 4 because it makes use of what I shall call the *parallel discourses* on real minds, such as cognitive science, psycholinguistics, psychology, and the philosophy of mind, in order to study what I shall variously call the *whole mind*, the *social mind*, and the *mind in action*. Real-mind discourses are invaluable here because they can be used to provide explanations that are fuller than those that are currently available within narrative theory as to how the reader can recuperate meaning from fictional texts. They are parallel discourses because they contain a very different kind of picture of consciousness from that provided by narrative theory, and as far as I know, the two pictures have not yet been brought together in quite the way in which they are here. For example, in chapter 4, "The Whole Mind," I attempt to enlarge our picture of the whole fictional mind in a number of the different directions that are suggested by real-mind discourses. These include the functionalist approach of cognitive scientists toward human mental functioning (that is, studying what thinking is for); how the views of psychologists and philosophers vary on the extent of the relationship between language and thought; the importance not only of non-verbal conscious events but also of entirely non-conscious mental states; the pivotal role of dispositions in any picture of the whole mind; the role of emotions in mental life and in particular their relationship with cognition; the lessons to be learned from the philosophy of action when considering the relationship between thought and behavior; and, finally, first-person ascription and in particular the unreliability of many self-ascriptions of motives and intentions. (Remember the *Friends* scene that was discussed earlier?)

I move the argument on in chapter 5, "The Social Mind," by considering the whole mind that is described in chapter 4 now put in its social context. I start by examining the considerable extent to which our thought is public and social in nature. I then pick up the discussion about unreliable first-person ascription at the end of chapter 4 and contrast it with the reliability of a good deal of third-person ascription (the *Friends* scene again). After a brief section on the work of Russian psycholinguists on the development of purposive thought, I continue with the Russian tradition by focusing on the insights of the great discourse theorist Mikhail Bakhtin on the dialogicality of thought. Finally, in a section entitled "The Mind Beyond the Skin," I explore the fascinating issue of the socially situated or distributed nature of much of our cognition, action, and even identity.

The purpose of chapter 6, "The Fictional Mind," is to relate this work more specifically to the fictional mind. I begin by building on the discussion in chapter 2, section 4 of cognitive frames and narrative comprehension by applying these issues in more detail to mental action in novels. I argue that one of the key frames for comprehending texts is what I refer to as the *continuing-consciousness frame*. In other words, readers create a continuing consciousness out of the isolated passages of text that relate to a particular character. In this way, we assemble what I call an *embedded narrative*: the whole of a character's various perceptual and conceptual viewpoints, ideological worldviews, and plans for the future considered as an individual narrative that is embedded in the whole fictional text. In using this term I am following the narratologist Marie-Laure Ryan, who introduces it in an article entitled "Embedded Narratives and Tellability" (1986) and later in her book, *Possible Worlds, Artificial Intelligence, and Narrative Theory* (1991). I then relate the embedded narrative notion to the concept of *teleology*, or the investigation of narrative in terms of its final purpose or ending. Finally, the various ideas introduced in this chapter are considered in the context of the aspectual nature of the storyworld, which is only ever viewed under particular aspects or from individual and therefore limited points of view.

In chapter 7, "The Fictional Mind in Action," I explore some of the specific implications of the general ideas that were introduced in the previous chapter. Using a number of examples from a specific text, Evelyn Waugh's *Vile Bodies*, I consider some of the subframes of the continuing-consciousness frame. One subframe concerns the relationships between fictional thought and fictional action and how these relationships are presented in fictional discourse. In particular, the term the *thought-action continuum* is introduced to draw attention to the fact that the distinction between thought and action in fictional texts is not as clear-cut as narrative theorists have assumed. Drawing on the work in chapter 5 on the social mind, I go on to discuss another subframe: the prevalence in novels of what psychologists call *intermental thought*, or shared, group, or joint thinking. In order to consider the third subframe, I introduce the term *doubly embedded narratives* in order to convey the idea that versions of characters exist within the minds of other characters and that the relationships between these versions determine to a great extent the teleology of the plot. To finish the book,

I devote the last chapter, "Further Applications," to some tentative suggestions for further historical applications of the ideas summarized earlier.

In summary, *Fictional Minds* describes a theoretical framework that considers the whole of a particular fictional mind, thereby avoiding the fragmentation referred to earlier; views characters' minds, not just in terms of passive, private inner speech in the modes of direct or free indirect thought, but in terms of the narrator's positive linking role in presenting characters' social engaged mental functioning, particularly in the mode of thought report; analyzes in functional and teleological terms the purposive nature of characters' thought: their motives, intentions, and the resulting behavior and action; highlights the role of the reader in constructing characters' embedded narratives by means of a series of provisional conjectures and hypotheses about their mental functioning; and shows how readers read plots as the interaction of those embedded narratives.

Several of the devices that are used in the constructions of fictional minds by narrators and readers, such as the role of thought report in describing emotions and the role of behavior descriptions in conveying motivation and intention, have yet to be defamiliarized. As Hegel puts it, what is "'familiarly known' is not properly known, just for the reason that it is 'familiar'" (1931, 92). The narratologist Manfred Jahn refers in a different context to a "number of interesting cognitive mechanisms that have largely remained hidden below both the reader's and the narratologist's threshold of awareness" (1999a, 168). In my view, this number includes some of the mechanisms that produce the illusion of fictional minds. However, within the embedded narratives framework, these devices can be fully defamiliarized and thereby made more visible.

3. Some Definitions and Assumptions

Narratology and narrative theory. I will use these terms interchangeably. Some theorists distinguish between them by reserving the former term for the type of thinking about narrative that arose from the structuralist movement of the 1960s, 1970s, and beyond and by using the latter term in a much broader sense to cover all theoretical writing on the nature of narrative. However, although this distinction may seem attractive in theory, I think that it would be difficult to maintain in practice.

The narrator and the implied author. I will use the term *narrator* to describe the agency responsible for the words on the pages of fictional texts. I shall not refer to the actual author, because I am studying only the fictional texts themselves and not their historical circumstances. The other term that is used in this context, *implied author*, was made famous by the literary critic

Wayne C. Booth in *The Rhetoric of Fiction* (originally published in 1961) and further developed by a number of narratologists since. The term is defined in Gerald Prince's *Dictionary of Narratology* (1987) as "the implicit image of an author in the text, taken to be standing behind the scenes and to be responsible for its design and for the values and cultural norms it adheres to" (1987, 42). Prince explains that the narrator must be distinguished from the implied author. The former recounts the situations and events and is inscribed in the text as a teller; the latter is taken to be accountable for the selection, distribution, and combination of the events and is inferred from the text. But, Prince concedes, while the distinction is clear in the case of first-person narrators, it can be problematical in other cases (1987, 42–43). The concept of the implied author is a valid and informative way to refer to responsibility for the values and cultural norms that can plausibly be inferred from a text, subject to the caveat that different readers may infer different implied authors from the same text. However, during the discussions of a wide variety of novels that are contained in the following chapters, I have not found it possible to maintain a coherent distinction between the agency that is responsible for selecting and organizing the events (as Prince describes the role of the implied author), and the voice that recounts them (the narrator). For example, which one decides that direct access is given to the thoughts of one character and not another? Which one decides on the length and extent of access or whether it is given in direct or free indirect thought or in thought report? Which one decides on the precise degree to which the language used in the discourse explicitly or implicitly conveys the motivation of a particular character? Because I have not been able to answer these questions, I will refer only to the narrator.

Non-narrated narration. Some narratologists believe that it is possible for narration to occur without a narrator. For example, in *The Fictions of Language and the Languages of Fiction* (1993), Monika Fludernik asserts that "there *can be* narration without a narrator. That is to say, in *pure* reflector mode narrative there cannot be any indication of a narrative voice" (1993, 443). (The term *reflector mode* describes a novel such as Henry James's *The Ambassadors* in which the action is reflected through the consciousness of a *reflector character*.) However, other narratologists are equally insistent that all narratives must necessarily have a narrator. For the narratologist Mieke Bal, as she explains in *Narratology* (1997), the statement "Elizabeth felt somewhat tired that day" should be read as "I narrate: . . . 'Elizabeth felt somewhat tired that day'" (1997, 25). There is a very complex and technical debate behind these two positions, and it would take me a long way out of my way to justify my belief that reflector novels such as *The Ambassadors* contain plenty of evidence of the presence of a narrator. For this reason, I will simply say that one of the assumptions behind this book is that Bal is correct to say that all narrative has a narrator. (For more on this issue, see the highly illuminating discussion in Richard Aczel's article, "Hearing Voices in Narrative Texts" [1998].)

The reader. I refer frequently throughout this book to the reader. Here I mean what is meant by the term *implied reader*: the theoretical construct of the ideal, informed, or model reader that is implied by or can be constructed from the text. Nevertheless, I hope that my generalizations are also true to a fairly large extent of the psychological activities of real readers. After all, it is necessary to presuppose a high degree of correlation between implied and real readers in order to explain the incontrovertible fact that most fictional texts are readily understood by real readers. However, I have to own up to the fact that I have done no empirical research at all on how real readers read.

Story and discourse. This is a standard narratological distinction. As defined by Prince, the *story* is the content plane of narrative, the what of a narrative, the narrated (1987, 91). The *discourse* is the expression plane of narrative, the how of a narrative, the narrating (1987, 21). The two elements are often referred to in Russian formalist terms as the *fabula* and the *sjuzhet*. There are also many other names for this pair of concepts, but as some terms are used by different people to signify both sides of the dichotomy, I will not confuse you by listing them here. It is a problematical distinction. Many theorists have pointed out that any attempt to tell the story simply results in another discourse. It is never possible to arrive at a pure unmediated story, and each reader's story will be subtly different from every other reader's. In some cases, say *Emma*, the differences might focus on the personality of the heroine. In other cases such as Henry James's *The Turn of the Screw*, readers might differ quite substantially over what events took place in the story. Also, the literary critic Jonathan Culler (1980) makes the important point that ultimately the two concepts are entirely incompatible planes of explanation. "Emma marries Knightley because she falls in love with him" is a story explanation; "Emma marries Knightley because that is the ending that brings to a satisfactory conclusion the various themes and meanings of the novel" is a discourse explanation; and these two explanations cannot be reconciled. Finally, I have found that it can often be difficult to decide whether an issue such as the motivation for an action belongs to the story plane or the discourse plane. Nevertheless, the distinction between the events and situations in the story and the presentations of them in the words on the pages of the fictional text is a valuable one. Some narratologists use models that contain three or even four elements, usually by splitting the discourse plane into such aspects as text, narration, and textuality. *The Fictions of Discourse* (1994) by Patrick O'Neill contains a good summary of the various models (1994, 20–21). I have added the concept of *storyworld*—see chapter 2, section 2—to the story and discourse distinction to create a three-part model.

The mind. Generally, I use the term *mind* in preference to alternatives such as *consciousness* and *thought*. The use of the latter two terms is often accompanied by a tendency to see mental life mainly in terms of inner speech. In addition, consciousness can have the implication of self-consciousness, which I want to avoid because it deflects attention from non-consciousness and latent states of mind. The important point is that the mind refers to much more than what is normally thought of as consciousness or thought. For example, it is possible to drive skillfully while thinking about something else. This is the mind in action, but it is not thought or consciousness in action. The terms *mental event* and *states of mind* are very useful. *Mental functioning* and *mental action* are particularly worthwhile for their emphasis on the functional nature of mental activity. For comments on the terms *stream of consciousness* and *interior monologue* see the next section. The inclusive use of the term *mind* embraces all aspects of our inner life: not just cognition and perception, but also dispositions, feelings, beliefs, and emotions. Of course, the term is so wide that its use can shade off into such notions as character and personality, but I regard its doing so as desirable. A range of terms, including thought and consciousness, will be used throughout the text for the sake of variety, but my paradigm term for the aggregate of mental states and events is the *mind*.

I am particularly interested in the various ways in which the interrelations between different types of thought are presented in fiction. I will anticipate my argument by mentioning a few random examples of what I have in mind. Psychologists such as Jon Elster in *Alchemies of the Mind* (1999) continually stress the interconnections between cognition and emotion and argue that in practice they are difficult if not impossible to disentangle. Cognitions tend to have a strong emotional element and vice versa. They also relate closely in causal terms: a character's anger might be caused by a cognition of some sort that in turn results in further emotions and then other cognitions. Also, both are necessary to will and motivation. Philosophers talk of actions arising from or being caused by (or however expressed) an interrelationship of desires and beliefs. "I *desire* x and I *believe* that I can achieve x by *doing* y." The philosophers John R. Searle and Daniel Dennett, the neuroscientist Antonio Damasio, and the psycholinguist Steven Pinker all suggest that our mental events and states, including cognitions, come with a particular mood, tone, or color. For example, Searle refers to the "pleasure/unpleasure dimension" to all consciousness (1992, 141). Damasio stresses the "continuity of the melodic line of background emotion" (2000, 93). I am sure that an investigation of these various relationships will illuminate a good deal of fictional thought.

Embedded narratives. As explained in the previous section, a central concept in this book is one that I label *embedded narratives*, the use of which has the undeniable drawback that many theorists attach a completely different meaning to the term. Its more familiar meaning is a self-contained narrative that is embedded within a so-called *frame narrative*. For example, in *The Arabian Nights*, the stories that Sheherazade tells her husband every night are embedded within the frame narrative of her attempts to delay her threatened execution. The creation of an additional use is regrettable but, on balance, justified because the term vividly illustrates a number of the important features of fictional minds to which I wish to draw attention.

Mimesis and diegesis. These two terms are staples of literary theory, but unfortunately both contain a wide variety of meanings. Prince's dictionary reflects some of the drift in use. His long entry for the term *mimesis* (1987, 52–53) contains, in summary, these three meanings: *showing* (as opposed to telling), which is defined elsewhere in his book as "a mode characterized by the detailed, scenic rendering of situations and events and by minimal narratorial mediation" (1987, 87); the direct speech of a character; and an accurate representation of life. One problem is that these completely separate meanings— together with several others, identified, for example, by the narratologist Meir Sternberg (1982)—are often confused with each other. Another problem is that the partner term, *diegesis*, is sometimes used in opposition to mimesis and sometimes used in completely separate senses. According to Prince (1987, 20), diegesis has two meanings: *telling* (as opposed to showing), which is defined as "a mode characterized by more narratorial mediation and by a less detailed rendering of situations and events than showing" (1987, 96), and the storyworld in which the narrated situations and events occur. Obviously, the first meaning for diegesis is used in opposition to mimesis but the second is not. A further complication is that some definitions of mimesis, Moshe Ron's, for example (1981, 18) and Fludernik's (1993, 459, 463), have inflated its meaning so far that it completely encompasses the notion of diegesis. For these reasons, it seems to me that the two terms are beyond precise definition. I will use them only when other theorists commonly do. For example, narratologists regularly refer to direct thought as the most mimetic mode of thought presentation, and thought report as the most diegetic.

4. What the Book Is Not

Occasionally you read book reviews in which the chief criticism is that the wrong book was written. Why oh why did the author not see that what the world really needs is a completely different study with, possibly, just the original title surviving? Typically, these reviews, following faint praise for the book for being so short, contain a long list of additional topics that if included would have tripled its size. Readers of these reviews often sense that the list is in effect the book that the reviewer would have liked to have written, had he or she thought of it or had the time to do it. The following section is intended to assist such a reviewer by providing a checklist of the topics that comprise the book that this is *not*. This checklist is particularly necessary as the title *Fictional Minds* is so general that it can be explored in a wide variety of very different directions.

Fiction and non-fiction. I will not be addressing the various issues relating to the definitions of and the boundaries between such categories as narrative, fiction, non-fiction, history, and the novel. Anyone interested in this fascinating topic should consult such authorities on narrative theory as Hayden White (1978, 1987), Michael McKeon (1987, 2000), Marie-Laure Ryan (1997), and Dorrit Cohn (1999). I have simply taken as a given the existence of a number of texts that are generally accepted as novels and have tried to see how they work.

Literary criticism. Literary critics are concerned with the wide variety of strategies that are used by novelists to give meaning and form to the narrative, such as the use of symbolic structures of motifs, metaphors, metonymies, and so on. They then frequently relate these symbolic structures to the historical circumstances of the novels that they are analyzing. A study of the relationship between these issues and the subject of this study would focus on the means by which narrators construct characters' embedded narratives and, therefore, in aggregate, the plot, in order to achieve these effects. It is my intention to theorize an aspect of the process of reading and not the end product. The embedded narrative approach is primarily an attempt to explore fully the workings of dense and complex fictional texts. This is the process. The end products are the various purposes to which these explorations might be put.

The historicized approach. I will not address the issue of how presentations of fictional minds have developed and changed over time. However, chapter 8 makes some suggestions about how it will be possible to historicize the new approach. For example, put simply, the device of direct presentations of characters' minds was the subject of a fierce debate in the middle to late eighteenth century, became naturalized in the early to middle nineteenth century, was problematized toward the end of the nineteenth century, and became the subject of various sorts of experiments in the twentieth century. However, the purpose of the present study is to establish and justify my basic approach first in order to ensure that as much evidence as possible on the presentation of fictional minds has been made available before attempting to trace these sorts of historical developments. Narratives from the Bible onward presented characters' minds by means of descriptions of behavior and action, and so embedded narratives can be established purely on this basis. It is only when the roles of the reader, narrator, and character in this process have been completely understood that the development of the device of detailed direct access in the late eighteenth and early nineteenth centuries can be put in its full historical context.

Reception theory. Reception theory is the attempt to "understand literary works in relation to specific readerships, reconstructing the changing expectations which condition the responses of successive generations, or of different sub-cultures at the same time" (Baldick 1996, 171). In my terms, reception theory is the study of the historical relationship between real and fictional minds or how real minds have in the past received presentations of fictional minds. This kind of study would be enriched by the theory suggested here, which could help to establish the precise means by which fictional minds have been constructed by the historical readers of particular periods.

Genres and intertextuality. Intertextuality may be defined as the sum of the myriad relationships that exist between different texts. These include adaptation, imitation, parody, as well as the less obvious relationships that have been explored by poststructuralist critics such as Julia Kristeva. Intertextual factors also include the role that readers' expectations with regard to genres such as the thriller, the romance, and the Gothic novel play in the constructions of the fictional minds that are contained within those fictional texts. In discussing briefly in chapter 2, section 3, the sensitive and imaginative analysis of intertextuality and genre by such critics as Umberto Eco in *The Role of the Reader* (1981) and Jonathan Culler in *Structuralist Poetics* (1975), I explain that in my view this vitally important perspective has been thoroughly explored and well acknowledged and that the purpose of this book is to go in some different directions.

Realism. As this book is about the relationship between real minds and fictional minds, it may appear that I am concerned with the issue of realism in the novel. For example, you might think that I will be arguing that fictional minds are "realistic" when they are similar in some specified way to real minds and "unrealistic" when they are not. This is not the case. I am arguing that the approach proposed in this book applies to all novels, apparently realist or not. I do not distinguish between realist and non-realist texts. A reasonably plausible definition of the concept of realism would consider the extent to which a fictional discourse is consistent with the dominant scientific and other knowledge-based discourses at the time of writing and at the time of reading. However, the issue of consistency is not one that I will be exploring here as it implies that the real-life discourses are to be regarded as the norm from which fictional-mind discourses may or may not deviate. My way of working is the other way round: as far as fictional minds are concerned, I regard fictional discourses as the norm, and I then investigate whether or not the use of real-mind discourses can illuminate our study of them. In my view real-mind discourses assist the study of such non-realist texts as the postmodernist novel and fantasy fiction just as much as the realist novel. It may appear that I am predisposed to realist fiction because, as it happens, most of my examples belong in that category. However, this is not significant as I am concentrating on canonical novels that just happen to be realist texts. See the next section for more on this point.

The unconscious. In chapter 4, section 4 I consider the non-conscious activities of the mind, but I say very little there about the *unconscious*, the central concept of Freudian psychoanalytical theory. This may seem surprising. One reason for the omission is that, as explained in the opening section, I see this book as a counterweight to the current biases in narrative theory, and as psychoanalytical approaches are well established within the theory, there is no pressing need for further comment here. The other reason is that I am personally quite skeptical of Freudianism and have always found it puzzling that a school of thought could become so well established on the basis of so little empirical evidence. However, to have argued this viewpoint would have been a distraction from the main purpose of the book, and so it seemed best simply to put the question to one side.

Stream of consciousness and interior monologue. I suppose these two terms might be the most surprising omissions. How can a book about consciousness in fiction have so little to say about them? The answer is simple: like mimesis and diegesis, they are beyond precise definition. Although the two terms have different origins, they have now become inextricably linked. *Stream of consciousness* was first used in 1890 by William James in *Principles of*

Psychology. It is thought that *interior monologue* was probably initially used to describe *Ulysses*. Interestingly, although the formal or theoretical definitions for these terms vary widely, the ostensive or practical definitions are very precise. That is to say, apart from occasional references to earlier novelists (for example, Edouard Dujardin), theorists define the two phrases in relation to the modernist novels of Joyce, Virginia Woolf, William Faulkner, and Dorothy Richardson. The examples used to illustrate the terms are invariably taken from *Ulysses* or, less often, from Woolf's *To the Lighthouse* or *Mrs. Dalloway*.

Some of the theoretical definitions describe the types of fictional thought that occur in the minds of characters in the story. Although most emphasize the random, associative, illogical, and seemingly ungrammatical free flow of thought, others mention more controlled and directed thought; non-conscious, but also conscious thought; verbal, but also non-verbal thought. Some specify cognition only, while others include various combinations of cognition, perception, sensations, and emotions. Confusingly though, other theoretical definitions refer to a completely separate issue: the techniques of thought and consciousness presentation in the discourse. Most of these definitions stress an apparently unmediated presentation in the mode of free direct thought. However, this can be misleading. Many illustrative passages contain a dense mixture, often in equal proportions, of surface description of the physical storyworld together with all three modes of thought presentation: thought report, free indirect thought, and direct thought. For example: "Made him feel a bit peckish. [thought report] The coals were reddening. [surface description] Another slice of bread and butter: three, four: right. [free direct thought] She didn't like her plate full [free indirect thought]" (Joyce 1986, 45).

To add to the confusion, there is no clear consensus on the relationship between the two terms. Some theorists use the terms interchangeably. Others regard one as a particular type or subset of the other. Some attach different and separate meanings to each. Perhaps the most common distinction is this: Stream of consciousness describes the thought itself and/or the presentation of thought in the sort of third-person passage that I have just quoted and that is characteristic of Woolf and the early episodes in *Ulysses*. Interior monologue describes the long continuous first-person passages or whole texts that contain uninterrupted, unmediated free direct thought such as "Penelope" (Molly Bloom's famous monologue in the last episode of *Ulysses*) or the first three sections of Faulkner's *The Sound and the Fury*. For example: "I suppose she was pious because no man would look at her twice I hope Ill never be like her a wonder she didnt want us to cover our faces" (Joyce 1986, 608).

Some writers, after commenting on the regrettable confusion, give firm advice about how the two terms should be used in the future. As these suggestions invariably go unheeded, the advice that I would otherwise have been tempted to give (do not use the two terms at all) will not be given.

5. A Note on the Texts

As my interest is solely in narrative fiction, all of my primary sources are novels. I will not be considering formal non-fiction narratives such as histories, biographies, autobiographies, and memoirs, or informal or natural narratives such as spoken life histories, testimonies, conversation, stories, and jokes. Narrative has become a very fashionable heuristic tool within such social sciences as sociology, cultural studies, and anthropology, and I would be very excited if my conclusions were of interest to scholars working in these fields, but, as I say, my focus is on fiction.

I have tried to make use of a wide range of canonical novels written in English from Aphra Behn to Thomas Pynchon. My claim, right or wrong, is that the aspect of the reading process with which I am concerned is fundamental to all narrative fiction. In talking about narrative as the description of fictional mental functioning, I may sound as though I am talking about the *consciousness novel* of Henry James or the stream of consciousness or interior monologue novels described earlier. But nothing could be further from the truth. I am talking about the novel as a whole because all novels include a balance of behavior description and internal analysis of characters' minds. In addition to the canon, I have made good use of thrillers. I read thrillers because I enjoy them. But I find that I cannot follow the plot of a thriller unless I have a fairly clear conception of the mental functioning of the main characters (who knows what and who is trying to achieve what at any given point in the story). It is this operation of attempting to follow the lines of their thinking that enables me to follow the logic of their actions and, therefore, the twists and turns of the plot.

In general, I will concentrate on third-person novels and will pay much less attention to first-person novels. That is to say, my priority is the *heterodiegetic narrator* (one who is not a character in the story being narrated) and not the *homodiegetic narrator* (one who is a character in the story being narrated). There are various complexities inherent in this apparently simple distinction. It is well known that some heterodiegetic narrators of third-person novels (the famous example is Henry Fielding's *Tom Jones*) do not let the fact that they are not participants in the storyworld inhibit them from making liberal use of the "I" pronoun when letting us have their views on a wide variety of subjects. Conversely, some homodiegetic narrators of first-person novels (such as Anthony Powell's *A Dance to the Music of Time* series) are so unobtrusive that there is frequently very little use of the "I" pronoun for long stretches of text. It is equally well known that there are always two first persons in any homodiegetic narrative: the one who experiences the events and the one who later recounts them. The Pip who is the narrator of Charles Dickens's *Great Expectations* is much older and wiser than the Pip who experiences the events. Other complexities include a first-person narrator disappearing and being replaced by a third-person narrator (as in Gustave Flaubert's *Madame Bovary*). Although, as I say, I discuss very few first-person novels, I think that it is quite likely that my approach will prove to be as well suited to them as to third-person novels. In particular, the variety of evidence that is available for the construction of character (action and behavior as well as direct access to thoughts) would explain how first-person narrators construct other characters. For example, it would show how both the older and the younger Pip differently construct the character of Joe despite neither having direct access to his thoughts.

In addition to the primary texts, a word of explanation is also required for the secondary texts. There has been a truly vast amount of work done on real minds in such fields as cognitive science, philosophy, psychology, and psycholinguistics. It would not be possible for a single work to do justice to it all. Any selection of the vast source material available in these fields is bound to be arbitrary. A large number of books could be written on my subject without any overlap at all in the choice of real-mind studies. You may finish this book saying, "Why on earth didn't he mention x or y?" (add name of philosopher, psychologist, or cognitive scientist of choice). If you do, my initial position is that I am referring to real-mind discourses only in so far as they are able to illuminate fictional minds and that the two phenomena, real minds and fictional minds, are very different things. My fall-back position is the Dr. Johnson defense: When asked by a woman of his acquaintance why he had incorrectly defined the word pastern as the knee of a horse, he replied: "Ignorance, madam, pure ignorance!"

Finally, I should add that I have made extensive use of MITECS, the encyclopedia of the cognitive sciences that I referred to earlier. It is an invaluable sourcebook, and I recommend it strongly—it is much less intimidating than it sounds!

Conclusion

In *Unspeakable Sentences* (1982), the narrative theorist Ann Banfield declares that "the language of narrative has the resources for a picture of the activities and states of the mind commensurate with the most sophisticated theories of knowledge and consciousness" (1982, 210). I believe that she is right. However, I also think that our theories about the presentations of the pictures of the activities and states of the mind that are contained in narrative fiction need to become more sophisticated than at present if they are to reflect the richness and complexity of current theories of knowledge and consciousness.

2

Some Narratological Approaches

Many of the problems that are discussed in this book arise from the fact that narratology has created clear boundaries between various aspects of fictional minds, even though the fictional texts themselves show that these boundaries are not clear at all. Examples include those between individual minds and their context, between thought and action, and also, within minds, between different types of thought. They have come about because different branches of the discipline of narrative theory have developed in different directions. Clear boundaries and rigorous typology are understandable and necessary, especially in the early stages of a discipline. However, disciplines mature, and when they do, the heuristic and pedagogic tools that have been historically useful have to be reconsidered and, if necessary, remolded. In the case of fictional minds, the time has come for the map to be redrawn.

1. Story Analysis

There is a discourse within narrative theory that is concerned with what is variously called narrative grammar, narrative structure, the analysis of story, the functional classification of action sequences, and so on. I will refer to this branch of narrative theory as *story analysis*. It is associated with the Russian theorist Vladimir Propp's seminal study of Russian folk tales, *Morphology of the Folk Tale*, which was originally published in Russia in 1928 and proved highly influential on the work of French high structuralists such as Claude Bremond (1973), A. J. Greimas (1983), and Tzvetan Todorov (1977) when it was belatedly discovered by them in the 1960s and 1970s. Propp's purpose was to identify the common elements in the narrative patterns contained in nearly two hundred Russian folk tales. The constant features were abstracted from the more contingent aspects of the stories and were described as *functions*. A function is an "act of a character, defined from the point of view of its significance for the course of the action" (Propp 1968, 21). Propp identified thirty-one such functions. They occur in various combinations in the tales but, interestingly, always in exactly the same order. He also devised a model of the dramatis personae who act in ways that embody these functions. During the 1960s and 1970s, structuralist theorists such as Bremond, Greimas, and Todorov developed various models that closely followed Propp in this respect and that were based on the concept of an *actant*: "A fundamental role at the level of narrative deep structure" (Prince 1987, 1). In essence, these models were typologies of the types of characters who fulfill the various recurring functions that are found in narrative. A typical model contains the following six actants: subject, object, sender, receiver, helper, and opponent. As is clearly apparent, this sort of analysis, which tries to identify features of all narratives, is necessarily carried out at a very high level of abstraction.

Before attempting to place this subject area within my argument, I would like to make a general point in passing: Propp analyzed some folk tales. He did not analyze all types of folk tales; he did not analyze other sorts of Russian narratives; he did not analyze narratives from other national traditions. It is my guess that he might have been surprised if he had known of the conceptual weight that now rests on his slim empirical findings. It would be interesting to know whether someone who did not know about Propp or the French structuralists and who attempted to construct a typology of narrative story forms could arrive at an account that would look nothing like Propp's but that would fit an equally large number of stories. I do not have anything in mind; I simply ask whether the thought is implausible. If no one has constructed such a typology so far, then that itself is an important piece of evidence, but I do not find the thought that someone could do so entirely inconceivable. This is certainly not a criticism of Propp. It is simply a suggestion that possibly too much use has been made of his pioneering and seminal work and that less reliance on it in the future might result in a richer and more complete picture of narrative form.

To return to my argument: a good deal of highly technical, rewarding, and original work has been done on the analysis of story structure. However, when narrative is considered from the point of view of fictional minds, story analysis can seem rather rigid, mechanical, and uninformative. There can be a tendency to force particular narratives into a straitjacket that does not necessarily illuminate them. How much does it help our understanding of *Madame Bovary* to be told that the actants in it are these: subject = Emma; object = happiness; sender = romantic literature; receiver = Emma; helper = Leon, Rodolphe; and opponent = Charles, Yonville, Rodolphe, Homais, and Lheureux (Prince 1987, 2)? It is tempting to wonder whether this is an obvious area in which the structuralist origins of the discipline have had a limiting effect. As David Herman explains, "[s]tructuralist narratologists, interested in formulating a 'grammar' of narrative, wanted to shift attention from characters as 'beings' to characters as regularly recurring, typifiable 'participants' in the syntagmatic unfolding of the narrated action" (1999b, 233–34). Also, the narratologists Ruth Ginsburg and Shlomith Rimmon-Kenan point out that in classical narratology characters "were related neither to world view nor to time-space, but—labelled 'functions'—were subordinated to the succession of events" (1999, 80). However, if the ways in which characters are constructed by readers are to be fully understood, they have to be regarded as fictional beings that are related to world view and time-space in a fuller and more holistic manner than story analysis envisages.

In particular, the way in which the concept of *action* is used within story analysis is rather limited and impoverished. Action is crucial to this study, and it is discussed at a number of points, for example, in chapter 4, section 7; chapter 5, section 5; and chapter 7, section 2. I explore different aspects of the concept of action at various stages in my argument in order to deepen and widen our understanding of the term beyond the story analysis use. The analysis of narrative structures is clearly dependent on a good deal of indirect inference about fictional minds through examinations of the function and significance of the physical actions caused by those minds. What was the purpose, motivation, intention, and so on behind the decision to take the action? However, this methodology is rarely explicitly described by story analysts in terms of mental functioning because the minds of characters tend to be regarded as a given rather than acknowledged as a discursive construct. This point is borne out by the following discussion of the story analysis notion of an *event*.

There is a noticeable emphasis on events in a number of proposed definitions of narrative. For example, a narrative is "the semiotic representation of a series of events, meaningfully connected in a temporal and causal way" (Onega and Landa 1996, 3); narration is "a discourse representing one or more events" (Prince 1987, 57); and narrative fiction is "the narration of a succession of fictional events" (Rimmon-Kenan 1983, 2). Mieke Bal defines an event as "the transition from one state to another state, caused or experienced by actors" (1997, 182). Bal's last point is an important one. Events only have significance if they are experienced by actors. It is difficult to imagine a narrative that consisted entirely, for example, of descriptions of natural events in which no person was present to experience those events. Onega and Landa refer to events being meaningfully connected in a causal way, and the causal links between events are nearly always formed by fictional minds. Events cause or are caused by mental states and mental episodes. In fact, one could argue that to talk of events does not accurately convey how fictional narrative works. In practice, nearly all of the physical events described in novels are perceived by characters and have an impact on their mental functioning. Otherwise, why mention them? Exceptions to this rule might include the historical events that are referred to by narrators in novels by writers such as Sir Walter Scott and George Eliot and that are not experienced by the characters, but in general, I would maintain that my generalization holds true. It would in a sense, therefore, be more accurate and more revealing about the function of physical event descriptions in narratives to refer to them not as events but as *experiences*. In addition, many events are actions that are performed by individuals who experience the mental episodes that constitute the motives, intentions, and so on that cause the action. These mental events have to be recovered (rightly or wrongly) by the reader from the discourse as part of the operation of assembling characters' purported mental functioning. This is an essential element in the reading comprehension process. For actants and functions to be understood, they must be translated into language that refers to the consciousnesses of the fictional beings in the story. A quest by a hero is not just a quest, it is a decision taken by the hero to go on the quest. In addition, the discourse may reveal that the decision is taken joyfully, regretfully, fearfully, or whatever.

Story analysis relates primarily to the structures contained in the story, while any comprehensive consideration of fictional minds must focus both on the action contained in the story and also on the presentation of the accompanying consciousness in the discourse. It is revealing that the language of actants and functions is totally alien to the language of fictional minds and consciousness. When characters are not seen as beings, issues of consciousness do not arise. Of course, characters are elements in the narrative structure as well as beings, but I suggest in chapters 6 and 7 that there is a way of acknowledging this aspect of fictional minds that is not reductive and mechanistic. The kind of perspective that I envisage addresses the gulf between the story and discourse sides of narratology. Onega and Landa suggest that most theories of narrative privilege either story or discourse (1996, 25). However, it is possible that further research might show that there is a way of bringing together the story and the discourse sides of the discipline. For example, the presentation of action in the discourse has received little attention to date because action is seen primarily as a story, not a discourse, issue. It is unfortunate that discourse analysts tend to give the appearance of not being interested in action, and story analysts appear to be equally uninterested in consciousness. Nevertheless, it is perfectly possible to create a theory of the presentation of consciousness and action in fiction that applies equally well to both the story and the discourse.

There is some evidence of potential skepticism toward the approach that I am advocating. In discussing definitions of narrative of the sort referred to above, the narrative theorist Meir Sternberg holds, in a discussion of how to conceptualize narrativity, that the "most popular approach since Aristotle . . . locates it in a represented action, event-line etc" (2001, 116). He then refers in a footnote to assorted variants of this approach and remarks, "Contrast the odd appeal to 'experientiality' instead in Fludernik" (2001, 122). (*Experientiality* is the term used by Monika Fludernik in *Towards a "Natural" Narratology* [1996] for subjectivity, consciousness, and what I call fictional minds.) But how can actions, event-lines and so on be understood except in terms of the experientiality of the characters involved in those actions and events? Where else does the logic in an event-line lie? I find it very difficult to conceive of a narrative that does not involve fictional mental functioning or experientiality, and I therefore find it odd that Sternberg finds it odd that Fludernik should argue that experientiality is fundamental to narrative.

In conclusion, I do not wish to sound too critical of story analysis, and it is important not to lose sight of the many insights that have resulted from it. It has an important place in the study of whole fictional minds. David Herman has pointed out that it has great value within the cognitive-science approach that is discussed in section 4 of this chapter: "Yet the concept of actants has prompted later researchers to argue that characters in a narrative can be viewed as constructs modelled on processors' pre-stored expectations about human beings and human behavior. . . . Narrative actants, in other words, can be characterized as the output of inferences triggered by grammatical cues in stories; those inferences are grounded in behavioral paradigms that form part of the broader cognitive repertoire of story-tellers and their audiences—of language-users generally" (1999b, 234). This use of the actants concept as a basis for the study of cognitive frames is an insight that I wish to explore in section 4 and in later chapters. It is a valuable example of how, by combining various approaches within innovative new perspectives, we can arrive at a clearer understanding of how fictional minds work. But to do this, we have to be as imaginative as possible about the precise extent and scope of these cognitive repertoires.

2. Possible Worlds

The concept of possible worlds began life within analytical philosophy. It was developed initially by such philosophers as Saul Kripke (1980) and David Lewis

(1973) in order to deal with various technical issues in modal logic, the branch of logic that is concerned with necessity and possibility. So, for example, necessity can be defined in terms of propositions that are true in all possible worlds; possibility in terms of propositions that are true in at least one possible world; and impossibility in terms of propositions that are not true in any possible world. The idea was then adapted and extended by such narrative theorists as Lubomir Doležel (*Heterocosmica*, 1998), Thomas Pavel (*Fictional Worlds*, 1986), and Marie-Laure Ryan (1991) to refer to the possible worlds that are created in worlds of literature and that are also known interchangeably as fictional worlds, narrative worlds, text worlds, and storyworlds. (See also Paul Werth's *Text Worlds* [1999] for a more linguistics-based perspective.) These theorists, however, together with others such as Ruth Ronen in *Possible Worlds in Literary Theory* (1994), are careful to emphasize the differences between the original philosophical model of possible worlds and the new narrative model of story-worlds. From now on, I will be considering only storyworlds. Discussions on how fictional minds are constructed have to be put in the context of possible-worlds theory. The purpose of this section is to make a few introductory remarks about the concept before later chapters develop the idea in relation to fictional minds in more detail.

Although the story analysis strand of narrative theory that was discussed in the previous section has as its basis the concept of story (as opposed to discourse), it is Doležel's view that the "basic concept of narratology is not 'story,' but 'narrative world,' defined within a typology of possible worlds" (1998, 31). Storyworlds are possible worlds that are constructed by language through a performative force that is granted by cultural convention. When a third-person narrator makes a statement about a character it is, according to speech act theory, a *performative utterance*: it creates what it says in the act of saying it. This is why the quote with which I started the book suggested that it is only fictional people about whom we get completely reliable information. Generally, third-person narrators never lie (although some self-conscious experiments in the French Nouveau Roman have played with the idea of the unreliable third-person narrator). The question of the unreliable narrator that was made famous by Wayne C. Booth in *The Rhetoric of Fiction* is a completely separate issue that relates to first-person narrators.

Possible-worlds theory has made a profound contribution to narratology in a number of ways. One relates to its focus on the question of access to fictional worlds. In other words, how do readers comprehend fictional texts sufficiently to be able to enter the storyworld that is described in the text? This line of inquiry builds on the work that was done within the earlier tradition of reader response theory. Within possible-worlds theory, reading—and therefore access to the storyworld—has three elements: the source domain, the real world in which the text is being processed by the reader; the target domain, the story-world that constitutes the output of the reader's processing; and the system of textual features that triggers various kinds of reader-held real-world knowledge in a way that projects the reader from source domain to target domain. The reference to the utilization of real-world knowledge in the reading process will bring us in section 4 to the contribution that cognitive science can make to an understanding of the reading process. Doležel maintains that "fictional worlds are accessed through semiotic channels and by means of information process-ing" and that readers can do this "by crossing somehow the world boundary between the realms of the actual and the possible" (1998, 20). The reconstruc-tion of the storyworld by the reader "integrates fictional worlds into the reader's reality" (Doležel 1998, 21). My thesis is that the main semiotic channels by which the reader accesses fictional worlds, and the most important sets of instructions that allow the reader to reconstruct the fictional world, are those that govern the reader's understanding of the workings of characters' minds. Once this central point has been established, then work can be done on the differences between the sets of instructions that are characteristic of various genres and subgenres such as, for example, the psychological novel and the thriller. The same point applies to different historical periods of the novel. See chapter 8 for further details.

Storyworlds differ ontologically from the real world because they are incom-plete. (Ontology is the study of existence, the nature of being, and the essence of things.) Every storyworld contains ontological gaps or "spots of indetermi-nacy" in a phrase of Roman Ingarden's (1973, 246) that was later borrowed by Wolfgang Iser (1978, 170). These gaps constitute the difference between, on the one hand, the combination of the story and the discourse that constitutes the text and, on the other hand, the storyworld. No discourse could ever be long enough to say in its story all that could be said about the whole storyworld. So, fiction is necessarily incomplete and full of blanks where nothing is said about a part of the storyworld and gaps where something but not everything is said. (I will use the term *gaps* to cover both blanks and gaps.) Obviously, the nature of the gaps varies. Some gaps are temporary (for example, the identity of the murderer in a whodunit) and are filled in later in the discourse; others are permanent, and it is these gaps that we are talking about here. Doležel dis-tinguishes between gaps in terms of implicitness. He states that "implicitness based on presupposition is a major source of fictional-world construction and reconstruction" (1998, 175). "The meaning of all texts is a composite of overt and covert semantic constituents" (Doležel 1998, 172). He then introduces a three-part distinction: "explicit texture constructs determinate fictional facts, implicit texture constructs indeterminate facts and zero texture creates gaps" (1995, 209). In terms of Emma Woodhouse's mind, it is explicitly stated at the end of the novel that she loves Knightley; it is implied throughout that she has always loved him; there is zero reference to her views on the French Revolution. Marie-Laure Ryan brings together the two issues of access and gaps by arguing that one important semiotic channel for accessing fictional worlds and for creating the implicit texture that closes ontological gaps is what she terms the *principle of minimal departure*; that is, while reading a text and reconstructing a storyworld from it, the reader assumes the minimal possible departure from the actual world unless such a departure is specified or strongly indicated by the text. So the reader will assume that Emma has one head, two arms, two legs, and so on unless told otherwise. I will explore in chapter 6 how the theoretical treatment of gaps has to take account of the special nature of fictional minds.

Doležel refers at some points to the semiotic procedures for the creation and re-creation of fictional minds, commenting that for the "semantics of fictional narrative, inferences regarding aspects and constituents of acting are of special significance" (1998, 175). He then cautions us in this way: "Yet many precautions have to be taken when inferring the mental traits of fictional persons from their actions" (Doležel 1998, 176). But is his warning necessary? Surely we take many precautions in inferring the mental traits of *real* persons from their actions. The taking of these precautions is second nature. It is precisely those inferential skills, an example of the real-world knowledge referred to above, that enable us to read at all. So why is the warning necessary? The answer is fairly obvious: Doležel is reinforcing the distinction referred to above between the explicit storyworld-creating knowledge that is infallibly supplied by the third-person narrator and the implicit knowledge that is all too fallibly inferred by the reader from the text. I am not querying this entirely valid distinction, but I do wonder whether too much emphasis on it can cause us to lose sight of the variety of ways in which readers construct fictional minds. Some of these ways are unique to the creation of fictional minds: the performative utterances of the narrator regarding individual characters and also the fact that readers have frequent direct access to fictional minds. Other ways have features in common with real minds: we weigh the views of others when coming to our view about an individual, and also, as Doležel says, we infer mental traits from actions. My concern is that possible-worlds theorists appear to privilege the first way, the self-creating statements of the narrator, at the expense of the others.

As storyworlds are called into being through the unrestricted creative power of fictional language, possible-worlds theorists lay a good deal of emphasis on the argument that the limits of the fictionally possible are the limits of the expressible or imaginable. It is quite true that the range of fantasy worlds created in imaginative literature is extraordinary. Science fiction, science fantasy, and magical realist novels are notable examples. However, I will suggest in chapter 6, section 4 that the special nature of fictional minds places limits on the extent to which storyworlds are able to depart from the actual world.

I referred in chapter 1 to different parts of narrative theory as different corners of a large field. Narrative theorists have been aware for some time of these divisions. Doležel has convincingly advanced the view that the concept of a storyworld "enables us to leave behind the split that traditional narratology created by separating story from character. A narrative semantics based on action theory radically psychologizes the story and, at the same time, features fictional characters as persons for and in acting" (1998, 55). The possible-worlds approach forms a promising way to unify previously divergent approaches to fictional minds. It is interesting that the foremost possible-worlds theorist should see the potential for that theory to deepen and enrich the story analysis treatment of fictional minds. In the following section I will show how narrative theorists such as Uri Margolin have made clear the implications of possible-worlds theory for the subject area of characterization.

3. Characterization

A good deal of illuminating work has been done within narrative theory on characterization by, for example, Umberto Eco (1981), Jonathan Culler (1975), Shlomith Rimmon-Kenan (1983), Mieke Bal (1997) and Uri Margolin (1986, 1987, 1989, 1990, 1995a, 1995b, 1996a). The following passage contains an excellent summary of the sort of work that has been done to date. Characters, it states, "can be more or less textually prominent, dynamic or static, consistent or inconsistent, and simple, two-dimensional, and highly predictable or complex, multi-dimensional, and capable of surprising behavior; they are classable not only in terms of their conformity to standard types (the braggart, the cuckold, the *femme fatale*) or their corresponding to certain spheres of action but also in terms of their acts, words, feelings, appearance, and so on; and their attributes can be directly and reliably stated (for example, in a set-piece presentation) or inferred from their (mental, emotional and physical) behavior" (Prince 1982,

124). However, theorists have consistently expressed dissatisfaction with the current state of characterization theory at the time of their writing. For example, according to Patrick O'Neill, the "multifarious ways in which characters emerge from the words on the page, in which storyworld actors acquire a personality, is one of the most fascinating and least systematically explored aspects of narrative theory and narrative practice" (1994, 49). Mieke Bal contends that "no satisfying, coherent theory of characterization is available" (1997, 115). In my view, these comments do not take sufficient account of the work done by Uri Margolin. In a long series of articles published between 1986 and the present, he sets out a complex, rigorous, and comprehensive conceptual framework for the study of character. These essays, which contain numerous examples of typologies that comprise the essential features of various different aspects of characterization, are a rich, full, and suggestive resource for future researchers in the field of characterization.

One of Margolin's major contributions is to explain how the various definitions of character have emerged out of contrasting textual approaches. These definitions can be summarized as follows (for more detail, see Margolin 1987, 107–8; 1989, 1–5; 1990, 843–47):

(a) *Grammatical person.* The character as a topic entity of a discourse, the subject of referring expressions such as noun phrases, proper names, and pronouns. Subject area: text linguistics. I will not be concerned directly with this approach except in so far as it underpins (c) speech position.

(b) *Literary device.* The character as part of the design of a literary work of art, one of many means of achieving aesthetic effects. Subject area: literary criticism. As I say in chapter 1, section 4, I will not be addressing the issues that arise from this subject area.

(c) *Speech position.* The character as a constitutive role in the process of narrative transmission or communication. These roles include textual speaker and also narrative instance or level such as narrator and focalizer. Subject area: narratology. I discuss focalization in section 5 of this chapter and the speech category approach in detail in the following chapter.

(d) *Semes.* The character as standing for a thematic element, a semantic complex, or macrosign composed of semes and unified by a proper name (as described in Roland Barthes's *S/Z*). Subject area: semiotics. Some aspects of this approach are discussed later in this section.

(e) *Actant.* The character as a role or element in the story structure. Subject area: story analysis. This approach was discussed in section 1 of this chapter.

(f) *Non-actual individual.* The character as a non-actual being who exists in a possible world and who can be ascribed physical, social, and mental properties. Subject area: possible-world semantics. This is the paradigm that was introduced in the previous section and that is adopted throughout this study.

The non-actual individual approach seems to me to be far richer and more informative than the others, although it must be acknowledged that they all have their place. While describing this approach, Margolin refers to the importance of the mental dimension, the features of which he lists as follows: cognitive, emotional, volitional, and perceptual events, and inner states such as knowledge and belief sets, attitudes, wishes, goals, plans, intentions, and dispositions. He calls the sum of these mental phenomena *interiority* or *personhood* (1989, 4). The same question applies to Margolin's notion of interiority as was applied to Fludernik's notion of experientiality in section 1 of this chapter. How can we come to a full understanding of how characters come into existence in the reader's mind without an acknowledgement of the importance of the mental dimension? And if the non-actual individual approach allows for a greater acknowledgement of the importance of interiority and personhood than the others, then it has a prima facie case to be considered as the best approach. Interiority, experientiality, and fictional minds are, after all, a good part of what we read novels for.

Margolin's views on the relationships between, and the relative merits of, the six approaches change over time, and it is instructive to follow the development of his thought. In "Introducing and Sustaining Characters in Literary Narrative" he does not comment on the relationships between the approaches or refer to their relative value: he says only that the discussion in the rest of his essay will focus on the non-actual individual approach (1987, 108). In "Structuralist Approaches to Character in Narrative" (1989), he is much more explicit in saying that the various perspectives have incompatible features and irreconcilable presuppositions (1989, 2). No two of them "can be translated into each other or reduced to a common denominator; nor can they be synthesized in any meaningful way" (1989, 5). He also appears to give them equal value: "each seems to command a certain degree of theoretical legitimacy, and each of them enables us to see and say things we could not have otherwise" (1989, 5). "No concept of character can consequently raise a claim to an ultimate, exclusive, or obligatory theoretical status" (1989, 7). On the other hand, he declares that the notion of a character as a non-actual individual "is arguably the closest to our cultural intuition, flexible and open-ended, and at the same time, theoretically well-grounded" (1989, 10), and so, as in 1987, he devotes the rest of his essay to it. However, by 1990 he seems to be more outspoken. While discussing three of the approaches he suggests that the non-actual individual approach is superior to the speech position and actant approaches in terms of conceptual comprehensiveness, theoretical depth, explanatory power, and the diversity of texts to which it is applicable. For example, unlike the other two, the non-actual individual approach can handle ontologically problematical as well as ontologically straight storyworlds; that is, it can account for postmodernist as well as for "realist" constructions of character. He describes the speech position and actant approaches as acceptable but highly partial, selective, and weak on the intuitive notion of character (1990, 845–46). He also comes to a different view on the relationship between the approaches and argues that, as the speech position and actant approaches implicitly presuppose the existence of storyworlds while the non-actual individual approach makes such an existence explicit, the possible-worlds approach can include as subsets the predicates of the other two (1990, 845).

Manfred Jahn certainly supports the subsuming of the actant approach under the non-actual individual approach, pointing out that, while in "early structuralist accounts, literary characters are just 'roles,' 'functions' or as Barthes calls them, 'paper beings,'" in fact, "a reader *must* project a pragmatic identity on fictional characters in order to understand description and narrated perception, speech, and action" (1999b, 17). I would put the point even more strongly in case Jahn's list implies that there are some aspects of narrative that do not need such a projection in order to be understood. In my view, there are essentially no aspects of narrative that can be understood without the semiotic operation to which Jahn refers.

Margolin makes the point that the non-actual individual approach is suitable for various different kinds of texts. It is my view this approach may be the only one that is suitable for *all* texts. As Margolin suggests, a theory of character change, or how characters develop in various ways over the course of a narrative, "should be based on a wide corpus, embracing a maximal number of types of narrative, ancient and modern, realistic and fantastic, high and popular, without privileging the realistic psychological model" (1995a, 5). The theory of character as non-actual individual is suitable for all of these and not just for the realistic psychological model because it explains how we read all narrative. Margolin's point about character change is a good example. It is a centrally important aspect of narrative, and it is much more amenable to the storyworld perspective than to the others because the others do not have the necessary flexibility, fluidity, and comprehensive reach. Characterization is a continuing process. It consists of a succession of individual operations that result in a continual patterning and repatterning until a coherent fictional personality emerges. Readers create fictional people on their first encounter with them, and these beings continue to exist until they leave the narrative, the narrative ends, or they "die." During an initial act of characterization, when we first meet a character, we might say to ourselves, "That was a selfish act." On the other hand, particularly if we have an expectation that this might be a character that we will meet again, we are also quite likely to say something like, "He must be a selfish person." The building of a whole personality starts happening immediately, even during the first act of characterization. Characterization is an inference from an individual action, then, toward a supposed disposition or trait, and these are states of mind that extend over time. In the same way, subsequent actions are interpreted by the reader in the context of the whole of the character's mind as hypothesized up until that point. Judgments are then adjusted by the interpretation placed on the action, and a new frame is formed within which future actions can be interpreted. This process is not easy to theorize within the non-storyworld approaches.

I mentioned in the previous section that much of the discussion of the role of the reader within the possible-worlds perspective echoed the conclusions of earlier reader response theory. It may therefore be helpful at this point to consider some of the aspects of that theory that are relevant to the reader's constructions of whole characters. Umberto Eco has used the thought-provoking phrase, "the cooperative principle in narrativity" (1981, 256). In effect, the meaning of a text will not unfold unless the necessary cooperation exists between the reader and the narrator, and this principle of cooperation applies in particular to the specific and central issue of the construction of characters' minds.

The main thrust of Wolfgang Iser's arguments in *The Act of Reading* (1978) is that a reading causes a work to unfold its inherently dynamic character. As the reader uses the various perspectives offered by the text in order to awake responses in himself or herself, the text may not go far enough, resulting in boredom for the reader, or may go too far, resulting in overstrain for the reader. The development in the mind of the reader of a network of the embedded narratives of various characters is an essential factor in the dynamic process that Iser describes. On the basis of the initial information contained in the text and obtained from the various sources described in this study, the reader will form initial hypotheses about the past (that is, the character's memories and feelings about the past), the present (the character's decisions about behavior and action), and the future (longer-term intentions, plans, and goals). These hypotheses will then be modified in the light of further information about the development of other embedded narratives and the relationships between them in the context of the whole storyworld. Too much information about fictional minds, as Iser says, means that the reader has too little to do to construct that mind. Poorly written novels often fail on this point. Too little information, and the construction of minds becomes difficult. This last point is, of course, not necessarily a problem. Thrillers and whodunits depend for their effect on the sense of mystery that results from a paucity of mental-life information. Many modern novels use a variety of modernist, postmodernist, and behaviorist techniques in which this information is at a premium. When readers say that such novels are "difficult," it is often this feature that they have in mind.

Iser argues that, as part of the dynamic process that he describes, the unwritten outlines of the text, its gaps, draw the reader into the action and influence the interpretation of the written text. The written text imposes certain limits on the unwritten in order to prevent the whole experience from becoming too hazy and blurred. However, the unwritten implications worked out by the reader's imagination endow the written text with far greater significance than it would otherwise possess (1978, 170–79). There is a large number of constraints on the amount of evidence that the narrator can make available in the discourse for any one character, even a protagonist. As only a certain number of the words on the pages of the text can refer to a particular character, it is part of the competence of the reader to construct, both from this written text and from the unwritten implications that comprise the gaps within the written text, a continuing consciousness for that character. Having accomplished that initial and basic task, the reader then has to interpret all the available evidence, not just that which is made available by direct access, in order to plot the detail and direction of that character's embedded narrative.

The topics of genre and intertextuality form the basis of a good deal of the discussions on character. In terms of the real-world knowledge that readers bring to an understanding of a storyworld, these issues relate to readers' knowledge of other storyworlds. It is much easier to access a storyworld if the reader can apply knowledge of other storyworlds that are constructed in similar ways. Genre is a common and useful basis of similarity between individual novels. For example, it helps to know that one is reading a romance rather than a thriller in order to use previously existing knowledge of other romances to interpret the various genre-related textual cues that invariably arise. Similarly, the wide-ranging and complex interrelationships between discourses that fall under the heading of intertextuality are of great benefit to the reader while attempting to construct coherent and satisfying fictional personalities. Jonathan Culler makes several very interesting points on characterization that are primarily concerned with intertextuality (1975, 230–38). Culler remarks that character is not simply a conglomeration of features, it is a directed, teleological set based on cultural models. We do not simply add together the actions and attributes of an individual character, drawing from them a conception of personality and role. According to Culler, we are guided by formal expectations about the roles that need to be filled. He emphasizes that it is not necessary that characters should precisely fit stock types, but that these models guide the perception and creation of characters, enabling readers to compose situations and attribute intelligible roles (1975, 235–37).

The notion of intertextuality makes an important contribution to our understanding of how readers construct characters. However, I would argue that the vitally important aspect of reader construction of character that has come to be known under this label has been given much more attention than the complementary and specifically textual approach that I have in mind. Culler, Eco, and others have convincingly explained the precise nature of such extra-textual material as the cultural and literary codes that readers use to construct notions of character, but I am aware of very little work on what might be called the intratextual evidence in the discourse that is used by readers for the same purpose. It might be a good idea to combine both approaches so that the intratextual evidence that is made available within the embedded narrative approach can be interpreted in terms of the intertextual models that Culler describes. Of course, it is an oversimplification to draw such a sharp distinction between the two. Culler indicates that the intertextual process is drawn both from non-literary experience and literary conventions. Revealingly, as an example of the former, he comments that, as soon as the basic outline of a character begins to emerge, one can call upon any of the languages developed for the study of human behavior in order to structure the text in those terms (1975, 237). This describes perfectly the use that I am trying to make of the parallel discourses of philosophy, psychology, and cognitive science. But, although I am using these discourses, in effect, as intertextual models, I would still maintain that a distinction can be made, as my approach encourages more attention to the evidence that is available within the discourse than the approaches that commonly come under the name of intertextuality.

Despite the first-rate quality of the research that has been done so far on characterization theory, only a fraction of which was discussed briefly earlier, a serious concern remains. It is that a fault line has developed within narrative theory between the study of characterization and the study of the presentation of consciousness. For example, in her excellent study, *Narrative Fiction* (1983), Shlomith Rimmon-Kenan devotes two fine chapters to the subject of characterization and one to speech representation that includes some discussion of thought presentation. However, there is no reference at all in the characterization chapters to thought presentation, apart from a passing reference to the fact that the consciousnesses of Mrs. Dalloway and Molly Bloom are "presented from within" (1983, 42). Equally strikingly, there is no reference at all in her chapter on speech and thought presentation to characterization. This seems strange. Take a sentence such as this: "As usual in these circumstances, he became angry and defensive." This is the sort of statement that recurs continuously in narrative texts and often fulfils a pivotal role in guiding the direction of the narrative. It presents an episode of immediate consciousness (the emotion of anger) within the context of the character's disposition to anger. The disposition in part causes the episode. The episode is a manifestation of the disposition. The event and the state are indissolubly linked. It is by interpreting episodes of consciousness within a context of dispositions that the reader builds up a convincing and coherent sense of character. It is through the central linking concept of dispositions that characterization and thought presentation can be seen as different aspects of the same phenomenon. However, within narrative theory, dispositions belong to the subject area of characterization, and mental events belong to the subject area of thought presentation. The absence of a holistic approach makes a recognition of the whole mind very difficult to achieve.

In 1989 Uri Margolin advanced the view that the theory of character as non-actual individual had, up until that time, been treated as ancillary and as some sort of *post scriptum* to more fundamental theories such as actantial patterns and narrative situations. He suggested, though, that the situation had recently improved due to the formulation of semantic models for fictional worlds and non-actual individuals, as well as the gradual elaboration of cognitive models for the selective representation of information frames for texts. He concluded with a fine flourish by saying that the "task is before us" (1989, 23). I hope that this book can, however imperfectly and incompletely, make a contribution to the response that is still required to Margolin's challenge.

4. Cognitive Science and Frames

It appears that the term *cognitive science* is used in roughly two senses, one narrow and one broad. In the broad sense, the term is used for the study of human cognition. It comprises those aspects of the disciplines of philosophy, psychology, neuroscience, artificial intelligence, linguistics, and, sometimes, anthropology that relate to cognition. The increasing use of the plural term *cognitive sciences* (as in the title of *MITECS*) seems to involve an acknowledgement of this broad usage. The development of this new discipline is often dated to the 1950s and linked to the emergence of Noam Chomsky's theory (1965) that the system of rules underlying our linguistic competence is "hard-wired" into our brains as part of our innate genetic endowment. In the narrow sense, the term refers specifically to the study of the computational theory of the mind; that is, it comprises only those aspects of the disciplines listed earlier that bear on how the neural information processing of brains can be studied in the same way that the information processing of computers can be studied. The brain is treated as though it is a kind of computer, although the extent of the claimed relationship between brains and computers varies from writer to writer. Views also vary on the nature of the relationship between the broad and narrow tendencies.

Broad cognitive science is uncontroversial. Everyone agrees that cognition should be studied and that there is still a good deal that we do not know about it. However, narrow cognitive science is very controversial indeed. Several writers, including John Searle in philosophy and Antonio Damasio in neuroscience, disagree with much of the computational theory of the mind. These and other writers say simply that the brain is not a computer. Or, in a more nuanced objection, they say that we do not learn very much about the brain by studying it as though it were a computer or similar to a computer. It is clear from Damasio's emphasis in *The Feeling of What Happens* (2000) on the importance of consciousness and the emotions that he feels that the brain is too complex and its nature too elusive for the computational theory of the mind to be of much help in describing how it works. Searle is a well-known skeptic, and in *The Rediscovery of the Mind* (1992), he asserts bluntly that there are "brute, blind neurophysiological processes and there is consciousness, but there is nothing else . . . no rule following, no mental information processing, no unconscious inferences, no mental models, no primal sketches, no 2 1/2D images, no three-dimensional descriptions, no language of thought, and no universal grammar" (1992, 228–29). His list of what does *not* take place in the brain is a cognitive-science tool kit. However, it seems to me that, notwithstanding Searle's concerns, broad cognitive science has a lot to offer narrative theory. Readers who are interested in exploring the diverse ways in which the two disciplines can enrich and illuminate each other are recommended to read *Narrative Theory and the Cognitive Sciences* (2003), edited by a pioneer in the field, David Herman. In Herman's very persuasive view, which is also explained in *Story Logic* (2002), narrative theory should be regarded as a branch of cognitive science (2002, 2). Taking the relationship between cognitive science and narrative theory in a related direction, Uri Margolin, in an essay in *Narrative Theory and the Cognitive Sciences* entitled "Cognitive Science, the Thinking Mind, and Literary Narrative," applies some of the conceptual tools of cognitive science in a most illuminating way to such traditional narratological notions as the narrator, the implied author, focalization, and defamiliarization.

I am concerned more specifically in this book with the ways in which cognitive science can add to our understanding of fictional minds. Luckily, I will be skirting around some of the more contentious and controversial issues that are raised by narrow cognitive science and will, instead, be focusing on some of the contributions that can be made to narrative theory by the broad variety. A number of philosophers and others (such as David Lodge in *Consciousness and the Novel*) have deep concerns that the issue of consciousness has become marginalized. For example, Searle wishes to rescue the notion of consciousness from the neglect or even hostility of cognitive science. It is his argument that "[m]ore than anything else, it is the neglect of consciousness that accounts for so much barrenness and sterility in psychology, the philosophy of mind, and cognitive science" (1992, 227). And one senses that cognitive science is chief among the barren and sterile culprits. It is fair to say that the jury is still out on this point. I will refer to Searle's concerns in later chapters, but it seems to me that an interest in cognitive science is not at all incompatible with a recognition of the importance and centrality of fictional consciousness.

Narratologists have made good use of a number of cognitive-science concepts that can help to explain the reading process. In 1986, Thomas Pavel wrote that "[c]ontemporary linguistics has gradually . . . shifted its attention from semiosis—the arbitrary link between meaning and sound—to language universals, innate grammars, and the links to cognitive psychology. This shift has failed to make itself felt in literary theory" (1986, 116). However, although he may have been right at the time of writing, cognitive science has had a substantial impact on literary theory in the years since. Theorists such as David Herman (1997, 2002, and 2003b), Gilles Fauconnier (1997), Mark Turner (1991), and Monika Fludernik (1996) have contributed a good deal to our understanding of the reading process by using the techniques of cognitive science. *Fictional Minds* is an attempt to build on their work by focusing on my specific area of interest. It will do this primarily by concentrating on the concepts of frames, plans, and scripts. In *Scripts, Plans, Goals, and Understanding* (1977), the cognitive scientists Roger Schank and Robert Abelson explain that we use "specific knowledge to interpret and participate in events we have been through many times" (1977, 37) and that "the reader brings a large repertoire of [these] knowledge structures to the understanding task" (1977, 10). They call the knowledge structures *frames*. Another very influential cognitive scientist, Marvin Minsky, according to MITECS, "proposed organizing knowledge into chunks called *frames*. These frames are supposed to capture the essence of concepts or stereotypical situations, for example being in a living room or going out for dinner, by clustering all relevant information for these situations together. This includes information about how to use the frame, information about expectations (which may turn out to be wrong), information about what to do if expectations are not confirmed, and so on" (Nebel 1999, 324). MITECS elaborates on the question of expectations and assumptions as follows: "Frames are knowledge structures that contain fixed structural information. They have slots that accept a range of values; each slot has a default value that is used if no value has been provided from the external world" (Brewer 1999, 729). We assume that a restaurant will serve food at a price unless we are informed otherwise. The default value of the food slot within the restaurant frame is availability for payment. Marie-Laure Ryan's principle of minimal departure is a description in different terms of the default values contained in the frames that we apply to texts. Our assumption that the storyworld will not depart from the real world unless we are told otherwise is a default position.

Other cognitive-science concepts have a number of similarities with frames. For example, *mental models*: "the mind constructs 'small-scale models' of reality to anticipate events, to reason, and to underlie explanation" (Johnson-Laird 1999, 525); *frameworks*: a "framework is an interconnected set of beliefs, notions and predispositions which 'frames our world-view'" (Freeman 1995, 79); and *inner maps*: we "navigate our way through our social and physical world by constructing an inner representation, an inner map of that world, and we plot our course from that inner map and from our representation of where we want to get to" (Sterelny 1999, 451).

Within our cognitive frames, we use scripts and plans to guide our everyday behavior. A script is a stereotypical sequence of events, and a plan is a stereotypical set of ways of reacting to stereotypical situations and events. There is a natural mixture of scripts and plans in day-to-day functioning. Scripts and plans also include the default mechanism that is characteristic of frames. For example, plans "provide the mechanism for understanding events about which there is no specific information" (Schank and Abelson 1977, 97). They do this by allowing us to use default assumptions about what is likely to happen in particular situations in the absence of specific information. It is only when our assumptions are proved wrong that we have to improvise.

It is significant that much of the description of frames, scripts, and plans is functionalist in the sense that the descriptions emphasize the function or purpose of these phenomena. See chapter 4, section 1 for more on the notion of functionalism. In particular, frames et cetera are linked to goals for the future. "Scripts and plans serve as guides for individual acting . . . and become indispensable in the pursuit of complex social activities" (Doležel 1998, 65). "A plan is made up of general information about how actors achieve goals" (Schank and Abelson 1977, 70). Scripts are "organized by goal structures that are used to make sense of the need for them" (Schank and Abelson 1977, 227). Finally and particularly interestingly, Schank and Abelson discuss this issue in terms that make real people sound like characters in novels or, in my terms, that make real minds sound like fictional minds: "In a role theme, a particular actor's goals are determined by his role. . . . Once a role theme is invoked, it sets up expectations about goals and actions" (1977, 132–33).

In chapters 6 and 7 I will explore the ways in which cognitive frames enable readers to comprehend the fictional minds contained in texts. The purpose of the present discussion is simply to indicate in general terms some of the ways in which frames work. My final point here is that cognitive frames explain how readers fill gaps in storyworlds. According to the well-known psycholinguist Steven Pinker, writing in *How the Mind Works* (1997), "the mind reflexively interprets other people's words and gestures by doing whatever it takes to make them sensible and true. If the words are sketchy or incongruous, the mind charitably fills in missing premises or shifts to a new frame of reference in which they make sense. Without this 'principle of relevance,' language itself would be impossible. The thoughts behind even the simplest sentence are so labyrinthine that if we ever expressed them in full, our speech would sound like the convoluted verbiage of a legal document" (1997, 552). You will notice that Pinker talks of the real-world gaps in our knowledge of other minds. He asks, What is the nature of the purported mental functioning that will make sense of other people's gestures? And he also asks of language specifically, What is the nature of the purported mental functioning that will make sense of other people's words? These questions apply equally well to fictional minds.

5. Focalization

Narratologists have developed and made much more systematic, rigorous, and comprehensive the concept that was once known as *point of view*, and have given it the name of *focalization*. Since the term was first introduced by Gerard Genette (1980), it has undergone a series of substantial adjustments suggested by such theorists as Mieke Bal (1997), Shlomith Rimmon-Kenan (1983), Patrick O'Neill (1994), and Manfred Jahn (1999c). David Herman has, for example, introduced a helpful new category entitled *hypothetical focalization* (2002, 310). This continual process of change has been accompanied by an undercurrent of skepticism from theorists such as Monika Fludernik, who thinks that focalization is a category "whose precise definition has . . . never been agreed upon and is still open to remapping" (1996, 344). "On account of these inconsistencies," she feels, "it may be well to scrap the concept of focalization in its traditional configurations" (1996, 346).

In summary, focalization is the perspective, angle of vision, or point of view from which events are related. In Genette's famous formulation, it must be distinguished from the act of narration in the following way: When you read a discourse and ask "Who speaks?" or "Who narrates?," you are concerned with narration. When you ask "Who sees?" or "Who thinks?" then you are concerned with focalization. Sometimes an agent sees and speaks at the same time, and sometimes the agent who sees is different from the agent who speaks. Various typologies of focalization have been created, but perhaps the best known is Genette's original model: *zero focalization* occurs in the traditional novel of the omniscient narrator where the events are not focalized through a single character but are clearly focalized through the narrator; *internal focalization* occurs when the events are, in general, focalized through a single character or characters in turn; and *external focalization* occurs when descriptions are limited to characters' external behavior (in what is called behaviorist narrative) (1980, 189–90). It is clear that the concept of focalization is crucially relevant to the study of fictional minds because it is concerned with the decisions that readers make about which consciousness is being presented in the text at any one time.

The concept of focalization has a good deal of potential as one tool among others for the examination of the presentation of fictional minds. In particular, focalization is an opportunity to explore in detail the precise methods by which a narrator uses a character's consciousness as the perceptual viewpoint or angle from which the narration takes place. Within the speech category approach, this technique is called *free indirect perception*. Take this example: "He sat on the bench. The train pulled away." At first glance, the second sentence looks as if it is as much a simple physical description as the first sentence. However, it can also be read as the character's perception of the physical event and, even more importantly, by extension, the character's experience of the psychological implications of the event. As I said in section 1 of this chapter, physical events should be considered as character experiences. The context may show that he was waiting for the person he loves who was not on the train. Free indirect perception involves the recovery of those parts of the discourse that initially appear to be pure narratorial report but that, on reflection, can be read as descriptions of events or states in the storyworld as experienced by a particular fictional mind. A free indirect perception reading takes responsibility for subjectivity away from the narrator, where it initially appears to be, and gives it to a character. Internal focalization readings can naturalize as a character's perception a good deal of discourse that appears at first sight to be pure narratorial description. By this means, the whole consciousnesses of characters can be expanded to include descriptions of aspects of the storyworld that are seen from their perceptual, cognitive, and evaluative point of view. This interface between characters and their storyworld is a highly informative way to link the internal consciousnesses of characters to their external social and physical context.

However, I think that there are some problems with the concept of focalization. For example, it was envisaged primarily for, and works very well for, one aspect of mental functioning—perception. It is noticeable that theorists of focalization are much more comfortable talking about perception than about other areas of mental life, and most of the examples used in explanations of focalization are of perception. However, the notion works much less well for the other aspects of consciousness that are described in chapter 4. When other types of thinking such as cognition or the emotions are discussed, the conceptual framework can become rather cumbersome, uninformative, and even misleading. For example, when thought presentation occurs, the character who is having the thoughts is both the focalizer and the focalized object. Within Bal's scheme, in first-person novels the introspecting character has three functions: as the narrator, as the internal focalizer (1997, 148), and as what she calls the *non-perceptible focalized object* (1997, 153). In the case of third-person narration, the narrator has at least one function: as external narrator. The character has at least one function: the non-perceptible focalized object. Opinion is divided on who has the external focalizer function.

In the case of "I felt happy" (first-person narration), this means that there is a lot of conceptual apparatus to explain a very simple sentence. There are three elements: the "I" who is reporting the feeling; the "I" who is having the feeling; and the "I" who is introspectively aware of the existence of the feeling. Intuitively, one feels that only two and not three elements are needed: the "I" who is reporting the feeling and the "I" who is both having the feeling and is aware of the feeling. Searle has convincingly demonstrated that introspection cannot be understood in terms of one entity doing the introspecting and another entity experiencing the object of the introspection. The "I" who is feeling happy cannot be separated from the same "I" who is introspectively aware of the feeling of happiness. In Searle's terms, such a view of the faculty of introspection "requires a distinction between the object spected [sic] and the specting [sic] of it, and we cannot make this distinction for conscious states" (1992, 144). To relate Searle's point to the language of focalization, the distinction between the internal focalizer and the non-perceptible focalized object is a false one.

In the case of "He felt happy" (third-person narration), as I said, there appears to be some confusion over who is the focalizer. Rimmon-Kenan says firmly that it is the external narrator-focalizer. However, other theorists argue that the narrative is focalized here from the point of view of the character. The difference is, I think, a result of the varying levels of fluidity in the concept. The first approach is to regard focalization as a feature that is fairly fixed and constant throughout the whole length of a text: then the focalizer in the case of "He felt happy" is considered to be the external narrator-focalizer. (An exception is the reflector novel, where the focalization is considered to be fixed with the reflector character for the length of the novel.) The second approach is to use the concept in a very flexible and fluid way: the identity of the focalizer often then changes from sentence to sentence. O'Neill uses the concept in this way. Take this example: "He felt happy and she felt happy too." Within the first approach, the focalizer is the external narrator-focalizer. Within the second approach, there are two focalizers: the internal character-focalizer "he" for the first part of the sentence; and the internal character-focalizer "she" for the second part of the sentence. This confusion over such a basic element in the conceptual framework seems to me to be unsatisfactory.

A further concern is that focalization is defined in terms of the distinction between the agent who speaks and the agent who sees. But is this distinction workable? How is it possible just to speak, as opposed to seeing then speaking? Surely speaking involves seeing what it is that you wish to speak about? It seems to me that the question "Who speaks?" should really be reformulated in part, and in the case of third-person texts, as "Who is the narrative agent who sees that a character agent sees?" That is, it may be the character who sees, but it is the narrator who sees that the character sees. It is only then that the narrator is able to speak. This issue arises in particular with the mode of thought report. This mode is usually described as character focalization, but in practice, it is often clear that it is the narrator who sees that the character is seeing (or not seeing). Narrators often report mental processes that a character is not aware of, or only dimly aware of. This point is an example of the fact that the concept of focalization can sometimes conceal a good deal of the complexity of narrative. The labeling can often be uninformative or even misleading. The statement, "the narration is focalized through character x," covers a very wide range of cases. At one end of the scale is the case where the narration follows a character around so that there are no scenes in which x does not appear; x is the perceptual viewpoint from which the narration takes place, but there is little information about the workings of x's mind. At the other end of the scale is the case where the reader is given a full and detailed analysis of every aspect of x's mental functioning, including not just perception but also cognition, dispositions, and so on. And, of course, there is an infinite number of gradations along this scale. What is needed, therefore, is a typology that distinguishes between cases in a much more sensitive and discriminating way than the conceptual framework does at present.

Focalization can be rewardingly reconsidered within the context of fictional minds. A good example is contained in Mieke Bal's famous story of the laughing mice (1997, 144–46). Bal describes a large bas-relief in India in which mice are shown laughing at a cat in a yoga position. She explains that it can only be understood once the narrative is focalized through the mice and the viewer realizes that they are laughing because they know that the cat will not now chase them. However, this point can also be made in terms of fictional minds. The viewer thinks that the mice think that the cat thinks and so the mice think . . . and so on. Most narrative theorists (although not, for example, Gerald Prince) accept that the concept of focalization applies to the discourse: the same story can be presented in different discourses from different points of view. However, what I will do in later chapters is to explore the wider concept of aspectuality (used in the philosophical and not the grammatical sense) as it applies to the storyworld. Mieke Bal explains that "whenever events are presented, they are always presented from within a certain vision" (1997, 142). Bal develops this insight into the discourse within the conceptual framework of focalization. My rather different point is that, whenever events occur in the storyworld, they are always experienced from within a certain vision. I will call this feature of the storyworld *aspectuality*, and I will take it in the various directions indicated by later chapters.

Conclusion

A recurring theme throughout this chapter has been that, although the approaches discussed earlier all have their own individual strengths, their value would be even greater if it was explicitly recognized that they were concerned with fictional minds. I will take three examples at random: Acknowledgements of the importance of causal connections between events in definitions of narrative become even more valuable when it is recognized that these causal connections relate to the workings of fictional minds. Also, the inferences and hypotheses to which reader response theorists give quite justified importance involve, in the main, readers' analyses and judgments of characters' thought processes. Finally, many of the cognitive frames that we use to enable comprehension of texts to take place are concerned with fictional mental functioning. The narratological approaches described in this chapter do not, taken together with the speech category approach described in the next chapter, form a coherent and complete perspective on fictional minds. However, they will make invaluable contributions toward one because they can all be integrated into the framework described in the later stages of this study.

3

The Speech Categories

1. Summary

Because the speech category approach of classical narratology is based on the assumption that the categories that are applied to fictional speech can be unproblematically applied to fictional thought, it is concerned primarily with the part of the mind known as *inner speech*, the highly verbalized flow of self-conscious thought. For this reason, it does not do justice to the complexity of the types of evidence for the workings of fictional minds that are available in narrative discourse; it pays little attention to states of mind such as beliefs, intentions, purposes, and dispositions; and it does not analyze the whole of the social mind in action. The purpose of this chapter is to show how narratological approaches to consciousness have been distorted by the grip of the verbal norm. Chapters 4 to 7 will be concerned with the areas of the mind that have been given insufficient attention within the speech category approach. They will adopt a functional and teleological perspective on those areas and will not simply try to find a taxonomic equivalent to the speech categories. The mind that is studied in this alternative way is not passive, but active; it is not isolated in individuals, but is social and contextual; it is not simply the object of discourse, but is the agent of action. Typical paragraphs of fictional texts tend to be made up of densely woven fragments of a wide variety of different modes. They are not streams of direct thought with interruptions, or flows of free indirect thought with intrusions. Quite simply, they are typically complex in their portrayal of the fictional mind acting in the context of other minds because fictional thought and real thought are like that. Fictional life and real life are like that. Most of our lives are not spent in thoughtful self-communings. Narrators know this, but narratology has not yet developed a vocabulary for studying the relationships between fictional minds and the social situations within which they function.

This chapter has been written with reluctance. Sections 2 and 3 are necessarily rather negative and occasionally rather exasperated in tone, and so, if you are willing to take my word for it that the distortions that I have referred to have occurred, you might wish to skip these middle sections and go straight to section 4 and the more positive chapters that follow.

One difficulty in discussing the speech category account is that there is a wide range of models to choose from. They go from two speech categories, to the standard number of three, to Brian McHale's widely adopted seven-level model as contained in his influential article "Free Indirect Discourse: A Survey of Recent Accounts" (1978, 258–60), and even to Monika Fludernik's particularly elaborate construct, which, in total, contains no fewer than thirty elements (1993, 311). Another problem, often referred to at this stage in the discussion, is that each category has several different names. Like Dorrit Cohn, I think that there are three fundamental categories to which, unlike her, I have given very simple names: direct thought, thought report, and free indirect thought. For reasons that should be clear by now, it is vital to use names for the thought categories that separate them from speech. I described the three categories briefly in chapter 1, section 2, but I will now discuss them again in more detail.

Direct thought is the narrative convention that allows the narrator to present a verbal transcription that passes as the reproduction of the actual thoughts of a character (for example, "She thought, Where am I?"). It became conventionalized in the formal, mannered, and stylized soliloquy of the eighteenth- and early nineteenth-century novel. Eventually it developed into free direct thought, in which quotation marks and tags (such as "she thought") are not used, during the early part of the last century with modernist writers such as James Joyce and Virginia Woolf. Direct thought is also known as *quoted monologue* and *private speech* (and also *interior monologue* and *stream of consciousness*, though remember the caveats in chapter 1, section 4).

Thought report is the equivalent of indirect speech, in which narrators present characters' thoughts in the narrative (for example, "She wondered where she was."). It is the most flexible category and can be used for a number of purposes, some of which are listed in section 4. One important feature is that it can present thought as mental action (for example, "She decided to walk."). This mode is also known as *psychonarration, internal analysis, narratorial analysis, omniscient description, submerged speech*, and *narratized speech*.

Free indirect thought is, to put it simply, a combination of the other two categories. It combines the subjectivity and language of the character, as in direct thought, with the presentation of the narrator, as in thought report. For example, "She stopped. Where the hell was she?" The second sentence can be read as free indirect thought because it presents the subjectivity of the character (the narrator knows where she is) and the language of the character ("Where the hell"), but in the third person ("she") and past tense ("was") of the narrator's discourse. *Free indirect discourse* (that is, referring to both speech and thought) is also known as *free indirect style, le style indirect libre, erlebte Rede, narrated monologue, substitutionary speech, represented speech and thought, dual voice, narrated speech, immediate speech, simple indirect thought,* and *narrated thought.* The length of the list of names shows the extent of the hold that this subtle, exciting, and flexible technique has exercised over the discipline of narratology.

McHale's seven-point scale, which has been adopted by Shlomith Rimmon-Kenan among several others, can be collapsed into the three-mode model in the following way:

Diegetic summary   > thought report
Less purely diegetic summary >
Indirect content-paraphrase   >
Indirect discourse   >

Free indirect discourse   > free indirect thought

Direct discourse   > direct thought
Free direct discourse   >

With regard to direct thought, I have combined direct discourse and free direct discourse because it is not important for my purposes whether or not direct thought is tagged. Many narratologists make a sharp distinction between the two types. However, I agree with Dorrit Cohn that the distinction that is made between the rhetorical, rational, deliberate soliloquy and the associative, illogical, spontaneous free direct thought unhelpfully obscures the two key factors that they have in common: the reference to the thinking self in the first person and the reference to the narrated moment in the present tense (Cohn 1978, 12–13).

With regard to thought report, I have combined the four points on the scale into one mode because the differences between the four points are not relevant to my argument, and in any event, they can be very difficult to tell apart. For example, the linguists Geoffrey Leech and Michael Short illustrate in *Style in Fiction* (1981) their subdivision of thought report into *indirect thought* and *narrative report of a thought act* with these examples: "He wondered if she still loved him" (indirect thought); and "He wondered about her love for him" (narrative report of a thought act) (1981, 337). Although it is dangerous to be too dogmatic about other readers' perceptions, I wonder whether some people would find this a fine distinction, and possibly a little too flimsy for the taxonomic weight that is resting on it.

The precise nature of free indirect discourse has been the subject of a lengthy, technical, and fiercely contested narratological debate for a number of years. Although it is a swamp that I had originally intended to avoid completely, I will—on reflection and probably against my better judgment—make one small intervention. I said earlier that free indirect thought combines the subjectivity and the language of the character with the discourse of the narrator. If neither the character's subjectivity nor the character's language is present, then it is clearly thought report. But what do we do if only one or the other is present? My suggestion is this: if the character's subjectivity is present but not the character's language, then the passage should be regarded as free indirect thought. For example, "She stopped. Where was she?" If the character's language is present but not the subjectivity, it should be regarded as *colored thought report*. For example, "She wondered where the hell she was." In this case, the narrator's language has been colored by the idiom of the character, but it is still thought report because it is still the narrator's subjectivity. I mention this point because, when I read initial definitions and subsequent explanations of free indirect discourse, I am often not clear whether the writer has subjectivity or language in mind.

The relationship between the three modes of thought presentation and the areas of the mind presented by them can be put in the following, very simple terms: *direct thought* can be used only for inner speech; *free indirect thought* is equally suitable for inner speech but in addition, according to some theorists but not others, can have an ambiguous, hypothetical quality that makes it suitable for the presentation of some other areas of the mind; and *thought report* is suitable for presenting all areas of the mind, including inner speech.

It is also worth explaining at this point the type of thought report known as *narratized speech*. Prince defines it as a "type of discourse whereby a character's utterances or verbal thoughts are represented, in words that are the narrator's, as acts among other acts; a discourse about words uttered (or thoughts) equivalent to a discourse not about words" (1987, 64). Genette describes it by saying that the narrator can condense verbal thoughts into mental events in "a narrative of thoughts," or "narratized inner speech" (1980, 171). This concept usefully describes one, but only one, of the many uses of the versatile technique of thought report: in this case, its ability to summarize inner speech and present it as mental action. Narratized speech can be an invaluable element in the discourse. For example, "He thought, 'I will lift the wheel.'" can seem rather clumsy unless there are particular reasons for that formulation. The alternative, in narratized speech, is "He decided to lift the wheel." This is sharper and will perhaps more often fit the needs of the narrative. However, there is a danger inherent in the concept of narratized speech. If one accepts the view that thought is indeed speech, then it must logically follow that all thought report is narratized speech and that this is its only function. However, there is very often no evidence in the narrative for the reader to suppose that examples of thought report are narratized speech. The second example was used as an illustration of inner speech, but it is unlikely that a reader would read it as such, because it is generally not important whether or not this mental event involved inner speech. It is more interesting to classify it as a decision and therefore as an example of mental functioning or mental action in a social and physical context.

2. The Prosecution
It seems to me that there are at least five problems with the use of the speech categories to analyze presentations of fictional thought.

1. *The privileging of the apparently mimetic and rather glamorous categories of free indirect thought and direct thought over the diegetic and seemingly uninteresting category of thought report.*
A good deal of brilliant, imaginative, and subtle work has been done on free indirect thought and direct thought but very little has been done on thought report. Only Dorrit Cohn in her seminal and still exciting study *Transparent Minds* gives equal weight to thought report despite the fact that it is the most significant mode in terms of amount of use. The words that narratologists tend to use about the role of the narrator and therefore about thought report are negative ones such as narratorial "interruption," "intrusion," "interference," and "distortion." Instances of thought report are regularly simply mistaken for free indirect thought. Passages of narrative that are labeled interior monologue or stream of consciousness often contain a good deal of thought report that is simply not generally recognized by theorists.

2. *The overestimation of the verbal component in thought.*
The favored categories of direct thought and free indirect thought tend to show only that part of a character's mind that is the highly verbalized and self-conscious flow of consciousness known as inner speech. So, inner speech becomes the paradigm of the mind, even though it is only a very small part of the total activity of fictional minds. Perception is the only other part of the mind that has been analyzed in any detail. The mind is seen in metaphorical terms primarily as a stream or flow of self-conscious mental events. But this

metaphor is too linear and one-dimensional. The mind is a three-dimensional container. Better still, given the existence of latent states that exist over time, it is actually four-dimensional.

3. *The resulting neglect of the thought report of characters' states of mind.*
Many of the episodes of current consciousness that occur in characters' minds are not inner speech. Consider, "He suddenly felt depressed." Examples of such mental phenomena include mood, desires, emotions, sensations, visual images, attention, and memory. Characters' minds also contain latent mental states. The truth or falsehood of general statements about these states is independent of the person's feelings at the time that the statements are made. Consider, "He is prone to depression." That statement can be true even if the person is happy at the time when it is made. Examples of such states include dispositions, beliefs, attitudes, judgments, skills, knowledge, imagination, intellect, volition, character traits, and habits of thought. Such causal phenomena as intentions, purposes, motives, and reasons for action can be either immediate mental events or latent states, depending on whether or not they are present in consciousness at any particular moment. I hope that these long lists give an indication of the vast areas of the mind that are not suitable for analysis under the speech category approach. Presenting these various phenomena is a large part of the role of the narrators of novels, but it has received very little attention within the speech category account because of the first two problems. A consequence is that narratorial references to latent states of mind such as dispositions and beliefs are usually discussed under the entirely separate heading of characterization. It is an important part of my argument to question this entirely artificial distinction. Characterization and consciousness should be brought together under the wider heading of *mind*.

4. *The privileging of some novels over others, and some scenes in novels over others.*
I referred at the start to Dorrit Cohn's "predilection for novels with thoughtful characters and scenes of self-communion" (1978, v) and for "moments of lonely self-communion minutely tracing spiritual and emotional conflicts" (1999, 84). If you were to rely on classical narratology's speech categories for your picture of fictional minds in English literature, you might find that it consisted to a surprisingly large extent of thoughtful characters in scenes of lonely self-communion. For example, eighteenth-century novels, Dickens, Thackeray, Hardy, and the formal conservatives of the twentieth century such as Graham Greene and Evelyn Waugh are underrepresented because they are not entirely suitable for speech category analysis, although they respond well to the approach that is described in the following chapters. Fludernik's argument that Aphra Behn has

a crucial role in the development of what she calls the *consciousness novel* (1996, 168–72) is a welcome exception. The way that narrators of Dickens's novels construct characters' minds is different from, say, the narrators of Jane Austen and George Eliot because the former use more surface behavior, gaps, and indeterminacies and less direct access. Therefore, different demands are made upon the reader.

5. *The tendency to give the impression that characters' minds really only consist of a private passive flow of consciousness.* (The final problem is perhaps the most important one.)
What is missing is an explicit recognition that much of the thought that takes place in novels is the purposeful, engaged, social interaction that is discussed in later chapters.

Monika Fludernik uses the following passage from *Tom Jones* to illustrate the use of thought report for what she describes as "general and distant descriptions of consciousness" (1993, 297). It describes Captain Blifil's plans for the future: "These Meditations were entirely employed on Mr. *Allworthy*'s Fortune; for, first, he exercised much Thought in calculating, as well as he could, the exact Value of the Whole; which calculations he often saw Occasion to alter in his own Favour: And secondly, and chiefly, he pleased himself with intended Alterations in the House and Gardens, and in projecting many other Schemes, as well for the Improvement of the Estate as of the Grandeur of the Place" (1995, 72, quoted in 1993, 297). Her comment on this passage can be related to the five problems with the speech category approach as follows:

1. The passage will seem "general and distant" if the paradigms for the presentation of thought are the modes of direct thought and free indirect thought.
2. Equally, it seems "general and distant" if the paradigm for thought is inner speech.
3. The comment does not take into account the riches to be discovered in the analyses of states of mind in the mode of thought report (see section 4 of this chapter).
4. Eighteenth-century novels such as *Tom Jones* do not benefit from speech category analysis in the way that later novels do.
5. When the passage is seen as a description of active mental functioning rather than as a summary of a private and passive flow of consciousness, it becomes the opposite of "general and distant."

Narrative theorists might say of the five problems, "But I don't think these things!" I am not saying that they do. My point is that, although narratologists

[handwritten marginal note:] characters's minds aren't just privately constructed — v. much publically constructed

might agree with my arguments if asked, the theory as written does not take sufficient account of them. Analyses of particular passages of free indirect thought or direct thought will necessarily reveal the social context of the thought under discussion. But I am saying that the relationship between the thought and the context is not explicitly theorized. Obviously no narratologist thinks that reading Jane Austen or George Eliot is the same as reading Virginia Woolf or James Joyce. However, is it too far-fetched to suppose that, because of the emphasis in the theoretical literature, a reader of speech category narratology who had not previously read any of these novels might be surprised to find that neither *Emma* nor *Middlemarch* was a Woolfian or Joycean stream of consciousness? Equally, no narratologist believes that *Ulysses* consists entirely of passages of stream of consciousness or interior monologue. However, a reader of speech category narratology who had not previously read the book would, I think, have difficulty recognizing it, particularly the latter two-thirds of it, from the theoretical descriptions. The chief characteristic of the book as a whole is the increasing prevalence of more and more outlandish and bizarre narratorial voices, but who would guess it from the theory?

The rest of this section is devoted to the first and second problems, starting with the first. Once those parts of the mind that are most verbal have been privileged over those that are least, then it follows that the speech categories that are most suited to the apparently mimetic representation of inner speech will be privileged over the category thought report that is most suitable for the presentation of all the other areas of the mind. For example, Derek Bickerton talks of the "supersession" of thought report by free indirect thought (1967, 236). Some theorists of free indirect thought such as Roy Pascal (1977) and Louise Flavin (1987) do not even mention the existence of thought report. Others use terms such as *narratorial description* and do not make it clear whether they mean surface description of the physical storyworld or thought report. Paul Hernadi argues that the signs of authorial narration in the mode of thought report are "arbitrary" in a way that the other two modes are not. The consequence, according to his revealingly hostile description of thought report, is that it treats mental events as though they are altogether non-verbal. For this reason, according to Hernadi, there is a "static, often lifeless quality" in much thought report (1972, 39). There are at least three problems here. First, thought report is able to describe inner speech in non-verbal terms when the technique of narratized speech is used, but this is not the same as treating inner speech as though it is non-verbal in origin. Secondly, some mental events *are* altogether non-verbal. Thought is a continuum, and thought report is flexible enough to present all the different varieties of it in a large number of different ways that are suitable to the needs of particular narratives. Finally, the result is static and lifeless only if it is done badly; it is full of movement and life if it is done well. Hernadi also suggests that by using free indirect thought the narrator "avoids" rendering thought from an external perspective and analytical distance (1972, 39). Why should this be a technique to be avoided? It is part of the function of the narrator to analyze psychic life and very often it is most appropriate for the narrator to do this by rendering thought from an external perspective and with analytical distance. These practices are not necessarily to be avoided.

While emphasizing that free indirect discourse is not unique to literature, Brian McHale suggests that it is "distinctively literary . . . because the essential character of literature itself is inscribed in miniature within it" (1978, 284). Michael McKeon, who lavishes similar praise on free indirect discourse in his *Theory of the Novel* (2000), refers to its "strictly 'literary' character" (2000, 486) and describes it as "an exclusively 'literary' style" (2000, 485) despite the large body of evidence to the contrary that is contained in Fludernik's *The Fictions of Languages and the Languages of Fiction*. As someone who uses free indirect discourse regularly in my (decidedly non-literary) work, I am able to say from personal experience that McKeon is mistaken. I labor the point only to stress that the high regard in which free indirect discourse is held can lead theorists into inaccuracy.

Much thought has been given to the gray area between free indirect thought and thought report. This debate arises because it is sometimes not clear whether the subjectivity being expressed in a particular passage is the character's or the narrator's. However, as far as I know, the issue is only ever discussed in terms of whether or not the passage is free indirect thought, not whether or not it is thought report. Interest is lost if it is established that it is not free indirect thought. No one ever refers to the delicious uncertainty and ambiguity of thought report in the same terms as free indirect thought. But why not? If free indirect thought tends to be fascinating and subtle and thought report is potentially static and lifeless, why can they be so difficult to tell apart? Of course, labels are just means to ends, and in itself, it is of little significance whether a particular passage is labeled in one way or another. In a sense, there may be no right or wrong about these decisions. Readers read discourses in different ways, and this is particularly true of a discursive phenomenon such as free indirect thought that is so dependent on the interpretive decisions of readers. However, it does become a problem when theoretical decisions are taken that contain a bias that impoverishes our understanding of the richness, subtlety, and variety of the various means by which characters' consciousnesses are presented to readers.

One result of the category bias is that the concept of free indirect thought grows and grows and is then applied inappropriately. Fludernik has rigorously analyzed one example (1993, 81–82). Manfred Jahn has discussed another. He says this about a study by Susan Ehrlich (1990) (I will use my own terms for the three categories in order to avoid confusion): "To make matters worse, [free indirect thought] is further extended by Ehrlich to cover even direct thought and indirect thought. . . . One of the immediate effects of Ehrlich's now seriously overextended [free indirect thought] is that, cuckoo-like, it has crowded out all its siblings. . . . But, it may be asked, is it not exactly Woolf's conscious modulation, her orchestration of *all* of the techniques, that produces the remarkable depth-effects and rhythmic quality of her novels? Extended [free indirect thought] not only provides no answer; the question itself is pointless if almost everything is [free indirect thought]" (1992, 360). Quite.

Discussions about the relative frequency of the three modes will have only a limited value until careful empirical studies are done that use precise and universally agreed criteria for the modes (for example, see Short, Semino, and Culpeper 1996). Nevertheless, it is still worth making one or two general points while we await the empirical evidence. Fludernik's perspective on the issue is that, in the representation of consciousness, "direct discourse is the least common technique (except in the interior monologue of the twentieth-century novel), with a traditional preponderance of [thought report] and, in second place, free indirect discourse, which comes close to competing with [thought report] in late-nineteenth- and early-twentieth-century fiction" (1993, 291). I agree with her view that thought report is the most common mode, but I would dispute the weight that she gives to interior monologue. In my experience, what is called interior monologue often contains as much thought report as the other two modes, as well a good deal of narratorial surface description of physical context. I would also dispute the weighting given to free indirect thought and would suggest that it can only be arrived at by classifying a good deal of colored thought report as free indirect thought. As I said, though, this can only be a very impressionistic discussion at this stage.

Following is a brief indication of the amount of attention that has been given to the three modes and to focalization in a random (honestly!) selection of classic narratological articles and full-length studies. This sort of approach is very crude, but it does give a fairly accurate indication of where the interest lies.

Free indirect discourse with a bias toward speech: Banfield 1982, Dillon and Kirchhoff 1976, Flavin 1987, Fludernik 1993, Hernadi 1972, McHale 1978, McHale 1983, Neumann 1986, Pascal 1977, Ron 1981, Weinberg 1984 (total: 11).

Free indirect thought: Bickerton 1967, Brinton 1980, Dry 1977 (total: 3).

Direct thought: Friedman 1955 (total: 1).

Narratology survey with direct thought bias: Chatman 1978 (total: 1).

Narratology survey with no bias: Cohn 1978, Fludernik 1996, McHale 1981 (total: 3).

Narratology survey with focalization bias: Bal 1997, Genette 1980, Genette 1988, O'Neill 1994, Prince 1982 (total: 5).

Thought report: none.

Narratology survey with thought report bias: none.

What this list shows is that there is, so far as I am aware, no book or article that is devoted specifically to thought report, and no survey of narratology that is biased toward thought report. Cohn is the only narratologist who is scrupulous in giving equal weight to all modes. In *Transparent Minds*, each mode is given a separate chapter. The chapter on thought report is first and is of the same length as the others.

Here are the results of another survey. I have identified ninety-five separate episodes of direct access to the thoughts of characters in chapter 29 of Thackeray's *Vanity Fair* and have classified them as follows: direct thought—1; free indirect thought—4; thought report—90. It is easy to see why there are few analyses of the presentation of the mind in *Vanity Fair* in the current narratological literature. If the response to this point is, "Well, the presentations of fictional minds in *Vanity Fair* are not that interesting," my response is, "How do we know?"

Concerning the second problem, there are numerous examples within narratology of the assumption that thought can be treated simply as internal speech. For example, the narrative theorist Seymour Chatman claims in *Story and Discourse* (1978) that the "most obvious and direct means of handling the thoughts of a character is to treat them as 'unspoken speech'" (1978, 182). Genette asserts that the "novelistic convention, perhaps truthful in this case, is that thoughts and feelings are no different from speech" (1980, 171). Genette also declares that "'Thought' is indeed speech" (1980, 178), adding, somewhat obscurely, "but at the same time this speech, 'oblique' and deceitful like all the others, is generally unfaithful to the 'felt truth'—the felt truth which no inner monologue can reveal and which the novelist must ultimately show glimpses of through the conceal-ments of bad faith, which are 'consciousness' itself" (1980, 178). Uri Margolin writes that "*[m]ental acts* share many features with verbal ones, especially in narrative, where they must unexceptionally be verbalized in the form of inner speech" (1986, 215). Margolin also refers to thought a number of times as "inner verbalization" (for example, 2000, 592) and as "subvocal" (for example, 1986, 218). Mieke Bal draws out a very important implication when she maintains that "[u]nspoken words—thoughts, interior monologues—no matter how ex-tensive, are not perceptible to other characters" (1997, 153). This statement shows very clearly how the verbal bias works against an understanding of the social and publicly accessible nature of thought. Remember how, in the scene from *Friends*, Rachel's thoughts *were* perceptible to Phoebe and the others?

With regard to the two statements from Genette that are quoted in the preceding paragraph and that are taken from *Narrative Discourse* (1980), he concedes in his later *Narrative Discourse Revisited* (1988), that "Cohn legitimately insists on making a place for the nonverbal forms of consciousness, and I was certainly wrong to classify as 'narratized inner *speech*' a statement such as 'I decided to marry Albertine,' which is by no means necessarily tied to a verbalized thought" (1988, 60). This is good. But he then comprehensively loses any ground that he might have gained by saying the following, which illustrates the grip of the verbal norm even better than any restatement of the original view could have done: "Dorrit Cohn's justifiable reservation about a possible nonverbalized consciousness holds good only *partly* for *one* of her three categories. Let us arbitrarily figure this part at 1/2: Cohn's reservation holds good for 1/6 of her own system" (1988, 61). He is making two points here, both of which are justified. It is the conclusion that he draws from them that is so revealingly mistaken. First, he is saying that direct thought and free indirect thought are necessarily tied to inner speech (though many theorists disagree with him about the latter), and so it is only with thought report that the issue of non-verbal thought arises. Second, the concept of narratized speech means that some of the thought presented in the mode of thought report could have been of verbal origin. He then arbitrarily suggests that this narratized speech might account for half of all thought report, and so the objection only applies to half of one-third of Cohn's system. To establish precisely how specious this argument is, it is best to approach the point from completely the opposite direction. I have emphasized throughout this discussion that there are vast areas of the mind that are not addressed within the speech category approach. As it is these areas that we are talking about here, from my perspective the problem looks much larger than one that affects just one-sixth of the whole. Reversing the proportions and saying that Cohn's reservations hold good for five-sixths of the fictional mind might be nearer the mark.

The verbal bias is clear when we look at some of the terms used by narrative theorists. The title of Shlomith Rimmon-Kenan's chapter on the subject is "Narration: Speech Representation," and within it, she never explicitly addresses the question of thought presentation as opposed to speech presentation at all. Roy Pascal uses the phrase *free indirect speech* throughout his book to refer to thought as well as speech. Another narrative theorist, Helmut Bonheim, explains the thinking behind this policy by saying that the "narrative mode *speech*, then, includes not only speech in the narrower sense of words supposedly spoken aloud but also a variety of ways in which thoughts and perceptions can be conveyed" (1982, 51). However, he also concedes that, since a particular character under discussion "is not supposed to be speaking . . . all the terms for [free indirect thought] which suggest speech are a little misleading" (Bonheim 1982, 53). Manfred Jahn has drawn our attention to a curious aspect of Ann Banfield's term for free indirect discourse, *represented speech and thought*: "Nothing, strictly speaking, is ever a representation of speech *and* thought. Thought, as opposed to speech, is non-discursive, private, non-communicative, non-pragmatic and semi-verbal, to list just a few differential properties" (1992, 350). Banfield's term is especially surprising because she is emphatic that she does not equate thought with inner speech. (Thought is "not linguistic in form" [Banfield 1982, 80].) As Jahn points out, for Banfield, "the assumption of 'inner speech' is a fallacy" (1983, 5). But if Banfield thinks that thought is never verbal, why does she yoke thought and speech together in the same term? I am not aware that she ever separates them out, sometimes as *represented speech* and at other times as *represented thought*. It might be thought that I would agree with Banfield about thought not being "linguistic," given the direction of my argument, but this is not the case. In my view, the position is very simple: sometimes thought is highly verbalized and can accurately be described as inner speech; sometimes it is not and so cannot. Banfield's dogmatic antiverbal approach is just as mistaken as the equally inflexible proverbal views discussed earlier.

As I said at the end of section 1, when texts are analyzed, the extent of the verbality of a character's supposed thought event is not only often unclear, it is usually not relevant. For example, "She felt excited." The temptation to regard the putative verbality of fictional thoughts as spots of indeterminacy (remember the discussion on gaps in the storyworld section in chapter 2?) should usually be resisted. In most cases, an attempt to close this particular gap is not necessary.

The reader does not need to speculate on the verbality of a fictional mental event such as "She felt excited." It is much more informative to analyze the thought in terms of motives and intentions, behavior and action. By contrast with such discussions, speculations on the verbality of putative mental events are rather sterile and scholastic. An extended example may be of value here. Derek Bickerton argues in his article "Modes of Interior Monologue: A Formal Definition" that the methods used to present inner speech are comparable to the methods used to present ordinary speech (1967, 232). In the case of direct thought, the link is obvious, as the use of direct thought in the example "He thought, 'I will lift the wheel'" is the exact grammatical equivalent of direct speech, as in "He said, 'I will lift the wheel.'" However, Bickerton goes further and maintains that thought report "is inner speech rendered in indirect speech" (1967, 238). There are two objections to this argument: One is that his reference to inner speech ignores the other areas of the mind. The other is that thought report only sometimes resembles the grammatical form of indirect speech. In the example "He thought that he would lift the wheel," the thought report does indeed resemble indirect speech, as in "He said that he would lift the wheel." However, in "He decided to lift the wheel," the grammatical form of the thought report bears no resemblance to indirect speech. It looks more like a report of a physical action, such as "He lifted the wheel" because "He decided to lift the wheel" is the thought report of mental functioning or mental action, not of inner speech. It is therefore not true that thought can only be represented by one of the methods for rendering spoken speech.

In the first paragraph of his article, Bickerton refers to the need for novelists to convey characters' inner lives. However, by his second paragraph, this need has become solely identified with the use of interior monologue (1967, 229). Bickerton uses a passage from George Eliot's *Middlemarch*, a summary of Lydgate's inner life, to conclude that in it "the inner speech is summarized" (1967, 235). I will quote the first paragraph of this passage, in my own formatting, in order to show that this identification of thought report with narratized speech is simply wrong. My comments apply equally well to the second paragraph, which is omitted solely for reasons of space:

(a) Lydgate believed himself to be careless about his dress, and he despised a man who calculated the effects of his costume;

(b) it seemed to him only a matter of course that he had abundance of fresh garments

(c) —such things were naturally ordered in sheaves.

(d) It must be remembered that he had never hitherto felt the check of importunate debt, and he walked by habit, not by self-criticism.

(e) But the check had come (1977, 406–7, quoted in 1967, 235).

The content of the thought in this passage is not inner speech, and the form in which it is presented is neither narratized speech nor the equivalent of indirect speech.

(a) describes Lydgate's states of mind, specifically his dispositions. The first statement is a belief, and the second statement is an attitude or preference. Both are true descriptions of his mental life whether or not he is consciously thinking about them. It is unnecessary to postulate an original occurrence of inner speech during which they may have been formulated.

(b) is also a state of mind and is even further removed from inner speech. It would be perfectly possible to preface it with a statement such as: "Without consciously thinking about it, it seemed to him . . ."

(c) has an uncertain status. It can be read as *indefinite free indirect discourse*: what the character might have outwardly said or inwardly thought, although no specific occurrence of inner or spoken speech can be identified. (There is more information on this phenomenon in the next section.) However, it can also be regarded as colored thought report.

(d) departs even further from inner speech than (a), (b), or (c). How can a sentence be described as a character's inner speech when it consists of the narrator reminding the reader first that something had never happened to that character, and then that he was in the habit of *not* thinking about such things?

(e) is the narrator's summary of the events that had happened to Lydgate to modify his dispositions.

The grip of the verbal norm is a very tight one indeed when an example of narrative discourse that is so far removed from summarized inner speech can be presented as such.

The three categories are value-free tools to be used when appropriate. It is perfectly possible to criticize an author for an unimaginative or unrevealing use of a discursive tool within the pragmatic needs of a particular discourse, but it is foolish to claim that two of the modes are inherently superior to the third. It is unclear why narrative techniques have to be valued at all except in the context of the specific and different narrative effects for which they are designed. The presentation of thought in Harlequin or Mills and Boon romances is substantially in free indirect thought and is static and lifeless; in Henry Fielding, it is substantially in thought report and is full of life and movement. However, this is no reason for me to claim that thought report is intrinsically superior to free indirect thought.

Margolin claims that "modern Western literary narrative . . . has a clear preference for the rich, detailed, and "unmediated" presentation of individual human inner life on all levels of consciousness" (2000, 606). I am not sure that I agree. I wonder whether it is more that narrative theory has that preference. The key is in the word "unmediated." Much of the confusion described earlier can be traced back to the privileging of showing over telling in the debate initiated by Henry James in his prefaces, continued by Percy Lubbock in *The Craft of Fiction* (1921), and criticized by Wayne C. Booth in *The Rhetoric of Fiction*. The Blifil and Lydgate passages quoted earlier are both blatant examples of the disgraceful practice of telling rather than showing. Rimmon-Kenan has perceptively commented on this preference for showing over telling: "However interesting this normative debate is, it is ultimately irrelevant for a theoretical and descriptive study of narrative fiction. . . . [T]here is nothing inherently good or bad in either telling or showing. Like any other technique, each has its advantages and disadvantages, and their relative success or failure depends on their functionality in the given work" (1983, 107–8). Theorists are quick to see the irrelevance of a normative debate when it is put in terms of showing and telling perhaps because those terms betray the historical context of that debate. However, there can be a tendency on the part of some to see less clearly the irrelevance of the fascination with direct thought and free indirect thought at the expense of thought report.

The context in which these difficulties can best be understood is that of the ideological distrust of the narrator. As Fludernik points out, mimesis, "particularly in the telling vs. showing opposition, then comes to privilege the seemingly 'unmediated' text of 'pure' mimesis in direct contrast to the Platonic groundings of the distinction, and this development relates directly to the discrediting of narratorial 'interference' at the end of the nineteenth century" (1993, 459). Fludernik also advances the view that, in the areas of both speech and thought representations, narratologists "distrust the narrator's discourse as a linguistically and ideologically distortive medium, placing a premium on 'objective' description and on the use of direct (or at least free indirect) speech" (1993, 459). It is in this way that the vital role of thought report is devalued. It is seen as a departure from the unmediated ideal, as distortion, as interference, and as interruption. Fludernik asserts that authorial narrative "is most familiar to us in the form of a reliable guide to human affairs. There is a consoling ability to know, to see into characters' minds . . . and to uncover life's rules and regularities. . . . It makes possible what is naturally impossible" (1996, 165–66). However, this consolingly reliable role of the narrator is now distrusted as authoritarian and repressive. It is in this context that Genette, in referring to free direct thought, argues that "one of the main paths of emancipation of the modern novel has consisted of pushing this mimesis of speech to its . . . limit, obliterating the last traces of the narrating instance and giving the floor to the character right away" (1980, 173). This is speech, according to Genette, that is "emancipated . . . from all narrative patronage" (1980, 174). These are very revealing expressions: "emancipation," "free," "obliterating," "patronage." This is a very clear expression of hostility to the controlling, distorting, interfering, and patronizing narrator who needs to be obliterated and from whom the reader requires freedom and emancipation.

Before the role of the narrator can be discussed in such value-laden terms, it must first be accurately identified and fully understood. The narrator has an essential and basic linking function that is fundamentally necessary to the way in which fictional narrative works and that can only very rarely be dispensed with. For example, it is not needed in "Penelope," the famous final episode of *Ulysses*, for the obvious reason that Molly is lying in bed in the dark. But this is a very rare case where the context in which the thought is taking place is so minimal and non-social that the linking function of the narrator is not necessary. It is this crucial, contextual function of the narrator that must be recognized before the ideological implications of other aspects of the role can be denounced. It is by such means as thought report and surface description of the storyworld that the narrator links the thought of characters to the social and physical context. This linking function has become so naturalized and familiarized that it is now partially invisible not only to ordinary readers but also to some analysts.

3. The Defense

The adjustment argument. While reading the next few paragraphs, you may be thinking that they have been put in the wrong place and that they should have gone in the previous section. With a defense like this, who needs a prosecution? My reason for putting these views here is that they form what might be called an *adjustment argument*, which goes as follows: all right, the fit between speech and thought is not a perfect one, and difficulties do arise, but when suitably adjusted, it is still informative to analyze thought in terms of the speech categories. It is this line of thinking that lies behind the phenomenon of narrative theorists referring to the disjunction between speech and thought, emphasizing the need for great care and then, in effect, carrying on regardless.

Dorrit Cohn has gone further than most in drawing attention to the difficulties that are inherent in the speech category approach. She argues that the "linguistically based approach . . . oversimplifies the literary problems by carrying too far the correspondence between spoken discourse and silent thought" (1978, 11). She mentions that one of the drawbacks of the speech category account is that "it tends to leave out of account the entire nonverbal realm of consciousness, as well as the entire problematic relationship between thought and speech" (1978, 11). Cohn says of thought report that "linguistic-structuralist critics, by reducing the technique to an unvoiced indirect discourse, disregard its various functions precisely because it is *not* primarily a method for presenting mental language" (1978, 12). She concludes, unsurprisingly, that thought report is "the most neglected of the basic techniques" (1978, 12). I include her views here, though because despite these reservations she has written the best account of the speech category approach.

Monika Fludernik is the narratologist who has the most radical reservations. In her view, the "scale model is quite unable to deal with the functional differences between the representation of utterances and that of consciousness. Although apparently the same means of linguistic expression are at one's disposal in the utterance and consciousness domains, their discourse effect is entirely incompatible" (1993, 310–11). Leech and Short also make the same point that the discourse effects produced by particular categories during the presentation of thought can be very different from their effects in speech presentation (1981, 318, 342–48). Fludernik observes that "the traditional tripartite schema . . . is hopelessly inadequate to the empirical textual evidence" (1993, 315) and explains that the "tripartite model breaks down entirely in relation to thought representation, where the parameters for the reporting of speech events are no longer operative" (1993, 78). Again, though, her views are contained in this section because her solution in *The Fictions of Language and the Languages of Fiction* is to create a very elaborate model of over thirty elements that is intended to remedy this inadequacy. Even so, it still involves a good deal of what she calls "fuzziness" (1993, 314–15). The moral appears to be that more and more elaborate taxonomies simply result in diminishing returns. Significantly, by 1996, Fludernik's solution in *Towards a "Natural" Narratology* is a much more radical one as it involves a recontextualization of the whole concept of narrative, and this recontextualization is based on the notion of consciousness. I hope that the arguments in my later chapters are consistent with hers.

I should mention here another of Fludernik's responses to the problem of speech category bias. Following Banfield (1982), she describes what she calls the *direct discourse fallacy* as "the mistaken (ingrained) belief that direct discourse is in every sense of the word *primary* or *originary* to other types of quotation" (1993, 281). In her view, fiction frequently subverts the convention that direct discourse is a primary source from which indirect quotation can be derived. The logical consequence is this argument: "Contrary to the standard approach to speech and thought representation, in which the characters' direct discourse is the most reliable part of the fictional universe and in which the narrator's or narrative's mediation is by definition always already a distortion, the approach that I have been advocating regards narrative *discourse* as a uniform one-levelled linguistic entity which by its deictic evocation of alterity—whether in the form of [direct thought, free indirect thought, or thought report, including colored thought report]—*projects* a level of language which is not actually *there* but is implied and manufactured by a kind of linguistic hallucination" (1993, 453). In other words, direct discourse is not to be privileged over the various indirect forms. On the discourse plane, this is a coherent and satisfying explanation. But the difficulty arises when it is considered in the context of the storyworld, where characters use speech, including sometimes inner speech. Within this perspective, there must be speech and inner speech events that take place in the storyworld, that can be directly quoted, and that form a primary verbal source from which indirect quotation is derived. It is regrettable that Fludernik's solution is not compatible with the concept of fictional worlds, but I cannot see any way round it.

The hypothetical argument. This argument has two aspects: although the discourse may appear to present the "actual" words of inner speech, it is in fact presenting a reconstruction by the narrator that is hypothetically based on what characters would have said that they were thinking, had they been asked; and although the discourse may appear to present an "actual" episode of inner speech, it is really presenting a summary of several possible such episodes. The hypothetical approach goes beyond the representation of individual episodes of the highly verbalized mental events of inner speech and describes the elusive, ambivalent quality of some passages of thought presentation, mainly in free indirect thought. This approach shows a partial way out of the exaggerated concern with the degree of verbality of the putative original mental event. It also goes part of the way toward an interest in more rewarding aspects of thought presentation such as the need for vivid presentations of states of mind and the role of the reader in building up a sense of stable and continuous characters. However, the limitation of the argument is that theorists tend to see the alternative to a single mental event as being a series of mental events, thereby missing the point that what hypothetical thought presentations often represent are states of mind.

Fludernik asserts that when free indirect thought is used to render a character's consciousness, it signifies more than just an internal speech act by that person, and no transcription of a thought act need be implied (1993, 77). Although she does not specify what this "more" might be, she appears to be edging toward a recognition that free indirect thought can be used as a summary of a number of inner speech episodes. But perhaps these episodes reflect a particular state of mind. Free indirect thought can appear, for the sake of vivid immediacy, to present a state of mind as though it is a single mental event. For example, during a passage of free indirect thought, the statement "She knew that he loved her" may occur. In that context, the reader can read this as a single mental event, say a sudden reawakening of that feeling, even though no specific mental event of this sort is explicitly described. But, in other contexts, it may be clear that the statement is simply the report of a permanently held belief.

Banfield argues that represented consciousness is not a realistic reproduction of the mind at work. In a rather pointed reference to the title of Cohn's book, she claims that narratives do not create transparent minds: "The mind is never transparent, not even to 'omniscient narrators.' Rather, its contents are hypothetically reconstructed and represented in a language sensitive to its various modes" (1982, 211). Dillon and Kirchhoff have a similar perspective. They feel that, in general, "the material that appears in [free indirect thought] is to be understood as a representation of a character's expressions or thoughts as he would express them, not necessarily as a 'verbatim' rendering of 'internal speech'" (1976, 431). The key phrase is "as the character would express them." They are suggesting that it is part of the narrator's role to reduce the complexity of the mind to a form that will meet the need for the fictional discourse to be understood by the reader. This form is the one that would result if the character could self-consciously respond to the question "What were you thinking just now?" But any such summary, to be a plausible picture of the whole mind, would have to include reference to states of mind as well as inner speech. Cohn feels that free indirect discourse, by leaving the relationship between words and thoughts latent, casts a "peculiarly penumbral light" on the character's consciousness, "suspending it on the threshold of verbalization in a manner that cannot be achieved by direct quotation" (1978, 103). This note of mystery encapsulates beautifully the inadequacy of the speech category picture of the mind. Cohn's point can be prosaically reworded by saying that free indirect thought is good at presenting states of mind such as beliefs and attitudes almost as if they are single mental events but without the narrator being specific as to the exact occasion on which these events might have taken place. In this way, free indirect thought can be used to solve the formal problem of how to present latent states of mind in an immediate, forceful, and active way. There is no mystery to this, and it is not necessary to shroud the discussion in peculiarly penumbral lights.

The narratologist Anne Waldron Neumann has attempted to provide a conceptual framework that can account for the hypothetical nature of free indirect discourse. Neumann defines free indirect discourse as "that mode of indirectly reported speech or thought which quotes what we feel could be at least some of the words of a character's actual utterances or thought, but which offers those words interwoven with the narrator's language . . . *without explicitly attributing them to the character in question*" (1986, 366). She explains that the study of reported speech and thought in fiction may necessitate reconstructing or hypothesizing what was "actually" uttered in the story from what is reported in the discourse. To read a sentence as free indirect discourse, we must use our ingenuity and infer who is quoted and which words in the sentence are quotations. We are left to guess whether the words in the discourse were ever uttered in the story and, even if we think that the words did occur, whether they were spoken or were thought (1986, 368–69). In her view, there are three types of free indirect discourse: *definite*, when we are certain that the words were used by the character; *almost definite*, when we know that words were used and that they were the sort of thing that the character would say or think in that situation; and *indefinite*, which uses language characteristic of the character but leaves it unclear whether the words were spoken or thought or whether it only reports the sort of thing that they would say or think. We can correctly identify it with the character in the discourse, but its status in the story is uncertain (1986, 370, 376).

I think Neumann's account is valuable for its strong emphasis on the active role of the reader, its awareness of the hypothetical nature of much free indirect discourse, and its acknowledgement that a good deal of narrative discourse is indeterminate in status. However, her ideas can be developed further. As with Cohn, the distance and ambiguity that Neumann refers to can be explained by the fact that what is being represented is states of mind. Also, the points that she makes regarding indefinite free indirect discourse can provide a starting point for an analysis of the precise means by which the reader builds up a sense of a stable and predictable fictional character. For example, how is a reader able to say whether or not language is "characteristic" of a fictional person, is "the sort of thing that they would say or think"? In the following section I will quote short passages of thought report that illustrate the relationship between the presentation of consciousness and characterization. This is the framework within which readers can make interpretive decisions about characters and thereby recuperate meaning from such discursive phenomena as indefinite free indirect discourse.

The pragmatic argument. This is the view that we are simply talking about convenient assumptions about how the mind works and the accepted conventions by which fictional minds are represented in narrative fiction. As quoted in chapter 1, section 2 and in section 2 of this chapter, Genette argues that the narrative convention is that "thoughts and feelings are no different from speech" (1980, 171). It is Bonheim's view that "thought may be, or at least in the conventions of narrative usually is represented as, a process which can be considered verbal" (1982, 70). The argument is that, in saying that it is a convention that all thought is verbal because it is assumed that thoughts and feelings are inner speech, we are simply relating convenient assumptions about the nature of consciousness to the particular needs of narrative discourse. Sternberg here makes explicit the assumptions behind the pragmatic approach: "nobody is likely to deny that much narrative thought shows elements other than verbal, and that all thought, in order to pass from unuttered to communicable form, must be mediated and given physical shape by a reporter. Not even the most speechlike interior monologue offers a pure, reporter-free transcript. Many such monologues involve transmuting impression and sensation into language; some are openly stylized, artificial, multi-voiced" (1982, 134). He is saying that, pragmatically, thought has to be treated as speech in order for it to be given "physical shape" in the discourse. See the earlier discussion on narratized speech on why this is not the case. Despite the apparent attractiveness of the pragmatic approach, it causes at least two problems. One is that, while narratologists may assume that the fictional convention is that all or most thought is indeed speech, it is simply not true to say that fictional narrators share that assumption. What is speechlike about the Blifil and Lydgate passages quoted earlier? The second problem is the danger that the observation of literary conventions can easily harden into convictions about how the mind actually works. Genette undermines his point by adding that the convention is "perhaps truthful in this case"(1980, 171); Bonheim is equally ambivalent. Care should be taken with notions of novelistic conventions. It is very easy for them to solidify initially into working assumptions and then into firm conclusions—for example, that thoughts and feelings really are no different from unspoken speech or that the obvious and direct means of handling fictional thoughts are the only means.

Chatman holds that what is "important for narrative theory is only what authors . . . and their audiences *assume* the mind to be like. Their assumptions may be quite wrong scientifically and still function verisimilarly, as a cultural commonplace" (1978, 181). Put bluntly, it is not a problem for readers and narrators to have a mistaken view of the way in which the mind works, as long as they share that view. I agree. However, it does become a problem when readers and narrators share a rich and complex view of the mind (that may be right or wrong), while the speech category approach imposes on narrative an oversimplified and impoverished mind picture that does not do justice to the practice of narrators and the experience of readers. As it happens, I think that the parallel discourses of cognitive science, psycholinguistics, and philosophy have a lot in common with the mind pictures of both readers and narrators—it is the speech category theory that appears to be out of step.

In summary, I have described three related defenses against the criticisms contained in the previous section. The three arguments appear to go some way to ameliorate the crudities of the speech category account. However, they do not affect the five basic problems that were described earlier (the privileging of free indirect thought and direct thought over thought report; the overestimation of the verbal component in thought; the resulting neglect of thought report of characters' states of mind; the privileging of some novels over others and some scenes in novels over others; and the impression that characters' minds really only consist of a private, passive flow of thought). The adjustment argument is little more than an acknowledgement of the existence of the problems; the hypothetical argument does not go far enough; and the pragmatic argument, though superficially attractive, has dangerous pitfalls. What is required is not to try to modify the speech category account, but to step outside its limitations altogether. The three viewpoints then become unnecessary. The reader does not need to adopt either a hypothetical or a pragmatic view toward the supposed verbality of the fictional mental events reported in statements such as "He was overjoyed" or "She decided to walk." Neither does the reader have to worry about how the speech categories can be adjusted to take account of these statements. They are simply reports of states of mind and mental functioning.

4. Thought Report

While reviewing Dorrit Cohn's *Transparent Minds*, Brian McHale drew attention to the neglect of thought report. "In the analysis of third person texts, [thought report] has always been the poor relation, neglected in favor of the more glamorous, more mimetic techniques of [direct thought and free indirect thought]. We have by and large been content to treat [thought report] as a sort of degree zero of psychological realism. Now Cohn has effectively legitimized [thought report], delimiting its boundaries, outlining its devices, functions, potentialities. She has put it on the map of psychological techniques once and for all" (1981, 186). This section is an attempt to build on Cohn's achievements. The concept of fictional minds transcends the speech category approach, but if it is to be considered in terms of the three modes, it privileges the mode of thought report. I will propose here an approach toward thought report that will, rather than marginalize it, put it at the center of the presentations by narrators to readers of the contents of fictional minds in their social and physical context. It is an approach toward narrators' presentations of the whole mind that focuses on both states of mind and inner speech and that acknowledges the indispensable and pivotal role of thought report in linking individual mental functioning to its social context. The presentation of the mind in narrative fiction is a dynamic process, a negotiated relationship between the narrator, the character, and the reader in which a set of formal conventions is given meaning by the reader. Much of what the reader does in using presentations of characters' minds to construct from the discourse those aspects of the story that relate to these minds is done by means of thought report.

With regard to the distinction between story and discourse, it is important to stress that the story contains mental as well as physical events. It consists of characters' reasons for action as well as the actions themselves. In fact, a distinction cannot really be made between the two, because the concept of an action necessarily contains within it mental phenomena such as intentions and reasons. These reasons, intentions, motives, and so on form an indispensable part of characters' embedded narratives that can be recovered by readers from the discourse, in part with the help of direct presentations of minds. A vital part of this whole process is the use of the mode of thought report. In particular, it has what I shall call a *linking function*, whereby the narrator, in presenting a character's consciousness, connects it to its surroundings. The use of this device emphasizes the nature of consciousness as mental action and thereby brings together consciousness and physical action. The mode of thought report is ideally suited to informative presentations of the purposive and directive nature of thought as well as its social nature. The other two modes are much less suited to this linking function, which forms such a large part of the richness and complexity of the novel.

When the mind is regarded as a private, passive flow of consciousness, the explicit presence of the narrator appears to be unnecessarily obtrusive and distorting. However, most characters' thought takes place in a social context of action and interaction with others. For this aspect of the novel, thought report is the most suitable mode of presentation. It is not an interruption, an intrusion, or a distortion. Because thought report provides a background, low-level flow of contextual information, its presence in the discourse is often overlooked. Theorists tend to see the use of thought report as increasing the audibility and prominence of the narrator. Since its presence in discourse is so often disregarded, my inclination is to draw the opposite conclusion. In any event, my chief concern is with the almost continuous form of thought report that unobtrusively and, it appears, almost inaudibly, links characters to their context. This is very different from the prominent judgments or commentaries that narratologists tend to identify with thought report. Part of the purpose of this section is to defamiliarize this completely naturalized device. The resonant last few words of Culler's *Structuralist Poetics* are "as yet we understand very little about how we read" (1975, 265). We will understand a little more once we pay more attention both to the presence and also to all the functions of thought report.

Thought report can of course go beyond the simple reporting of thought and shade into commentary or ethical judgment on that thought. However, the two activities, reporting thought and commenting on it, are logically distinct from each other. I am concerned only with the issues raised by the apparently simple device of the reporting of thought and not with the other questions raised by narratorial judgments. This point is important because, as I have said, it is possible that much of the prejudice against the "obtrusive" narrator can be traced back to a dislike of the judgmental and moralizing narrator. But because insufficient care has been taken to distinguish between the different functions of the prominent narrator, this dislike has also attached to the entirely separate function of the reporting of thought. The irony of the intrusion prejudice is that the sort of thought report with which I am particularly concerned is so low level that it is all but invisible. It is almost paradoxical that I am trying to raise the visibility of thought report while combating the widespread perception of its alleged intrusiveness!

The mode of thought report is normally assigned what might variously be called a default, supplementary, safety net, or stopgap function. It appears to be assumed that the narrator uses thought report only when the more preferable techniques are not suitable for a particular context. It is necessary to turn this

[handwritten margin note: thought-report captures social context of action / interaction w/ others]

negative approach on its head and explore positively the real and important functions of thought report. Thought report is a mediation by the narrator between the character and the reader. At certain points in the text, the pragmatic requirements of the narrative may indicate the need for a high level of mediation, for example, when it is necessary for the narrator to indicate to the reader the various contexts in which the thought of the character is taking place. At other times, lesser levels of mediation are required, for example, when the context is not important, or when it has already been established or is to be kept deliberately vague. The other modes can then be used. But, within this approach to mind presentation, the mode of thought report is the norm because the linking function is such a vital contribution to what can plausibly be described as the purpose of the novel: the exploration of the relationship between individuals and the societies within which they live.

Thought report is not the only means of placing characters' minds in context. For example, the narrator may use a passage of external description that sets the scene, followed by a passage of direct thought that relates in some way to that scene. The relationship between the two will be implicit but can still be perfectly clear. Also, I refer to the linking function of free indirect perception later. However, although thought report is not the only way to connect thought with context, it is the mode that is most suited to this function. So, the questions to ask are functional ones: What factors affect the decisions of the narrator relating to presentation of context? Why are different levels of mediation required at different points in the narration? What are the different ways in which the three modes contribute to the linking function? What effects relating to mediation and context are specific to thought report?

Some theorists have commented briefly and in passing on the linking function, though without giving it the emphasis that it warrants. Chatman implicitly refers to the need for it, observing that critics "have noted the difficulty of unrelieved pure interior monologue, of conveying the outer action and situation of a character if the text is totally locked up in his mind. Inferences can only go so far" (1978, 185). But notice that "pure" unmediated thought presentation is the norm and that thought report is the departure from the norm that is required only when inferences can finally go no further. Bickerton also refers to the contextual function in a rather negative way, stating that it enables "the narrator to incorporate background and narrative material into the monologue" (1967, 235). Again, the norm is the character's monologue, and thought report is sometimes necessary in order to "incorporate" other material into it. The relationship between consciousness and situation is a process that can be analyzed in a much more dynamic and positive way than simply the incorporation of background material into a monologue.

Cohn draws attention to what she calls the dovetailing function as it relates to the presentation of characters' perceptions on the borderline between thought report and free indirect perception. She comments that descriptions of characters' perceptions blur the distinction between the external and the internal scene and neatly dovetail the representation of both inner and outer reality (1978, 49). This point is pursued with great subtlety and insight in Georges Poulet's article, "The Circle and the Center: Reality and *Madame Bovary*" (1955). He uses the famous discussion by Erich Auerbach in *Mimesis: The Representation of Reality in Western Literature* of a paragraph from *Madame Bovary* that vividly expresses Emma Bovary's perception of, and consciousness of, her physical environment. The passage is this one: "But it was above all at mealtimes that she could bear it no longer, in that little room on the ground floor, with the smoking stove, the creaking door, the oozing walls, the damp floor-tiles; all the bitterness of life seemed to be served to her on her plate, and, with the steam from the boiled beef, there rose from the depths of her soul other exhalations as it were of disgust. Charles was a slow eater; she would nibble a few hazel-nuts; or else, leaning on her elbow, would amuse herself making marks on the oilcloth with the point of her table-knife" (quoted in Auerbach 1953, 483; Poulet 1955, 392). It is a complex mixture of thought report (the feelings rising from the depths of her soul), free indirect perception (her awareness of the room), and action (nibbling, making marks) that is highly informative about Emma's states of mind. Poulet's view is that, if Flaubert had simply decided to paint Emma from the outside, she would merely be an object among objects. If, on the other hand, he had wanted to make her a purely subjective being, then nothing would have been left except the sensations and emotions caused in Emma by the surrounding objects. There would then have been no awareness on the part of the reader of Emma as a person standing against a background of things, since she would have been reduced to the status of a stream of thoughts and feelings (Poulet 1955, 393). Poulet's argument is that Flaubert succeeded in devising a new way of presenting the relations between the mind and the surrounding reality (1955, 405). He contends that *Madame Bovary* has an inner coherence because things are constantly fused together in the unity of a single, perceiving mind and also because this mind, conversely, is kept from disappearing into its own consciousness by the objectivity of a world with which it is in constant touch. There is not only a theoretical representation of reality, there is also a concrete medium through which this representation has been received (that is, Emma's perceptions) (Poulet 1955, 393). Poulet argues that Flaubert achieves his purpose of conveying vividly the interrelation of a consciousness and its environment by showing something purely and intensely subjective, Emma's mind, located within a place and surrounded by a long enumeration of details of the environment that are objective in themselves but are also endowed with affective powers (Poulet 1955, 393–94).

Poulet's point is that narrators have to find ways of combining two very different objectives: the need to convey the subjective process of a single consciousness and the need to describe the social and physical environment within which that consciousness is functioning. The narrator has to present a consciousness as fully as possible while conveying the surroundings within which it is placed. The combined use of thought report and free indirect perception allows the two objectives to be met simultaneously. Minds do not function in a vacuum. Not many fictional minds are at work while completely divorced from any interaction with other minds or the stimulus of an active physical environment (like Molly Bloom in the "Penelope" episode in *Ulysses*). There are many ways in which this linking can be done, and not all of them are by thought report. As I said, this passage includes free indirect perception. While the narrator is describing Emma's perception of her environment, he is simultaneously describing her consciousness, her physical environment, and the complex and dynamic relationship between the two. Another way of tying together consciousness and environment is the description of action, which is both a private mental event (Emma amusing herself) and a physical happening in the public world (making marks). Emma makes marks on the tablecloth as a response to her intolerable situation. The distance between the narrator and the character that is created by thought report, as opposed to the two less-mediated modes, is often the way in which a fictional consciousness can be situated within its environment. Furthermore, this situating process is usually an integral part of the plot-forming aspect of narrative. Emma's feelings about the environment within which she is situated so vividly by the narrator will lead to the tragedy at the end of the novel.

Here are some of the specific ways in which thought report can fulfill the linking function that I have just described. Some of my comments are very sketchy because I explore the related issues in more detail elsewhere in the book. It seemed useful nevertheless to group together some of the key attributes of thought report in one place.

Presentation of variety of mental events. Section 2 contained a long list of mental events—including inner speech, perception, sensations, emotions, visual images, attention, tone or mood—that are suitable for presentation in the mode of thought report. Many are less or not at all suitable for presentation in the other two modes. This is particularly noticeable in the case of emotions. The narratological neglect of the importance of the emotions is extraordinary until it is remembered that they cannot occur as such in inner speech. I develop this point and the following two points in the next chapter.

emotions

Presentation of latent states of mind. Again, as listed in section 2, the fictional mind consists of a large number of areas or aspects that include attitudes, judgments, evaluations, beliefs, skills, knowledge, character traits, tendencies of thought, memory, intellect, volition, mood, imagination, and desires. The philosopher Daniel Dennett uses the memorable phrase "mind-ruts" (1991, 300) to describe the way in which groups of mental events can coalesce into tendencies of thought.

latent states of mind

Presentation of mental action. This point arose during the discussion of narratized speech. More generally, it is related to the mental causal network behind actions that includes motives, intentions, and reasons for action. Thought report is the mode that is best suited to the ascription of particular motives, intentions, and so on. A particularly unfortunate consequence of the speech category account is the assumption that the division between thought and action is unproblematical. A good deal of the interest that novels have for us lies precisely in the problematical complexities that arise when the relationship between thought and action is studied. The following quote from *The Monk* by Matthew Lewis is a good example of the amount of information on motives and intentions that can be conveyed in just a few words by thought report: "The lady was perfectly satisfied with the conversation which had passed between them; she looked forward with satisfaction to the prospect of his becoming her son-in-law; but prudence bade her conceal from her daughter's knowledge the flattering hopes which herself now ventured to entertain" (Lewis 1998, 190). If you cast your mind back to the Blifil passage, you will see a similar picture of goals and intentions being worked into plans for the future.

motives, intentions, etc.

Presentation of character and personality. In the Blifil and Lydgate quotes used earlier in the chapter, and also in the passage from *The Monk*, you will see that thought report is starting to shade into characterization. In fact, putting it in those terms is misleading. How could we go about establishing where the thought report ended and the characterization began? Within my approach to fictional minds, this sort of passage is the norm and not the

shades into characterization

meeting of boundaries between two different phenomena. It is one of the key strategies for reading texts because it links the present thoughts of the character with earlier judgments and hypotheses regarding that character and, in this way, provides the basis for predictions regarding the future course of the narrative. It is difficult to imagine what reading narrative would be like without the use of this strategy.

Summary. Cohn points out that thought report is the most flexible mode, particularly in temporal terms, because it is suitable both for summary and for the expansion of a significant moment (which is referred to later). It can summarize an inner development over a long period of time using a panoramic view or telescopic perspective. Cohn refers to three different rhythms of time condensation: *iterative*, which organizes events into a pattern of recurrence (for example, "very often," "occasionally"); *durative*, which organizes events into a pattern of persistence (for example, "continued," "still"); and *mutative*, which, unlike the others, refers to changes over a time span (1978, 35). Cohn describes the capacity of thought report to present "mental descriptions in a large time frame" (1978, 34) and also refers to it as a "kind of panoramic view of [an] inner self" (1978, 34), "an inner development over a long period of time" (1978, 34), "a distant perspective, looking over the entire time span" that the narrator recounts (1978, 35), and "a psychic syndrome continuing over an extended time period" (1978, 36). States of mind such as beliefs and dispositions necessarily exist over time, and so for their presentation in narrative, summary becomes the norm. A lengthy time period will seem "general and distant," to use Fludernik's description of the Blifil passage, only if you are approaching the mind in terms of a series of discrete mental events.

Presentation of background information. This is a wide category that includes such features as negative knowledge, physical context, presupposition, and other contextual information.

Negative knowledge. This is what the character does not know but the narrator does, and it is particularly significant in the context of motives and intentions. Sometimes it is clearly signaled as in, "He had not realized yet how much he loved her." At other times the issue is less straightforward: "He left because he was angry." Here, it is not clear whether it is the narrator or the character who is establishing the causal relationship. People who act when they are angry often do not know until afterward, if then, that they acted *because* they were angry. It is very common in passages of this sort to find that the character's self-conscious knowledge of their own states of mind, and in particular of the causal relationships between them, is difficult to establish with precision. The use of thought report leaves the question open. The other two modes are much less flexible: their use makes it clear that the character is self-consciously aware of the state of mind.

Physical context. A good example appears in the opening paragraph of *The House of Mirth* by Edith Wharton: "Selden paused in surprise. In the afternoon rush of the Grand Central Station his eyes had been refreshed by the sight of Miss Lily Bart" (1979, 5). It is very common for sentences to consist both of thought report and also of surface description of the physical storyworld. There is more in chapter 7 on this point.

Presupposition. Chatman defines presupposition as the part of a sentence that is a given, that goes without saying, and that is already understood. For example, this is the first sentence in Edmund White's *The Married Man* that directly describes the main character's consciousness: "Austin thought there might be more action in the pool and the shower rooms, but he didn't like swimming and he'd sort of given up on cruising" (2001, 1). It is legitimate to presuppose that Austin is gay. A clichéd example of presupposition is the question: "When did you stop beating your wife?" Chatman remarks that it is a powerful device for hinting that the character whose consciousness is being presented is deluded and self-deceiving (1978, 209–11). Presupposition is, therefore, an important element in the interpretation and judgment subfunction that is mentioned later. Other forms of presupposition, this time involving characters rather than readers, are illustrated with examples from *Vanity Fair.* In one example, "they understood each other perfectly well" (1994, 287), a state of affairs is described—an agreement or understanding between two characters—that presupposes knowledge by both characters of the other's mind. Presupposition can also relate to the feelings of an individual: "the pair, whose conduct has so chafed the jealous General" (1994, 285). The description of the actions of two people presupposes the mental functioning of a third person. Another example that is also closely related to action is "George said to his wife, whom he could leave alone with less scruple when she had this society" (1994, 282). A relationship between two characters that results in a course of action being taken in certain circumstances is mentioned in passing. It presupposes the prior knowledge of both their minds that would explain the context to this arrangement. These examples show that the device of presupposition is often closely related to intermental thinking.

Presentation of intermental thinking. I will argue in chapter 7, section 3 that the use of thought report for the presentation of intermental or group, joint, or shared thought is one of the most important aspects of the construction of fictional minds. It has been neglected because of the verbal bias.

[margin note: thought report & surface desc. often captured in same sentence]

[margin note: are there parts of the sentence that are already understood?]

Expression of consensus. In commenting on a particular example of thought report, Chatman notes that it contains "the suggestion of a kind of 'in'-group psychology . . . a sense of the broader social context." It is "indistinguishably the thought of one or all of the family, or what one of them said to the others, or the narrator's judgment of the situation" (1978, 207). The reason why it is not possible to distinguish between the various possibilities for the source of what is expressed is because everyone is in agreement. Looked at another way, there is a certain sort of double-voiced discourse that may look like an expression of opinion by an intrusive narrator but that on closer inspection turns out to be the expression of a consensus, a shared view within a particular social group. Leech and Short say of an example of thought report that "it need not be associated with a particular character, but may be the expression of [a] communal point of view" (1981, 349–50). McHale calls this phenomenon "the idiom of the group" (1978, 270). In "Discourse and the Novel," Bakhtin talks about "the common view" (1981, 301–2). Margolin, in discussing Fludernik's idea of the "typification, schematization, or contraction of recognizable shared stances, perspectives, views, or common opinions held by numerous members of the group," unfortunately refers to it as "collective inner speech" (2000, 605–6). Fludernik also uses the term "communis opinio," but she seems more interested in the implicit use of this concept as a deictic center, or viewpoint on action, rather than the explicit expression of communal opinion by a narrator (1996, 192). David Lodge quotes the following sentence from *Middlemarch*, "And how should Dorothea not marry?—a girl so handsome and with such prospects?" and asks where the question comes from. Not from Dorothea, he suggests, and not even from the narrator. Lodge concludes that "it is the voice of Middlemarch that is evoked here by the narrator, the voice of provincial bourgeois wisdom" (1990, 85).

Vanity Fair contains several similar examples of the apparently intrusive narrator in reality simply expressing a communal view: "a little troop of horsemen, consisting of some of the very greatest persons in Brussels" (1994, 281) and "It was almost like Old England" (1994, 282). One way to identify the consensus type of thought report is to listen for the note of irony that it often contains. In these two examples, it is quite likely that the narrator does not think that the horsemen *were* the very greatest persons in Brussels or that it *was* almost like Old England. The expression of the view of the consensus is another aspect of the presentation of intermental thinking.

Interpretation, analysis, and judgment. I will not discuss these uses here as they have been well covered already in a number of studies, particularly in Seymour Chatman's *Story and Discourse* (1978, 226–53).

In all of these subfunctions of the linking function of thought report, the thought processes of individual characters are connected by the narrator to their environment, thereby illustrating in very concrete and specific ways the social nature of thought. These various aspects of thought report also tend to emphasize the active nature of thought as mental functioning. As I said earlier, it is much less easy to explore these aspects of consciousness while using other modes because it is in thought report that the narrator is able to show explicitly how characters' minds are operating in a social and physical context.

For the sake of completeness, and to emphasize the versatility of the mode, I will also briefly mention another function of thought report, which is not mentioned earlier because it is not related to its linking function. It is what Cohn calls the *expansion of the moment*. As Cohn explains, thought report can expand or elaborate a mental instant that is of particular significance. This technique is popular in the modern novel. Proust is the obvious example. Expansion is often achieved through the use of what Cohn terms *psycho-analogies*. These are tropes that are used to express consciousness. She quotes this example from Virginia Woolf: "As a person who has dropped some grain of pearl or diamond into the grass and parts the tall blades very carefully" (1978, 44). Cohn suggests that it is sometimes difficult to tell whether the analogy is being used by the narrator or by the character (although not perhaps in the case of that Woolf example). Psycho-analogies are often sprinkled into passages of what is otherwise free indirect thought, when in Cohn's words the narrator "is unwilling to entrust the presentation of the inner life to the character's own verbal competence" (1978, 44). The expansion of the moment is particularly useful for Cohn's favorite use of thought report—the exploration of what she calls the "nether depth" (1978, 140).

Conclusion

I hope that I have not given the impression that I think that the speech category approach is beyond repair. On the contrary, as with the other approaches considered in chapter 2, I think that it has an essential place in the study of fictional minds. My point is simply that it is only one among a large number of perspectives on this crucially important aspect of narrative discourse. The distortions arise when it is thought to be the only one. There is time for one last hymn to the virtues of thought report. It tends to be centrifugal in nature, while direct thought and free indirect thought tend to be centripetal: it directs the reader's attention outward into the context of social situation and action, while the others direct the reader's attention inward into scenes of thoughtful self-communion. Let us now travel further in the centrifugal direction indicated by the mode of thought report and go on to consider first the whole mind and then the social mind.

4

The Whole Mind

Our mental business is carried on much in the same way as the business of the State: a great deal of hard work is done by agents who are not acknowledged. – George Eliot, *Adam Bede*

I will now begin the process of widening and deepening our concept of the fictional mind beyond the phenomenon of inner speech. Although this chapter and the next are mainly about real minds, I try to relate the arguments at regular intervals to the fictional sort. It is in order to obtain a variety of perspectives on the means by which readers construct fictional minds that the parallel discourses of cognitive science, philosophy, psychology, and psycholinguistics are examined in this chapter and the next. As Lubomir Doležel remarks, in order to "build a theory of interacting in fictional worlds, narrative semantics has to tap other sources of inspiration—social psychology, sociology, cultural semiotics, and so on" (1998, 97). In addition, I hope that these two chapters are of interest in themselves to students of literary theory who may not previously have encountered some of the real-mind discourses discussed in them. The notion of balance will recur throughout this chapter. In attempting to bring together parallel discourses, each of which tends to emphasize one aspect of the mind at the expense of others, I am trying to achieve a full picture of fictional minds. I suggest that the best way to produce a rich, informative, and genuinely heuristic perspective on the consciousnesses of characters in novels is to find a balance between these different views.

1. Functionalism

This section describes a functionalist approach toward the areas of the mind that are considered later in this chapter because it is within a functional perspective that these aspects of the mind can best be understood. Lubomir Doležel points out that "[a]ll mental faculties, from sensory perception to emotionality to thinking to remembering and imagination, operate between the poles of intentional acting and spontaneous generation" (1998, 73). It is the latter pole, which embraces such phenomena as contemplation, daydreams, fantasies, and free associative thinking, that has been the focus of attention within traditional narratology. Think of the deep interest in stream of consciousness and interior monologue. The attempt to redress the balance a little with a functional focus on the pole of intentional acting starts here.

Broadly speaking, there are two uses for the term *functionalism*. Strong functionalism is the doctrine that "[f]unctional kinds are not identified by their material composition but rather by their activities or tendencies" (Maloney 1999, 333) and that minds are functional kinds. Strong functionalists conclude from this that it is possible for robots or computers to have minds, even though the machine supporting this mental functioning is made from a completely different substance than that of human brains. So brains can be made out of machinery. Within cognitive science some theorists adopt a bottom-up approach that is determined by the biology of the brain: this is the way the brain works and that is what we will study. Conversely, strong functionalists adopt a top-down approach that is derived from the computational theory of the mind. It considers the outputs of mental functioning and studies the brain only in a very abstract manner as, in effect, the information-processing machine that produces those outputs. This is a contentious and controversial position to which there are a number of cogent objections. Searle, for example, regards strong functionalism as one of a number of approaches to the mind that deny the reality of subjective consciousness. I am not using the term *functionalism* in this very strong sense, but in a much weaker sense to mean an emphasis on the activities and tendencies of minds that asks the question What is thinking *for*? Strong functionalism is not relevant to the purpose of this book because, as fictional minds exist only in a semiotic and not in a physical sense, the question of what they are made of does not arise. Weak functionalism, however, is very relevant indeed.

It is a basic, operational, working assumption of cognitive scientists that the mind is an information-processing device. Daniel Dennett, one of the foremost philosophers of cognitive science, suggests that what "makes something a mind . . . is not what it is made of, but what it *can do*" and that "what minds do is process information" (1996, 68). Steven Pinker uses very similar words: "The mind is what the brain does; specifically, the brain processes information, and thinking is a kind of computation" (1997, 21). These comments illustrate the functional view of the mind that analyzes what it does and what it is for, rather than asking what the brain is made of. Within this context, the approach of cognitive science toward the phenomenon of consciousness is very illuminating. The first surprise is that cognitive scientists see consciousness as only a small part of their study. The second surprise is that they can even entertain the possibility that the centrality and importance of consciousness can be questioned at all. Most of us unthinkingly regard it as a given: consciousness is what makes us what we are, what makes us human. It just happens. But cognitive scientists are aware that many organisms survive perfectly well without consciousness in the human, self-conscious sense, and so they ask, What is consciousness for? I am sure that this would strike most of the rest of us as a very odd question. However, you will be relieved to hear that the answer is a positive one. For example, the neuroscientist Antonio Damasio's answer to the question is that the "devices of consciousness handle the problem of how an individual organism may cope with environmental challenges not predicted in its basic design such that the conditions fundamental for survival can still be met" (2000, 303). Consciousness allows us to adapt intelligently to our environment. We would not adapt so well without it. This is what it is for.

The psychologist William James is now famously associated with the phrase *stream of consciousness*. This term is related to the pole of spontaneous generation that Doležel refers to. But *MITECS* stresses his interest in the opposite pole of intentional acting. James "emphasized the *adaptive* nature of cognition: the fact that perception, memory, and reasoning operate not simply for their own sake, but to allow us to survive and prosper in our physical and social world." Furthermore, James "recognized that the hallmark of an intelligent being is its ability to link ends with means—to select actions that will achieve goals" (Holyoak 1999, xlii).

It is ironic that James's actual approach is a long way from the narrative term now associated with his name. It is noteworthy that James applied this functional perspective to the concept of intelligence, which Steven Pinker defines as "the ability to attain goals in the face of obstacles by means of decisions based on rational (truth-obeying) rules . . . [that is,] specifying a goal, assessing the current situation to see how it differs from the goal, and applying a set of operations that reduce the difference" (1997, 62).

Intelligence clearly requires a minimum amount of knowledge about the environment and appropriate planning to change the environment. Goal-directed action of this sort involves not only close attention to context but also a clear focus on the future. The concept of a goal involves a gap between an actual and present state of affairs and a counterfactual and future state of affairs that is more desirable. As Dennett puts it in two very striking phrases in *Consciousness*

Explained, "the fundamental purpose of brains is to produce future" (as the poet Paul Valéry originally said), and "all brains are, in essence, *anticipation machines*" (1991, 177). This kind of interaction with the world is clearly not a private or passive process. It is engaged and interactive. "Cognition is neither copying nor constructing the world. Cognition is, instead, the process that keeps us active, changing creatures in touch with an eventful, changing world" (Reed 1996, 13).

I suggest a functional approach toward fictional minds. Take Pip in *Great Expectations*. He is an adaptive, goal-directed, information-processing device. This sort of talk may seem deeply alienating, depressingly mechanistic, and chillingly antihumanist, but why? Information processing is concerned with perception, daydreams, and contemplation as well as with an active engagement with the social and physical context. The language may be unfamiliar and possibly even repellent, but the reality is known to us all. Pip's mind processes the information that he receives from the other minds around him and from other aspects of his physical and social environment. He learns, in particular from Estelle and Miss Havisham, that he wants to be different. He develops goals, such as wanting to be a gentleman, that conflict with his current situation. He then learns from Herbert, Mr. Jaggers, and so on how to adapt and how to become a gentleman. His mind adapts differently to all of the various minds with which it interacts. Finally, he learns the most difficult lesson of all—that becoming a gentleman is not enough and that he has another goal: he has still to learn how to be a good person. At every stage he establishes what his present situation is, what his desired situation is, and how best to reconcile the two. Pip has plans for the future, but these have to be adapted and continually updated to deal with the various surprises that confront him. The surprises are linked, and become a plot, through the plans that he adapts in the light of them. Of course, you will be thinking by now, Pip is not an information-processing device at all! He is a character in a novel, a collection of words on the page. So what I am really saying is that the reader must read those words *as if* they refer to an information-processing device. How else can we follow the plot of the novel?

Once this point is grasped, it is clear that a functional perspective on real minds is the basis of a teleological perspective on fictional minds. Teleological analysis is the study of narrative in terms of its ultimate purpose and overall design. The teleological analysis of a text is based on the assumption that its parts function coherently toward a comprehensible end purpose. The plots of novels are goal-directed in the sense that they have, or should have, coherent and satisfying endings or, alternatively, they deliberately frustrate readers' desires for such endings. The changing gaps between Pip's current situations and his various goals define the structure and design of the narrative. They comprise its teleological shape.

Once the unfamiliarity of thinking of fictional minds in terms of cognitive science has worn off, the parallels continue to be instructive and a rich source of insights into mental functioning in novels is revealed. The theorists in the parallel discourses themselves are aware of the value to be gained from pursuing these parallels. This is Steven Pinker again: "Once the fictitious world is set up, the protagonist is given a goal and we watch as he or she pursues it in the face of obstacles. It is no coincidence that this standard definition of plot is identical to [my] definition of intelligence. . . . Characters in a fictitious world do exactly what our intelligence allows us to do in the real world" (1997, 541). Equally, some narrative theorists are also aware of the value of a similarly functional approach to fictional minds. Doležel describes very clearly the pole of intentional acting that is referred to earlier by stating that the concepts of "intentionality and motivation define the 'outwardly' oriented domain of the mind, the practical mind directing, controlling, and monitoring acting and its results. . . . The operations of the practical mind, such as practical reasoning, decision making, calculation, planning, scripting, and the like, are prototypes of mental acts" (1998, 72–73). Marie-Laure Ryan has divided the repertory of mental registers of characters into five categories. Two of them, (the epistemic world of characters containing their beliefs, projections, and introspections and the desires, fears, likes, and dislikes of characters) are at the private and introspective pole. The other three (the individual obligations of characters that are created by promises and the social obligations of characters that are created by laws; the active goals of characters; and the plans through which characters seek to fulfill their active goals) (1991, 224) are functional in that they relate to how people plan ahead, adjust in the light of circumstances, and operate generally in a social context.

Finally, I would like to end this section with a tentative suggestion. Writers sometimes complain about the tyranny of teleology and the artificiality of careful plotting. *Realism* is, of course, a notoriously slippery concept, but, for example, the modernist emphasis on stream of consciousness and interior monologue has often been described as more "realistic" than writing that is geared to the intentional acting pole. However, perhaps the time has come for a re-evaluation of this debate. It is possible that the functionalism of real-mind discourses suggests that the teleological nature of traditional fictional-mind representations may not be so "unrealistic" after all.

2. Language

This section will consider a range of views on the relationship between language and thought and, in particular, on the importance of language in the formation and development of the mind. It shows that there is a good deal more skepticism within the cognitive sciences regarding the role of language than there is within literary theory. In his book *Literary Theory* (1983), Terry Eagleton refers to language, with its problems, mysteries, and implications, as both paradigm and obsession for twentieth-century intellectual life (1983, 97). The first sentence of *Language and Materialism: Developments in Semiology and the Theory of the Subject* (1977) by Rosalind Coward and John Ellis is this: "Perhaps the most significant feature of twentieth-century intellectual development has been the way in which the study of language has opened the route to an understanding of mankind, social history, and the laws of how a society functions" (1977, 1). This is a large claim and one that I certainly do not feel equipped to comment on. My argument is simply that, whatever the value of the study of language generally, an undue emphasis on the role of language has inhibited our understanding of fictional mental functioning. The previous section provided a good illustration of this point. The functional approach is not primarily interested in the degree of verbality in thought. I am sure that you noticed that there was not a single reference to inner speech in the discussion of the mind in the previous section.

There is a continuing debate on the extent of our need for language in order to learn about the world and, therefore, its role in forming the conceptual framework for our thought. What is at issue is the extent to which the whole of our cognitive universe is determined by the language and culture within which we are socialized and, therefore, the extent to which all of the thought of an individual is culture-specific. The position that an individual's thinking is to a large degree determined by his or her culture is often called the *Sapir/Whorf hypothesis*, after the American anthropologists Edward Sapir and Benjamin Lee Whorf. I am not primarily concerned with this debate but with the much more limited point that inner speech is just one part of the whole mind. To use again the simple example of driving a car: inner speech is not necessary to the workings of the mind while driving, but it is not possible to learn to drive a car without language. I am interested, then, not in the role of language in how we learn to think, but in the supposed verbality of fictional mental events.

First, I will describe some perspectives on the nature of thought that down-play the role of language. The skepticism that exists within cognitive science regarding the extent to which language is involved in day-to-day thought is not a new phenomenon and has existed within psychology throughout the twentieth century. As the popular-science writer John McCrone points out, the "belief that words can only clothe thought has seemed so axiomatic that until a rediscovery of Vygotsky's work in the late 1980s, it was exceptional to find a recent Western philosophy or psychology text that even mentioned the possibility that language might make a difference. And in truth, introspection seemed to suggest that words are indeed mostly secondary" (1999, 289). The reference to introspection here raises an interesting point. Some people's introspections seem to tell them that, on the contrary, words are indeed mostly primary. Introspection is clearly a tricky business. Also, although Lev Vygotsky (a Russian psycholinguist active in the late 1920s and early 1930s) brought the notion of inner speech to the center of psychology, he acknowledged that, "even if recorded in full with the help of some supersensitive phonograph, the inner speech would remain abbreviated and incoherent" (1986, 235) and admitted that inner speech becomes so fragmented that it is barely language at all. He refers to inner speech as "practically wordless" (1986, 243), "speech almost without words" (1986, 244), and "to a large extent thinking in pure meanings" (1986, 249). I say more about Vygotsky in chapter 5, section 3.

A number of psychologists have asked whether the loss or reduction of intellectual functions invariably accompanies a major impairment of language competence, and so whether thought is dependent on an intact linguistic function. The importance of this question is that if the two can be separated, then thought is possible without inner speech. Several studies of groups of patients with aphasia (that is, loss of speech) have reported that the patients have unimpaired levels of non-verbal reasoning and intelligence. There are several well-known cases of severely aphasic people who are unable to understand or respond to even the simplest words or phrases and whose speech is babble, but who can undertake a variety of complex tasks, learn new skills, and maintain good social relations. The Russian psycholinguist Alexander Luria reported the case of the composer Shebalin, who suffered a serious stroke, the result of which was severe difficulty in speaking and understanding speech, but who continued to produce remarkable music (Ellis and Beattie 1986, 271–72). It appears that a person can be virtually robbed of language yet still perform intelligently in other areas.

The language of cognitive science refers to mental spaces, blends, scripts, frames, plans, and so on. This is not a conceptual framework that allows with any ease for a central role for language in thought. None of these concepts is concerned with inner speech. This point can be illustrated very easily. There are 471 entries in MITECS, but only a very few of them consider the role of language in thought, apart from the small group of entries that are specifically concerned with language. In particular, the entry on consciousness (Davies 1999, 190–92) does not refer to language in general or inner speech in particular at all apart from a brief passing reference to spoken speech. In a book of 313 pages on the working of the brain, *Going Inside: A Tour Round a Single Moment of Consciousness* (1999), John McCrone does not get around to talking about language until page 278. Terry Au's entry in MITECS on language and thought is also quite cool on the impact of the Sapir-Whorf hypothesis: "While the jury is still out for the Sapir-Whorf hypothesis, it is probably safe to say that important aspects of our worldview are unlikely to be at the mercy of arbitrary aspects of our language" (1999, 445). He reinforces the point by asserting that recent findings on language-specific impairments "suggest that language and cognition can be decoupled. . . . [T]here is some evidence for our cognition and perception shaping the evolution of our language. Evidence for influence in the opposite direction, however, seems more elusive" (1999, 444).

There is astonishingly little about inner speech in Antonio Damasio's book about consciousness, which shares the relentlessly unconvinced tone of other real-mind discourses. For example, language, he maintains, is a "translation of something else, a conversion from nonlinguistic images which stand for entities, events, relationships, and inferences. . . . [T]here must be a nonverbal self and a nonverbal knowing for which the words 'I' or 'me' or the phrase 'I know' are the appropriate translations, in any language" (2000, 107–8). He also refers to the "core self [that] must be in place for its translation into a suitable word to occur" (2000, 186) and to "the imaged, nonverbal narrative of core consciousness" (2000, 187).

Here I will quote a long passage from *The Language Instinct* (1994) in which Steven Pinker explains his views on the matter in no uncertain terms. It is worth quoting in full in order to give a flavor of the depth of the hostility that exists amongst some cognitive scientists on this issue.

The idea that thought is the same thing as language is an example of what can be called a conventional absurdity: a statement that goes against all common sense but that everyone believes because they dimly recall having heard it somewhere and because it is so pregnant with implications. . . . Think about it. We have all had the experience of uttering or writing a sentence, then stopping and realizing that it wasn't exactly what we meant to say. To have that feeling, there has to be a "what we meant to say" that is different from what we said. Sometimes it is not easy to find *any* words that properly convey a thought. When we hear or read, we usually remember the gist, not the exact words, so there has to be such a thing as a gist that is not the same as a bunch of words. And if thoughts depended on words, how could a new word ever be coined? How could a child learn a word to begin with? How could translation from one language to another be possible? (1994, 57–58)

[handwritten margin note: do thoughts produce words or do words produce thoughts?]

To get around these difficulties, some cognitive science is based on the controversial and contested assumption that we think in a very abstract, symbolic language form that is called *mentalese*. According to Pinker, we do not think in a natural language such as English because natural languages are full of ambiguities and whatever we think in cannot be ambiguous because that is not the way our mental functioning works. Also, spoken languages are full of what he calls "grammatical boilerplate," which is not necessary for the language of thought. "So," Pinker concludes, "the statements in a knowledge system are not sentences in English but rather inscriptions in a richer language of thought, 'mentalese'" (1997, 70).

As I said, this is a continuing debate, and there are some cognitive scientists who emphatically stress the centrality of language to thought, although these views are often related more to the powerful role that language plays in forming our minds, rather than the role of language in everyday thought. Daniel Dennett makes the point about cognitive formation that language "infects and inflects our thought at every level. . . . The structures of grammar enforce a discipline on our habits of thought, shaping the ways in which we probe our own 'data-bases.' . . . [W]e can see how the powerful voices that a language unleashes in a brain can be exploited" (1991, 301). Cognitive scientists have drawn methodological conclusions about the study of the mind from this argument. Ray Jackendoff observes that "any theory of the semantic structure of language is ipso facto a theory of the structure of thought" (1983, 209) and that "to study semantics of natural language *is* to study cognitive psychology" (1983, 3). Gilles Fauconnier makes a similar point. "Because we know language to be intimately connected to some important mental processes, we have in principle a rich virtually inexhaustible source of data to investigate some aspects of mental processes" (1997, 2–3). However, Fauconnier also offers this important caveat: "Language data suffers when it is restricted to language, for the simple reason that the interesting cognitive constructions underlying language use have to do with complete situations that include highly structured background knowledge, various kinds of reasoning, on-line meaning construction, and negotiation of meaning" (1997, 7–8). It is surely deeply significant that this warning, although it relates to the study of the real mind, uncannily echoes the argument of this book regarding the need to study the fictional mind in the context of the complete situations that are described in novels.

I mentioned earlier that the results of introspection can vary wildly. Dennett evocatively describes the sensation of inner speech in a way that, to me certainly, rings very true: "Not only do we talk to ourselves silently, but sometimes we do this in a particular 'tone of voice.' Other times, it seems as if there are words, but not *heard* words, and at still other times, only the faintest shadows or hints of words are somehow 'there' to clothe our thoughts" (1991, 59). However, in a way that is characteristic of philosophers when discussing consciousness, he provides a familiar reservation: "In any event, the phenomenology of vivid thought is not restricted to talking to oneself; we can draw pictures to ourselves in our mind's eyes, drive a stick-shift car to ourselves, touch silk to ourselves and savor an imaginary peanut-butter sandwich" (1991, 59). My experience of works of philosophy and psychology is that they tend to sound more comfortable when describing, for example, the visual aspects of consciousness than when they are discussing the linguistic aspects.

An important characteristic of the pro-language perspective is its functional emphasis on the purposive nature of language: the use we make of language to direct and manage our thought and action. Here are four different perspectives on this issue: From a neurological perspective, it appears that scanner images show that the structure of language penetrates many parts of the brain and not just Broca's and Wernicke's areas, the two that are most closely associated with the use of language. In the normal course of events, when we learn language while young, when the brain is fairly plastic, the hardwiring of the brain is crucially affected by language. From a developmental perspective, Dennett suggests that "the practice of asking oneself questions could arise as a natural side effect of asking questions of others, and its utility would be similar: it would be a behavior that could be recognized to enhance one's prospects by promoting better-informed action-guidance" (1991, 195). That is, talking to oneself is "a way of building a 'virtual wire' between the relevant subsystems" (1991, 196). Here Dennett follows the Vygotskian line of thinking on how outer, directive speech goes underground and becomes inner speech. He concludes that "the greater virtues of sotto voce talking to oneself would be recognized, leading later to entirely silent talking to oneself" (1991, 197). This idea is discussed in greater detail in chapter 5, section 3.

From the perspective of situated, distributed, or shared cognition (see chapter 5, section 5), the philosophers Andy Clark and David Chalmers assert in their article "The Extended Mind" (1998) that "the major burden of the coupling between agents is carried by language. Without language, we might be much more akin to discrete Cartesian 'inner' minds, in which high-level cognition relies largely on internal resources. But the advent of language has allowed us to spread this burden into the world" (1998, 18). I discuss in chapter 5 the insight that language is one cognitive tool among others, albeit the most important of them. Finally, the narratological perspective. According to Lubomir Doležel, "[i]nner conflict is located in the mental domain of the acting person; it arises from contradictory intentions, desires, goals, strategies, and so forth. It manifests itself in the form of interior monologue, a basic verbal expression of mental tension" (1998, 109). This is a welcome functional approach toward the role of language in fictional thought. However, the verbal expression of mental tension is only one form of expression among a wide range of others, and we miss a good deal of other evidence of fictional mental functioning if we place excessive reliance on the purely verbal kind.

It is interesting to note that none of the theorists discussed earlier consider the possibility that the extent of verbality of thought, the importance of inner speech, may vary from individual to individual. There is an illuminating discussion on this point by Ann Waldron Neumann in which she compares the tags used to describe Elizabeth Bennet's and Lydia Bennet's thought processes in Jane Austen's *Pride and Prejudice*. Neumann comments that the narrator uses the term *saw* frequently when conveying Lydia's inner life in order to suggest a very simple primarily visual consciousness, while Elizabeth's thought is more highly developed and sophisticated and much more closely related to inner language. Although this is a useful idea, I am not sure that I would accept these value-laden terms, and it is predictable that Neumann should conclude with the remark that "Lydia suggests a nearly total absence of *thought*" (1986, 383). Thought that occurs in highly visual terms is still thought.

3. Non-verbal Consciousness

I drew attention in the previous section to the non-verbal nature of the terms that are used by cognitive science theorists to describe aspects of consciousness. There are several other examples of similar terms. One that is frequently used by philosophers is the term *qualia*: "The felt or phenomenal qualities associated with experiences, such as the feeling of a pain, or the hearing of a sound, or the viewing of a colour" (Blackburn 1994, 313). Note the non-linguistic nature of the three examples. Philosophers also use the term *what it's like* as a near synonym for qualia. Another example is this repeated reference to *feelings*:

"Consciousness begins as a feeling . . . consciousness feels like a feeling . . . a feeling of knowing. . . . The mysterious first-person perspective of consciousness consists of newly-minted knowledge, information if you will, expressed as feeling" (Damasio 2000, 312–13). The term *images* is yet another example. Many of us, I think, will have experienced a deeply unpleasant memory as a visual image combined with an almost physical pain. Damasio talks repeatedly of mind events as images, and although he stresses that these need not be visual, his terminology undoubtedly marginalizes the role of language in thought. According to MITECS, "imagery played a central role in theories of the mind for centuries" (Kosslyn and Rabin 1999, 387). Also, "[s]till other evidence for thinking without language has to do with mental images. Scientists and writers as well as visual artists have claimed that some of their most creative work was inspired by their mental images. . . . It seems, then, brilliant as well as mundane thought is eminently possible without language" (Au 1999, 444). Finally, with regard to purposive and functional mental activity, Dennett's view is that "[t]alking aloud is only one possibility. Drawing pictures to yourself is another readily appreciated act of self-manipulation" (1991, 197). For example, "Doc McCoy had a fairly good map of the United States in his mind, surprisingly detailed, and as up-to-date as he could keep it" (Thompson 2002, 99).

In the following taxonomies of consciousness, notice how little attention is given to the linguistic elements. Steven Pinker identifies three different uses of the term *consciousness* as follows:

1. *self-knowledge*: self-awareness or self-consciousness.
2. *access to information*: the information relating to mental events that can be accessed by the systems' underlying verbal reports, rational thought, and deliberate decision-making. This kind of consciousness has four features: a rich field of sensation (colors, shapes, sounds, smells, pressures, and aches); portions of this information falling under the spotlight of attention, getting rotated in and out of short term memory, and feeding deliberative cogitation; sensations having an emotional flavoring (pleasant or unpleasant, interesting or repellant, exciting or soothing); and an executive, the "I," which makes choices and pulls the levers of behavior.
3. *sentience*: or qualia, subjective experience, phenomenal awareness, raw feelings, what it's like to do something and so on. (Pinker 1997, 134–39)

In what Daniel Dennett refers to as a "brief tour of the phenomenological garden" (1991, 45), he picks out the following items: "experiences of the 'external' world such as sights, sounds, smells, slippery and scratchy feelings,

feelings of heat and cold, and of the positions of our limbs"; "experiences of the purely 'internal' world, such as fantasy images, the inner sights and sounds of daydreaming and talking to yourself, recollections, bright ideas, and sudden hunches"; and "experiences of emotion or 'affect' . . . ranging from bodily pains, tickles and 'sensations' of hunger and thirst, through intermediate emotional storms of anger, joy, hatred, embarrassment, lust, astonishment, to the least corporeal visitations of pride, anxiety, regret, ironic detachment, rue, awe, icy calm." Dennett stresses that "this taxonomy owes more to superficial similarity and dubious tradition than to any deep kinship among the phenomena" (1991, 46), and his book is in fact an attempt to replace this "folk-psychology" version of the mind with a more counterintuitive version. Nevertheless, I refer to it here because, like Pinker's, it is a widely accepted view of the mind in which the emphasis is very much on the non-verbal aspects of consciousness.

The rest of this section is taken up with a fairly detailed exploration of a third taxonomy of consciousness together with illustrations from a fictional text. John Searle lists in *The Rediscovery of the Mind* (1992) what he calls twelve gross structural features of normal everyday mental reality (1992, 128). It is his attempt to describe what the experience of consciousness is actually like. I have reorganized and simplified his list in order to sharpen its relevance to narrative. It is significant that only one part of one of Searle's twelve features refers to inner speech. I have illustrated Searle's categories with quotes from *The Crying of Lot 49* by Thomas Pynchon. I noticed after I had chosen the examples that they are all in the mode of thought report, although one or two are on the borderline with free indirect thought.

Searle refers first to what he calls *finite modalities*. These include the six senses, including balance; bodily sensations such as pain and the sensory awareness of the position of one's body; and the stream of thought. The stream of thought contains feelings and emotions such as a sudden surge of anger; words; visual images; and other elements that are neither verbal nor images. For example, a thought can occur suddenly in a flash and in a form that is neither words nor images (Searle 1992, 128).It is significant that, even within the aspect that Searle calls the stream of thought, he emphasizes non-verbal elements such as emotions and visual images at the expense of inner speech, which is completely marginalized.

The next feature is *unity*. Searle argues that conscious states come to us as part of a unified sequence. Without a sense of unity, we could not make sense of our experiences. (Searle and Damasio tend to emphasize the unity given by the sense of the self; conversely, Dennett and also Galen Strawson [1997] stress the "gappiness" and discontinuity of consciousness.) Vertical unity is the binding of disparate elements into a unified column: I have simultaneous experiences of various separate things as part of one and the same conscious event. Horizontal unity is the remembered present, the organization of conscious experiences through short stretches of time: I am aware of the beginning of the sentence that I am now finishing (Searle 1992, 129–30). Example of vertical unity: "Oedipa stood in the living room, stared at by the greenish dead eye of the TV tube, spoke the name of God, tried to feel as drunk as possible" (1996, 5). Example of horizontal unity: "Through the rest of the afternoon, through her trip to the market . . . then through the sunned gathering of her marjoram . . . into the layering of a lasagna . . . eventually, oven on, into the mixing of the twilight's whiskey sours . . . she wondered, wondered, shuffling back through a fat deckful of days" (1996, 5–6).

This feature could be used to ask several questions of fictional texts: What techniques, if any, does the narrator use to convey this sense of the unity of characters' consciousnesses? What are the difficulties in conveying vertical unity, given the relentlessly linear nature of narrative discourse? Do some narrators convey it more than others? If these differences exist, what would be their significance? For example, a good deal of twentieth-century fiction can be understood in terms of its evident desire to disrupt or problematize the sense of the unified nature of experience and to portray clearly non-unified states of consciousness. This comment also applies to several of the other features later described.

Searle then discusses the technical, philosophical concept of *intentionality*. In this context, intentionality means that a conscious state is directed at, or is about, something or other. Most consciousness is intentional, but not all. If I am depressed about something, this is an intentional state. If I am depressed, but not about anything in particular, then this state is not intentional (Searle 1992, 130–31). He elaborates further and introduces a concept that will assume greater and greater importance within this study. He says that every intentional state has what he calls an *aspectual shape*. This means that my conscious experiences are always from a particular point of view, are always perspectival. Seeing an object from a point of view consists of seeing it under certain aspects and not others. All seeing is seeing as (Searle 1992, 131). Example of an intentional state: "working hours were exquisite torture to him" (1996, 7). Example of a non-intentional state (where the context makes it clear that the state is not a response to the surroundings): "He gazed at her . . . [his] face now smooth, amiable, at peace" (1996, 99). The narratological implications of this analysis are fascinating. Intentional states of consciousness would tend to relate to events and situations that have already been established in the story. These events and situations would form reasons, causes, and motives for the resulting states of mind and would therefore have an obvious teleological value. For example, a character may be depressed because of a reversal in fortunes. Non-intentional states would work in a different way because they would not have external causes but could themselves function as causes of future events. For example, because the character was depressed for no reason, he went on a journey that made him feel better.

One of the most pervasive features of ordinary conscious awareness is the aspect of *familiarity*. Searle argues that the prior possession of an apparatus that is sufficient to generate organized consciousness automatically guarantees that the aspectual features of conscious experience will be more or less familiar. When I walk down the street, objects are familiar to me as trees, houses, and so on. Perhaps most important of all, I have an inner sense of what it feels like to be me, a feeling of myself (Searle 1992, 133–34). This aspect of familiarity makes possible much of the organization and order of my conscious experience. Consciousness involves categorization, but the categories have to exist prior to the experience because they are the conditions of possibility of having the experience. They enable us, to varying degrees, to assimilate our experiences, however novel, to the familiar (Searle 1992, 135–36). Example of familiarity: "She knew the pattern because it had happened a few times already" (1996, 30). Of course, narrators tend to be more interested in a character's lack of familiarity with their surroundings. This sort of unfamiliarity has a good deal of potential for various sorts of psychic disturbance and conflict with others. Example of unfamiliarity: "She moved through [the campus] carrying her fat book, attracted, unsure, a stranger, wanting to feel relevant but knowing how much of a search among alternative universes it would take" (1996, 71).

Searle also comments on what he describes as the *figure-ground* or *gestalt structure of conscious experience*. Gestalt psychology shows that our perceptual experiences come to us organized as a figure against a background. For example, I see the sweater against the background of the table on which it is lying. I do not perceive mere undifferentiated shapes, because our normal perceptions are always structured in this way. However, Searle argues that this seems to be true not only of perception but also of consciousness generally. When I focus my attention on something, it is against a background that is not the center of attention. All seeing is seeing as; all perceiving is perceiving as; and all consciousness is consciousness of something as such and such (Searle 1992, 132–33). It is within this context that Searle focuses on the question of attention and introduces the notions of *the center* and *the periphery*. Within the field of consciousness, some things are at the center of our attention, and some things are at the periphery. We are conscious of a very large number of things that we are not attending to or focusing our attention upon. Nonetheless, all of these phenomena are part of our conscious awareness (Searle 1992, 137–38). Searle emphasizes that we need to distinguish the center of attention/periphery distinction from the conscious/unconscious distinction. When I drive, my attention may be on other thoughts, but I do not drive unconsciously. There are different levels of attention within conscious states. During a drive, my highest level of attention is on my thoughts; at a lower level, but still attention, I am paying attention to my driving; in addition, there are many other things that I am peripherally aware of but that are nowhere near the center of my attention. However, it is not true to say that I am unconscious of these things. He concludes in a functionalist manner that attention goes to where it is needed and goes away from where it is not needed (Searle 1992, 138–39).

Example: "She stood in a nearly deserted parking lot, watching the headlights of Metzger's car come at her, and wondered how accidental [a previous incident] had been" (1996, 54). Her wondering is at the center of her attention, and the car is at the periphery. But if the car were to come too close, attention would go to where it is needed, and the car would then become the center of her attention. Another example: "She got in and rode with him for two miles before realizing that . . . the disc jockey talking was her husband, Mucho" (1996, 54–55). The radio program is at the periphery of her attention but comes into the center once the aspect of familiarity is recognized. Searle's use of the philosophical concept of attention is flexible and illuminating in part because it is a continuum, not a dichotomy. It is often not possible and not interesting to say how conscious or unconscious a character is of a particular mental event. It may be easier and more rewarding, as in these examples, to analyze fictional thought in terms of the center and periphery of attention. Although I have used the term *non-consciousness* in the heading to the next section because it is the generally accepted term, I think that Searle's terminology is in many ways preferable.

Another important feature of everyday mental reality with extensive implications for narrative discourse is the existence of *boundary conditions*. During the stream of thought, I tend not to think about where I am located, what day of the month it is, and so on. This is part of the situatedness, the spatio-temporal, socio-biological location of my present conscious states. Any state of consciousness is characteristically located in this way, although the location may not be the object of consciousness, even at the periphery. The pervasiveness of the boundary of consciousness is most noticeable in cases of breakdown. A sense of disorientation occurs when one cannot remember where one is or what day it is (Searle 1992, 139). Novels tend to be about crises in characters' lives, and so the boundaries that Searle describes are often reached. Therefore, the description of fictional minds experiencing this breakdown is common in a wide range of novels. In particular, it is not surprising that a postmodern novel such as *The Crying of Lot 49* has several examples. "[S]o in her first minute of San Narciso, a revelation also trembled just past the threshold of her understanding" (1996, 15); "At some point she went into the bathroom, tried to find her image in the mirror and couldn't. She had a moment of nearly pure terror" (1996, 27); "Something came to her viscera, danced briefly, and went" (1996, 53); "feeling like a fluttering curtain in a very high window, moving up to then out over the abyss" (1996, 105); and "She stood . . . in the night, her isolation complete, and tried to face towards the sea. But she'd lost her bearings" (1996, 122).

Searle also refers to the *overflow*. By this he means that conscious states tends to refer beyond their immediate content. They spill over to connect with other thoughts in long, associative series. If I look out of the window at the trees, the lake, and so on, and I am then asked what I have seen, my answer will have an indefinite extendibility (Searle 1992, 137). Examples: "What the road really was, she fancied, was this hypodermic needle, inserted somewhere ahead into the vein of a freeway" (1996, 16) and "But she'd only been reminded of her look downhill this noontime. Some immediacy was there again, some promise of hierophany: printed circuit, gently curving streets, private access to the water, Book of the Dead" (1996, 20). It is in these ways that narrators make regular use of associations in thought processes such as the chains of correspondences in which memories and sensations accompany immediate experiences. It can form an important part of the presentation of mind, not just in stream of consciousness novels, but also in more plot-oriented fictions such as *The Crying of Lot 49*.

Finally, Searle comments on *mood*. A mood, by itself, never constitutes the whole content of a conscious state. Rather, it provides the tone or color that characterizes the whole conscious state. We are always in a particular mood if the word is defined broadly enough to include a tone to our experiences, even if it is sometimes a neutral tone. It is characteristic of moods that they pervade all of our conscious experiences, and it is typical of normal conscious life that we are always in some mood or other. Moods need not be consciously directed at any intentional conditions of satisfaction (Searle 1992, 140). A related feature is the *pleasure/unpleasure dimension*. If we take the whole of a conscious state, a slice out of the flow of consciousness that is big enough to have some unity and coherence, then there is always a dimension of pleasure or unpleasure (Searle 1992, 141). Sometimes this can be intentional (in the philosophical sense described earlier) such as finding it unpleasant to see something disgusting and sometimes not as in bodily sensations (Searle 1992, 129). The description of characters' moods is clearly an important element in narrative discourse. Examples: "There had hung the sense of buffeting, insulation, she had noticed the absence of an intensity, as if watching a movie, just perceptibly out of focus, that the projectionist refused to fix" (1996, 12) and "She could carry the sadness of the moment with her that way forever, see the world refracted through those tears, those specific tears" (1996, 13). However, I found it significantly more difficult to illustrate this feature from the Pynchon novel than I did the others. This may be because it should often be unnecessary for the narrator to specify in literal terms a character's mood. It can emerge naturally for the reader from information on all aspects of that character's embedded narrative. For example, in a subtle and oblique novel such as *The Crying of Lot 49*, it would be inappropriate for the narrator to state in bald and explicit terms that Oedipa's moods progress from restlessness, curiosity, excitement, and unease to anxiety, fear, and terror.

4. Non-consciousness

Now we can move beyond the question of immediate consciousness, which can become a straitjacket. There is much more to the mind than consciousness, as the next three sections will show in some detail. This point is particularly important because, as the philosophers Andy Clark and David Chalmers point out, "many identify the cognitive with the conscious" (1998, 10) and so will find the idea of the *extended mind* unconvincing. This term relates to notions of social and intermental thinking, which are explained in chapter 5, section 5 and which are pivotal concepts within the structure of this book. Therefore, an appreciation at this stage of the importance of a wide variety of states of mind in mental functioning will help to make the idea of the extended mind, when it is explained in more detail later, more palatable.

I have deliberately used the term *non-consciousness* and not the more familiar term, the *unconscious*. I mentioned in chapter 1 that I wish to get away from the Freudian overtones of the latter term. There has been a tendency in the past to identify the two, and this has hampered a full understanding of how much can be encompassed within the broader heading of non-consciousness. However, it is noticeable that theorists are careful to acknowledge the debt to Freud in this area. As Freud emphasized, "much of information processing takes place at an unconscious level. We are aware of only a small portion of our overall mental life, a tip of the cognitive iceberg" (Holyoak 1999, xlii). Antonio Damasio is very informative about the range of the non-conscious and also puts this wide range in the context of the familiar notion of the unconscious:

> The unconscious, in the narrow meaning in which the word has been etched in our culture, is only a part of the vast amount of processes and contents that remain nonconscious, not known in core or extended consciousness. In fact, the list of the "not-known" is astounding. Consider what it includes:
>
> 1. all the fully formed images to which we do not attend;
> 2. all the neural patterns that never become images;
> 3. all the dispositions that were acquired through experience, lie dormant, and may never become an explicit neural pattern;
> 4. all the quiet remodeling of such dispositions and all their quiet renetworking—that may never become explicitly known; and
> 5. all the hidden wisdom and know-how that nature embodied in innate, homeostatic dispositions.
>
> Amazing, indeed, how little we ever know. (2000, 228)

Items three, four, and five of Damasio's list are dispositions that are dealt with in the next section.

The points that I wish to make on non-consciousness can perhaps best be illustrated by the narratologist Ann Banfield's comments on Bertrand Russell's *An Inquiry into Meaning and Truth* (1940), from which she quotes as follows: "Suppose you are out walking on a wet day, and you see a puddle and avoid it. You are not likely to say to yourself: 'there is a puddle; it will be advisable not to step in it.' But if somebody said 'why did you suddenly step aside?' you would answer 'because I didn't wish to step into that puddle.' You know, retrospectively, that you had a visual perception . . . and . . . you express this knowledge in words" (Russell 1940, 49, quoted in Banfield 1982, 197–98). Banfield uses this example to illustrate the conceptual distinction between what she calls reflective or verbal thought and what she calls non-reflective consciousness, which she appears to identify primarily with perception. Her uncontroversial argument is that perception is not dependent on verbal or conscious thought. As she and Russell agree, people do not say to themselves, "There is a puddle and I wish to avoid it." However, the rigidity of the verbal bias prevents Banfield from taking the example further. She misses the full force of it by focusing only on the visual perception of the puddle as an example of non-verbal thought. The much more interesting conclusion to be drawn from this example is that the individual does not just have a *perception* of the puddle and thereby acquires the *knowledge* that it is a puddle that they see. The person also adopts the *belief* that stepping into the puddle will be unpleasant, forms the *intention* to avoid the puddle for the *purpose* of not getting wet, makes a *decision* to avoid the puddle, and then performs the *action* of walking around the puddle. It is very significant that Banfield edits out of her quote from Russell a reference by him to action. The original passage reads: "You know, retrospectively, that you had a visual perception, *to which you reacted appropriately*" (Russell 1940, 49; emphasis added). This is an example, not just of passive, private perception, but also of mental action in a physical context. This mental functioning involves a sophisticated cognitive process, comprising several elements, involving various areas of the mind in addition to perception, and all taking place at the periphery of the subject's attention.

According to Banfield, what forces consciousness to become reflective is the subject being asked what he or she is doing: a request for linguistic information is the catalyst because to speak of something always implies reflective consciousness of it (1982, 198). Though true, this is very misleading. In the case of the very artificial and highly unlikely example of a conversation about a puddle, it is the request for information that forces the mental event to become conscious and therefore highly verbal. However, in reality, there is an infinite number of other reasons why non-self-conscious mental events become conscious and why they then cease to be self-conscious by no longer being at the center of an individual's attention. There is a wide spectrum of attention along which mental events move, and this movement to and fro along the scale of attention is very fluid. The rigid dichotomy of reflective and non-reflective thought does not reflect the complexity and the fluidity of the mind that was shown in the Searle taxonomy, which was discussed in the previous section. Banfield's example is also interesting with regard to the presentation of action in the discourse. Most attempts to list episodes of presentations of mind in a particular passage of fiction would not include a sentence such as "She avoided the puddle." It is much more likely that this statement would be classified simply as a narrative description of an event in the storyworld. This is probably why Banfield leaves out of her quotation the words that relate to the action taken. But I will argue in section 7 of this chapter and also in chapter 7, section 2 that descriptions of actions should be regarded, in part, as descriptions of the network of mental states and events such as intentions, beliefs, and decisions that lie behind the physical behavior and form part of the philosophical concept of action. It is through descriptions of actions that narrators portray the social minds of characters in their public and physical context. The distinction between descriptions of action and of consciousness can often be difficult to see.

Antonio Damasio is very good on the sensation of realizing that non-conscious processes have been at work within our minds without our "knowing" it. He reminds us that "we often realize quite suddenly, in a given situation, that we feel anxious or uncomfortable, pleased or relaxed, and it is apparent that the particular state of feeling we know then has not begun on the moment of knowing but rather sometime before" (2000, 36). The non-conscious includes not only feelings that we belatedly become aware of and the processes involved in automatically avoiding puddles but also large and important mental events. For example, sometimes we make up our mind about a big decision without realizing it. Consciously, we are torn between choice A and choice B. However, we begin to notice that, unconsciously, all our planning about the future is predicated on the assumption that we will choose B. When we then finally and consciously choose B, we know instantly that it is the right thing to do. We do not experience the doubts that we thought we would have. We feel a sense of lightness and relief because we had made up our mind some time ago but had not realized it. For example, "She had feared that being on her own again would be painful; instead, she had begun to realize, she felt rather like that gull: it hadn't liked the way it was treated, so it had taken flight and soared away" (Leon 2001, 115). When we say, "I did that without thinking!" and "I didn't put much thought into it!" what we often mean is that all the thought was put in beforehand. Picasso, near the end of his career, when asked how long it had taken him to do a very simple sketch, replied that it had taken him sixty years. On a less exalted plane, this is how skills of many sorts are developed. Indeed, "[m]any of our unthinking activities, such as driving a car, could become unthinking only after passing through a long period of design development that was explicitly self-conscious" (Dennett 1996, 155). Our dispositions, beliefs, and attitudes are unconscious for most of the time unless activated for some reason: "Religion, Brunetti reflected, as he stood on the steps, though he had never realized this until Paola had pointed it out to him, always made him uncomfortable" (Leon 2001, 150).

Much of the non-conscious nature of our mental functioning can be explained by the functional approach to the notion of attention. Cognitive science

brain's preference is to make as much as possible of its activity
This kind of "management by exception" is more efficient than
ing involved in activities for which it is not required. As Searle
's to where it is needed. This way, consciousness is reserved
...ses and can deal with the unexpected. Damasio observes that only a
fraction of what goes on mentally is really clean enough and well lit enough to
be noticed." In fact, it is "advantageous not to notice yourself knowing" (2000,
129–30). Dennett and Damasio both make this point in slightly different terms:
"Most of our intentional actions are performed without [elaborate practical
reasoning], and a good thing too, since there wouldn't be time" (Dennett 1991,
252). "The lack of dependence on conscious survey automates a substantial
part of our behavior and frees us in terms of attention and time—two scarce
commodities in our lives—to plan and execute other tasks and create solutions
for new problems" (Damasio 2000, 300). This emphasis on the need to reserve
attention for when it is required to deal with surprises fits in well with the need
for narrators to focus on fictional events that, in order to form a plot, will "surprise" (in the widest sense) the characters. Pip is living a settled and uneventful
life that does not require all his attention until he experiences the surprise that
Magwich's return gives him. His dilemma requires his full attention, and the
plot becomes eventful.

5. Dispositions

Philosophical behaviorists maintain that mental events are logical constructions
out of dispositions to behave in certain ways. This is a very strong claim that
amounts, in non-philosophical language, to saying that, when we talk about
mental events, we are talking *only* about dispositions to behave. I am not concerned with the truth or falsity of this position or with whether or not its truth
or falsity could ever be established. I simply want to point out that it is odd
that narrative discourse analysis has neglected phenomena such as dispositions
that are so central to other discourses that are also related to the mind. Dispositions play an especially important role in the workings of the fictional mind
because they are the primary link between the study of characters' immediate
consciousnesses and the area of characterization. Currently, as I said in chapter
2, there is surprisingly little cross-fertilization between these two areas, and
I hope that this state of affairs will come to seem increasingly strange as we
continue through this chapter. I wish to build up a perspective on the mind in
which it is seen, in Patricia Highsmith's words, as "not an event, not a moment,
but a condition" (1968, 173).

The term *dispositions* covers a very wide range of mental phenomena. As Damasio remarks, what we "usually describe as a 'personality' depends on multiple contributions . . . anything from trivial preferences to ethical principles" (2000, 222). Clifford Geertz contends that the term *mind* denotes "a class of skills, propensities, capacities, tendencies, habits" (1993, 58). These are states of mind or dispositions that, Damasio claims, are "records which are dormant and implicit rather than active and explicit, as images are" (2000, 160). In the vivid and very informative phrase that I used in chapter 3, Daniel Dennett calls them "mind-ruts" (1991, 300). Equally important to an expanded narratological view of fictional states of mind is Searle's concept of the *background*, which has something in common with the notion of dispositions. He points out that some mental states sound unnatural when described as beliefs. For example, I may have a belief that the system of congestion charging that has recently been imposed in London (that is, charging motorists to drive into the center of the city) will benefit the center of London. But I do not, in the same way, have a belief that objects are solid. I simply behave in such a way that I take the solidity of objects for granted. It is part of my network of background suppositions. What Searle calls the *background* consists of the mental capacities, dispositions, stances, ways of behaving, know-how, and so on that manifest themselves in, for example, intentional actions, perceptions, and thoughts (1992, 196). Searle is talking about some basic states of minds that, together with more sophisticated states such as beliefs and attitudes, are as much a part of whole fictional minds as immediate consciousness. To take Searle's concept in a slightly different but related direction, it is necessary for readers to make use of a similar network of background suppositions in order to put together coherent fictional minds out of scattered references to particular characters in the text. Some aspects of the background were included in the alternative approach to consciousness that was discussed in section 3.

Antonio Damasio describes the differences between immediate, single mental events and states that continue over time in terms of two selves: "the seemingly changing self and the seemingly permanent self" (2000, 217), which he also refers to as the *core self* and the *autobiographical self*. He suggests that, in "core consciousness, the sense of self arises in the subtle, fleeting feeling of knowing, constructed anew in each pulse." On the other hand, "[e]xtended consciousness still hinges on the same core 'you,' but that 'you' is now connected to the lived past and anticipated future that are part of your autobiographical record" (2000, 196). In the context of this discussion, mental events happen to the core self, and states are attributes of the autobiographical self. Incidentally, Damasio uses this notion of the two selves to shed a little light on one of the great mysteries of life: why we feel that we are always changing while simultaneously feeling that we always stay the same. In his view, it is the core self that causes the feeling of change and the autobiographical self that causes the feeling of sameness.

Memory is clearly an important aspect of the picture of the mind that is described in this chapter, including both memory stores that hold information for very brief periods of time and long-term memories that we carry with us always but may never retrieve for years at a time. Searle argues against a simplistic view of memory, pointing out that both language and culture tend to force on us a picture of memory as a storehouse or library of propositions, images, and representations. Searle thinks that it is more complex than that. We should think of memory rather as a mechanism for generating current performance, such as conscious thoughts and actions, based on past experience (Searle 1992, 187). This notion of memory as a mechanism rather than a big storeroom is completely consistent with the functional and dynamic conception of characters' minds as embedded narratives. Both convey a sense of the causal process or relationship that exists between memories of the past, behavior in the present, and plans for the future. In both cases the past is seen as actively causing, or generating, the present and the future.

Notwithstanding Searle's warning that we should be careful about an over-simplistic use of mental metaphors such as storerooms, the fact remains that we do use metaphors of this sort in order to conceptualize mental functioning. Given that we do, the metaphor that is most suitable for the whole mind is not that of the stream or flow of consciousness, but that of the mind as a container. The former tends to lead us to think of immediate consciousness as the norm while the latter makes room for all aspects of the mind. For example, "speakers often talk about ideas as if they were physical objects at different physical locations in the mind conceived of as a physical container. This commonsensical view is the well-known MIND-AS-CONTAINER metaphor. It is manifested in sentences such as 'Yolanda put the idea into Xavier's mind' and 'In some dark corner of his mind, Xavier knew he was wrong'" (Barnden 1995, 248). A number of other metaphors are also derived from the container model. It is significant that we talk of having something "at the back of" our minds. This is a folk-psychology recognition of the fact that the mind is a three- or four-dimensional, not a two-dimensional phenomenon. There are other folk-psychology formulations that are equally revealing: "turn my mind to it," "it went out of my mind," "he was out of his mind," "in my mind's eye," and "off the top of my head." Interestingly, many of them lend themselves very well to third-person formulations. The tendency to conceptualize the mind as a multidimensional container, not as a two-dimensional stream, gets support from Damasio, who says that in the brain there is an image space and also a dispositional space. "The *dispositional space* is that in which dispositions contain the knowledge base and the mechanisms with which . . . the processing of images can be facilitated." In other words, they are "abstract records of potentialities" (Damasio 2000, 331–32).

The terminology already exists within narrative theory that can reflect the distinction between immediate mental events, and dispositions and states of mind that exist over time. As a number of dichotomies are available for this purpose, it makes it all the more surprising that the opportunity has not been taken to apply the terminology in any systematic way to mental life. The event/state, event/existent, and the dynamic/static oppositions are standard ones in narratology. States and existents are those things that exist through time, and events are the changes that occur to existents. Thoughts are *dynamic events* and states of mind or dispositions are *static states* or *existents*. The same distinction can be put in terms of *stasis* (in this context, states of mind) and *process* (mental events). To illustrate this relationship, I will use two examples from *Vanity Fair*: First, "Away went George, his nerves quivering with excitement at the news so long looked for, so sudden when it came" (1994, 292). Here, process modifies stasis. The stasis is the state of anticipating the news; the process is the reaction to the news. Second, "Our Emmy, who had never hated, never sneered all her life, was powerless in the hands of her remorseless little enemy" (1994, 289). Here, stasis is the cause of process. The stasis is the disposition not to hate or sneer; the process is the current feeling of powerlessness.

The current bias within the study of fictional minds toward events at the expense of states appears to be a reflection of a wider bias that affects the presentation of fictional worlds generally. Marie-Laure Ryan has pointed out that, while "events are usually represented in great detail in narrative discourse, the configuration of states is hardly ever fully explicited [*sic*]" (1985, 718). Equally significantly, from my point of view, Ryan argues that, although "events get more attention on the level of discourse . . . they receive their meaning from the states between which they mediate, and the specification of the latter is of equal importance on the level of plot" (1985, 719). Although she is talking generally here, this sounds to be like a very accurate description of the relationship between mind events and mind states. Not all narrative theorists are fixated on mental events, however. Richard J. Gerrig, when considering the factors that influence characters' actions, draws a sharp distinction between the dispositional factors that are internal to individuals and the situational factors that are external to individuals (1993, 54). This distinction raises fascinating questions such as, What exactly are the means by which we build up the detailed and coherent sense of a character's disposition that enables us to make the distinction? A response to this question might then blur Gerrig's distinction because it may be that it is often characters' dispositions that get them into particular situations. It is this rich and complex relationship between events, dispositions, and contexts that is at the heart of novel reading. We ask ourselves continually, Given the sort of disposition that this particular character has, how will he or she react in this specific situation? The answers to this question will then modify to a greater or lesser extent the initial hypotheses that we have formed regarding that character.

6. Emotions

In this section I will attempt to demonstrate the importance of the emotions in any analysis of the whole of the fictional mind and to suggest some of the ways in which fictional emotion can be studied. In the context of fictional minds, Doležel maintains that emotions have "regained their status as powerful motivational factors but continue to elude theoretical grasp" (1998, 65). While discussing real minds, Damasio refers to "the scientific neglect of emotion" (2000, 39) but reassures us that, in recent years, "both neuroscience and cognitive neuroscience have finally endorsed emotion" (2000, 40). Now is the time for narrative theory to follow suit.

After the Box Hill expedition in *Emma*, Knightly reprimands Emma for being rude to Miss Bates: "Emma recollected, blushed, was sorry, but tried to laugh it off" (1996, 309). When he has finished his reprimand, this happens:

He had misinterpreted the feelings which had kept her face averted, and her tongue motionless. They were combined only of anger against herself, mortification and deep concern. She had not been able to speak; and, on entering the carriage, sunk back for a moment overcome—then reproaching herself for having taken no leave, making no acknowledgement, parting in apparent sullenness, she looked out with voice and hand eager to show a difference, but it was just too late. He had turned away, and the horses were in motion. . . . She was vexed beyond what could have been expressed—almost beyond what she could conceal. Never had she felt so agitated, mortified, grieved, at any circumstance in her life. She was most forcibly struck. The truth of his representation there was no denying. She felt it at her heart. How could she have been so brutal, so cruel to Miss Bates!—How could she have exposed herself to such ill opinion in anyone she valued! And how suffer him to leave her without saying one word of gratitude, of concurrence, of common kindness!

Time did not compose her. As she reflected more, she seemed but to feel it more. She never had been so depressed . . . and Emma felt the tears running down her cheeks almost all the way home, without being at any trouble to check them, extraordinary as they were. (1996, 310)

This passage contains very vivid descriptions of several strong emotions. There are no descriptions of Knightley's feelings, but the reader will probably infer from the context that he feels anger and disappointment mixed, perhaps, with a little self-righteousness. A large number of Emma's feelings are explicitly labeled: sorrow, anger, mortification, concern, self-reproach, vexation, agitation, grief, and depression. Several conclusions can be drawn from the passage:

- The emotions are reported in the mode of thought report because this is the mode best suited for the presentation of emotion. Emotions explicitly contained in the other two modes become first-person ascription and the problematical issues surrounding this form of ascription are discussed in section 8 of this chapter. There is some free indirect discourse in the passage (the sentences beginning "The truth," "How could she," and "And how suffer") that is used for Emma's remonstrations with herself.
- Her feelings are visible and public: they result in outward signs of behavior such as turning away, being unable to speak, blushing, and crying. However, they are also inaccessible and private: Knightley misinterprets her feelings and thinks that she is unconcerned.
- The emotions are inextricably linked with cognition. Knightley's (implicit) emotions arise out of his beliefs about Emma's conduct and his decision to share them with her. Emma's emotions arise out of her belief that Knightley is right and that she has acted badly. She thinks that Knightley has misinterpreted her actions. She decides on the basis of her feelings to behave differently in future and so on.
- The passage also shows that the presentation of emotion plays a vital part in the creation of character. Knightley's anger and disappointment arise from his high standards of conduct. It is a demonstration of his love for Emma that he allows these feelings to show. It also shows that Emma is basically a good person who regrets the results of her high spirits and her desire to show off. She will try harder in future to be more considerate and to help Knightley to think better of her.

• Finally, the passage has an important teleological value in that, though the argument temporarily drives them far apart, it will ultimately bring them to their marriage at the end of the novel.

One noticeable feature of work in psychology on the emotions is that there are numerous typologies that tend to be similar to one another but not identical. Although I will mention two here briefly, out of interest, I will not pursue the point as I am not sure that a collection of typologies is the most interesting approach to the subject. A more functional approach, which considers how emotions link with cognition to produce mental functioning and how these interrelations are presented in fictional texts, seems to me to be a more rewarding perspective. According to Damasio, a distinction can be made between *primary, secondary* (or *social*), and *background emotions*. The primary emotions are happiness, sadness, fear, anger, surprise, and disgust. The secondary or social emotions include embarrassment, jealousy, guilt, and pride. Damasio collects together a long and very interesting list of background emotions that includes the feelings of well-being, malaise, calm, tension, fatigue, energy, excitement, wellness, sickness, relaxation, surging, dragging, stability and instability, balance and imbalance, harmony and discord, edginess, discouragement, enthusiasm, down-ness, lowness, and cheerfulness (2000, 50–53, 286). Jon Elster takes a more minimalist approach in *Alchemies of the Mind* and limits himself to the following: anger, hatred, fear, shame, pity, indignation, gloating, envy, malice, and contempt (1999, 61). Elster comments with commendable understatement that this is a "mostly dark" list (1999, 61). Doležel lists a number of other lists in *Heterocosmica* (1998, 67–69).

Emotions last for varying periods of time. When they are short-term, they are emotional events; medium-term, they tend to be called *moods*; as long-term states, they are closer in nature to dispositions. Emotions therefore fit easily into the event/state framework established earlier: "He was angry" is an event; and "He is an angry person" is a state. In the construction of a fictional mind, different sorts of information play different roles. Emotions can be explicitly labeled or inferred from mental events that appear to embody an emotion such as anger. For example, if one character says of another, "He's angry," this has a different status from a direct presentation by the narrator of a stream of angry thoughts. Implicit information or explicit information such as a single-word label like *selfish* may have more or less impact on the reader, depending on the context. Certainly, the explicit labeling in the Emma passage has a very dramatic effect.

In the view of Antonio Damasio, "consciousness and emotion are *not* separable" (2000, 16). I think we should pause for a moment here and consider the implications of this statement. A good deal of work has been done within narrative theory on fictional consciousness, and as far as I am aware, very little has been done specifically on the emotions. But, according to an eminent neuroscientist, the two are not separable! Of course, one could argue that the many discussions of consciousness in narrative theory necessarily involve a consideration of emotions, but that is not my point. The issue of fictional emotion has not been *explicitly* recognized as an indispensable element in fictional consciousness. To reinforce his point about inseparability, Damasio stresses the pervasiveness of emotion. "Some level of emoting is the obligate accompaniment of thinking about oneself or about one's surroundings. . . . [V]irtually every image, actually perceived or recalled is accompanied by some reaction from the apparatus of emotion" (2000, 58). For example, "we continuously have emotional feelings . . . sometimes low grade, sometimes quite intense, and we do sense the general physical tone of our being" (Damasio 2000, 285–86). His attempt to convey some of the "what it's like" quality of consciousness is very reminiscent of the Searle typology and the examples from *The Crying of Lot 49* in section 3 of this chapter.

As we saw in the *Emma* passage, emotion is one of the more obvious ways in which our thought can become public. Both MITECS and Damasio draw a distinction between the public and the private aspects of the concept. The former states that in "current usage, the concept of emotion has two aspects. One pertains to a certain kind of subjective experience, 'feeling.' The other relates to expression, the public manifestation of feeling" (Brothers 1999, 271). Damasio proposes that "the term *feeling* should be reserved for the private, mental experience of an emotion, while the term *emotion* should be used to designate the collection of responses, many of which are publicly observable" (2000, 42). Doležel is also preoccupied with the importance of behavior and draws attention to the fact that emotions are "often accompanied by spontaneous physiological events. . . . When the events are observable (blushing, sparkling eyes, gestures) or audible (laughing, crying, exclamation of pain, tone of voice), they become signs (indices) of emotions" (1998, 68). As with all such ideas, I am not sure that the suggestion of different uses for the terms *emotions* and *feelings* is workable, but the distinction is certainly worth making. In the next chapter I will talk more generally about the public nature of thought.

The relationship between cognition and emotion is worth exploring further, as "most philosophical work on emotions has been cognitive" (Oatley 1999, 274).

Cognition causes emotion. Emma's emotions arise from her beliefs about what she has done. Consider a situation in which I am swimming, see a shark, and feel the appropriate emotions of fear, horror, and so on. Here, the emotions arise out of cognitions (the belief that the shark will eat me), physiological reactions (increased blood pressure), feelings (say, of terror), and action (getting away from the shark). The emotion of fear is playing a cognitive role: it is a rational and appropriate response to the situation. Emotion can be a mode of vision or recognition. Also, as Damasio and Searle suggest, cognitions nearly always have some sort of emotional component. In addition, theorists lay stress on the directive and cognitive role of attention when discussing the emotions. Damasio tells us that sometimes "we become keenly aware of [emotions] and can attend to them specifically. Sometimes we do not, and attend, instead, to other mental contents" (2000, 286). I referred in the discussion on non-consciousness to the importance of the notion of attention and to the fact that it goes to where it is needed. Any mental functioning that can efficiently be dealt with without attention tends to proceed as non-consciousness. However, when something unexpected happens, when we are surprised, we attend to our response. Emotions often have a role to play in this process. Fear is obviously a major factor in directing attention to possible danger, so the emotion has a cognitive function here. Less dramatically, although stress is often considered to be an inhibiting factor with regard to performance in examinations, its enabling role is less well recognized. Personally, I cannot sit at a desk and write continuously for three hours without the presence of stress!

Revealingly, the subtitle of Elster's book *Alchemies of the Mind* is *Rationality and the Emotions*. This link is pursued to the point where even the distinction between emotion and reason is questioned. According to Damasio, "the presumed opposition between emotion and reason is no longer accepted without question. For example, work from my laboratory has shown that emotion is integral to the processes of reasoning and decision making" (2000, 40–41). Patients who have "lost a certain class of emotions" have also "lost their ability to make rational decisions" (2000, 41). "These findings suggest that selective reduction of emotion is at least as prejudicial for rationality as excessive emotion" (2000, 41). "Well-targeted and well-deployed emotion seems to be a support system without which the edifice of reason cannot operate properly" (2000, 42). Damasio provides this simple but very telling example of the cognitive significance of emotion: "if you are told two stories of comparable length that have a comparable number of facts, differing only because in one of them the facts have a high emotional content, you will remember far more detail from the emotional story than from the other" (2000, 294). Novels tend to be stories with a high emotional content and are therefore often deeply memorable for that reason. Even stories that are written in a flat unemotional style often use this stylistic device to heighten the emotion (for example, to emphasize the fear and horror in Kafka's "Metamorphosis"). Also, novels such as Camus' *L'Etranger* gain their power by contrasting a notable lack of emotion in a character (in this case, lack of sorrow at the death of a mother) with a strong social norm (the expectation that one should feel sorrow at the death of a mother).

Emotions are important in guiding our goal management, and this fact has important teleological implications for fictional minds. We obtain our goals through action, and Jon Elster considers emotions as "action tendencies" (1999, 60–61, 281–83). Much of the literature on the emotions stresses their importance for the formation and achievement of goals. Steven Pinker, while making this point, also agrees with Damasio that the distinction between thought and feeling should be questioned: "The emotions are mechanisms that set the brain's highest-level goals. Once triggered by a propitious moment, an emotion triggers the cascade of subgoals and sub-subgoals that we call thinking and acting. . . . [N]o sharp line divides thinking from feeling, nor does thinking inevitably precede feeling or vice versa" (1997, 373). These views are examples of the complex interrelatedness of mental phenomena that I have drawn attention to several times already. Emotions, cognitions, goals, action, context, and so on, they all flow into one another until, as Pinker and Damasio argue, the distinctions are difficult to maintain.

In chapter 5, section 5 I will discuss what is called distributed or situated (or joint, group, or shared) cognition and action. I will just briefly mention here the notion of distributed or situated emotion. Consider the following: "Lutz argues that the Ifaluk of Melanesia do not conceive of emotions as something occurring within an individual person, but as a relation between several individuals in which the emotion exists independent of (and outside) the psyche of any one person. The notion of persons as unique self-oriented entities, in its turn, has been analyzed as arising from the specific cultural and political-economic environments of North America and Europe" (Sperber and Hirschfeld 1999, cxxvii–cxxviii). The suggestion that emotions can be socially distributed among individuals in a group just like other aspects of the mind such as cognition is reminiscent of the writing of such anthropologists as Edward Sapir, Benjamin Lee Whorf, Margaret Mead, and Ruth Benedict, all of which is now deeply unfashionable. As Sperber and Hirschfeld point out, like "all relativist ideas, these views are controversial" (1999, cxxviii). At one time, it appeared that the idea that the Inuit Eskimos had a hundred words for snow (or however many— it grew in the telling!) was the academic equivalent of an urban myth, and it was thought that in fact they had the same number as we do. However, there seems to have been a backlash, and it is now claimed once more that they do have many more words for snow than we do. Whatever the truth of the matter, I think that it is worth recognizing that these ideas are sufficiently plausible for well-respected anthropologists to have held them. As such, narrative theory should be conceptually well equipped to take account of them. Some of the work that I do in chapter 5 and chapter 7 on real and fictional intermental thinking might, I hope, make the idea of socially distributed emotion seem less outlandish than it may do at the moment.

7. Action

This section provides an introduction to the philosophy of action. In section 5 of the following chapter I will look at the sociocultural approach to action, and in chapter 7, section 2 I will introduce a novel approach to descriptions of action in narrative discourse that I hope will be of value to future research in the field.

Action arises when an agent wants to change some aspect of their environment and believes that an action will successfully bring about that change. The agent sees both the world as they believe it to be and also the world as they desire it to be. Action is required when there is a disparity between the two, and it is necessary to align the world as it is believed to be with the world as it is desired. Philosophers sometimes refer to this process as *practical reasoning* and also as the *action planning/decision system*. The action planning system can be run *on-line*, while we are taking action in the present, or *off-line*, when we are planning action for the future. Obviously, novels are full of examples of characters who act on-line and who also go through hypothetical, what-if situations in their mind while planning future action. It is common for characters in thrillers to run through a variety of scenarios in their minds in order to anticipate potential obstacles.

The philosophy of action separates the class of actions from the more general class of doings or bodily movements. For a doing to be an action, the physical movement must be brought about by the conscious individual himself or herself and not, say, by someone else causing their unconscious body to move. Doings are not actions if they are performed without the intention to perform them and without having a specific purpose. An action consists of both a mental event of intention and a bodily movement. Because a definition of action in purely behavioral terms such as bodily movement is impossible, mental notions such as awareness, knowledge, belief, desires, intention, and purposes are necessary. One issue that is of particular interest in the philosophy of action is the difficulty of defining an action. In the case of a death by shooting, do you define the action of the killer as the twitching of the finger, the pulling of the trigger, the firing of the gun, the killing of a person, or the murdering of a person? These descriptions differ to the extent to which they ascribe consciousness to the agent, take account of the consequences of the physical movement, and assign responsibility to the agent for those consequences. The philosophy of action approaches these questions by looking at the technical issues relating to the network of mental events that lies behind the physical events of action and behavior. Any analysis of descriptions of consciousness, behavior, and action in fiction needs to take account of these issues because they relate to the questions of personal responsibility that are at the heart of readers' responses to novels. It is part of our reading of *Emma* that Emma initially refuses to take responsibility for the consequences of her actions but then learns how to do so. Hurting Miss Bates was an unintended consequence of Emma's action at the Box Hill picnic, but it was still her responsibility. The novel can be read as the process by which she learns, ultimately, to take responsibility in this way. This is uncontroversial, but it is important to have a theoretical framework for establishing in precise and rigorous terms exactly how the reader is able to use the concept of action in order to read the novel in this way.

Any theoretical account of action has to unite the physical and mental sides of the concept and acknowledge that the relationship between the physical and mental is motivational. In other words, the mental side has to provide the motive, reason, intention, and so on for the physical movement. Within the mental domain, philosophers typically isolate two basic types of thought processes that go to make up intentions to act: beliefs and desires. Desires can include immediate volitions, settled objectives, and goal-directed action plans. Desires move you in wanting to take the action, and beliefs guide you in how to take it. A distinction can be made between intrinsic and extrinsic desires: the former we want for their own sakes, the latter as a means to an end. As is frequently pointed out, the concept of intention is a complex and slippery one. Dennett holds that it must involve consciousness: "Mere bodily complicity does not make for an intentional action, nor does bodily complicity under the control of structures in the brain, for a sleepwalker's body is manifestly under the control of structures in the sleepwalker's brain. What more must be added is consciousness, the special ingredient that turns mere happenings into [actions]" (1991, 31–32). But even within conscious action, there are different sorts of intentions. Intending to do A is different from doing A intentionally. The latter can be a side-effect action that is an undesired consequence of an intended action. In slamming a car door, we do not intend to disturb the neighbors, but we still slam the car door intentionally. Emma intended to say what she did, but she did not hurt Miss Bates intentionally.

In contrast to the belief/desire breakdown of intention, Doležel's position is that the notion of intention should be considered as an irreducible primitive that cannot be broken down any further into constituent elements. He feels that "intention is a puzzling notion, and its logical status and psychological correlative have caused much disagreement. The needs of narrative semantics will be satisfied if 'intention' is accepted as a primitive notion, irreducible to other mental factors of acting, such as desires, reasons and beliefs" (1998, 58). It is understandable why Doležel should feel this way, although the analysis of intention into desires and beliefs does seem attractive and is surely useful in analyses of narrative texts. Pip's intention to help Magwich escape comprises his desire that Magwich should get away, together with a set of beliefs regarding the best way for him to do so.

In the *Philosophical Investigations*, Ludwig Wittgenstein quotes the sentence, "I noticed that he was out of humour," and asks, "is this a report about his behavior or his state of mind?" (1958, 179). I will return to this question throughout the book. He is drawing attention to the fact that the mental and physical sides of action and behavior coexist and interpenetrate to the point where they are difficult to disentangle. Ultimately, as Clark and Chalmers suggest, it can become impossible to separate physical actions from the mental network that lies behind them. In considering what is involved in playing Scrabble, they claim that, in "a very real sense, the rearrangement of tiles on the tray is not part of action, it is part of *thought*" (1998, 10). I refer to this phenomenon in chapter 7, section 2 as the *thought-action continuum*. The mental structure behind action includes memories of the past, motives and reasons related to the present, and intentions and decisions related to the anticipated consequences in the future. In this way, a continual process of action—and, therefore, of thought—is created by narrators and by readers when, between them, they construct characters with continuing consciousnesses. A key feature of this mental decision making is that the performance of an action requires that we make assumptions about the actual situation in which we are acting, the future situation that is the intended result of the action, and also the future but counterfactual situation that would be the case if we do not act. To use some of the examples suggested by the linguist Teun van Dijk, I try to prevent a glass of wine falling because I can see that it is tipping over (actual situation), because I want to drink it later (desired future situation), and because I do not want it to stain the carpet (counterfactual future situation) (1976, 295). The counterfactual nature of embedded narratives is significant because characters spend much of their time imagining the consequences of alternative courses of action. The fact that characters think in terms of these stories is part of the reason why Marie-Laure Ryan chose the term *embedded narrative* to describe a fictional mind. Characters create their own narratives, their own perspectives on the storyworld of the novel; and the extent to which their own narratives are consistent with the narratives of the narrator and of readers will obviously vary. What will also vary is the relationship between the various counterfactual embedded narratives of characters as they relate to the future ("What would happen if I did this?") and what actually does happen in the series of events in the storyworld.

I will now consider the more specific issue of descriptions of actions in narratives. Intention is a crucial concept in this context, but it has been neglected by narrative theory. As Doležel has noticed, we are "faced with a curious discrepancy: while in the philosophy of action the problem of intentionality is at the center of interest, empirical studies of acting, including narratology, have hardly noticed its existence" (1998, 63). Van Dijk describes narrative discourse as a form of "natural action description," and therefore "an interesting empirical testing ground for the theory of action" (1976, 287). He shows that this is so by relating the concept of action to the observation and resulting descriptions of actions. Notice that Wittgenstein's question was about the *reporting* of behavior. This perspective on action can be used to highlight the role of the narrator in presenting such observations and descriptions in the discourse. The relationship between the actor and the observer, in the case of "natural" action, is similar to the relationship, in the case of fictional action, between the character and the narrator and also the character and the reader. Our knowledge of the structure of action is closely linked to the way in which we describe actions and doings. An action for which an observer does not have a concept remains for that observer a mere doing. It is significant that a number of the discussions of actions by philosophers refer to onlookers (for example, O'Shaughnessy 1997, 56). This insight can be related to the role of the narrator, the reader, and of other characters in considering a character's actions. All three are onlookers in very different senses. By ascribing an action to someone, we either have access to their intentions and purposes, or we make informed assumptions about their intentions and purposes based on conventional inferences. Of course, in fiction narrators can if they wish use direct access to characters' minds in order to make motivation explicit, but they need not do so, because the motivation will often be clearly implicit.

Van Dijk argues that examples of what are clearly action descriptions necessarily imply purpose and intentionality (for example, Ann carefully cleaned, Barbara accused him, and Larry refused). Examples that are clearly not descriptions of actions include state descriptions (leaves are green, Peter is ill); motion verbs without an animate subject (the Paris train arrives soon); process verbs (John recovered quickly); and patients of event verbs (Mary could not pay). Dubious and less obvious cases include descriptions of mental events (Sheila never realized); events where there is some doubt over the degree of control exercised by the agent (Harry found a briefcase); and bodily states that may or may not have been brought about intentionally (Laura stared, George hesitated) (van Dijk 1976, 300). These distinctions can be related to the role of the reader. To adapt the remark made earlier, an action by a character for which a reader does not have a concept remains for that reader simply a doing. It is part of the competence of the reader to ascribe consciousness to surface behavior. Therefore, the decisions made by the reader on van Dijk's marginal examples will depend on the willingness of the reader to ascribe the necessary mental events to the character. Context will often help. It may be clear from the situation in which they are acting whether Laura's staring and George's hesitating are actions or doings. With regard to his clear examples, I argue in chapter 7 that there is a continuum and not a sharp divide between action descriptions and consciousness descriptions, and it seems to me that these cases are edging toward the middle of that continuum.

The mental events, processes, and states that distinguish actions from mere doings are crucial to the concept of embedded narratives. A description by a narrator of a character's action is a description of the development of that character's embedded narrative. The reasons, motives, intentions, purposes, and so on behind the action may be explicitly specified by the narrator, they may be implicit but understood by the reader, or they may remain mysterious. However, they are always there in the storyworld. The core of the embedded narrative approach is the systematic analysis of the structure of mental events that lies behind the decisions that lead to actions and, specifically, of how this is presented in the discourse by the narrator. This causal, mental process is the embedded narrative in action. In addition, physical action is the point at which different characters' embedded narratives entangle. Descriptions of joint actions in particular reveal the enmeshing of the various mental networks of two or more characters.

I will finish this section with a few words about action and characterization. Lubomir Doležel has explained very clearly the link between the two. Motivational factors, he says, because they are "habitual features of a person's character, produce regularities in acting, modes of acting characteristic of individuals and personality types. . . . [M]otivation is the key to understanding the diversity of acting, the why and how of actions. The study of motivational factors is to become an important part of a semantics of fictional narrative" (1998, 63). As Doležel explains, one highly informative way of forming a sense of a fictional character or personality is by observing regularities in behavior and then by building up hypotheses about the likely motivation for the behavior. However, analyses of action can be handicapped by the occasional invisibility of the concept of action within narratological discourse analysis. You will remember how, in the Bertrand Russell puddle example discussed in section 3, Ann Banfield edited out Russell's reference to an action. Here are two more examples: In chapter 3, section 4, I discussed a short passage from *Madame Bovary* that has become famous from discussions of it first by Erich Auerbach and then by Georges Poulet. You might think, therefore, that there is little left to add, and nothing of any significance left to squeeze out of it. However, I would like to make one further comment on it. It consists of two sentences. The first, on which nearly all of the commentary has concentrated, consists of Emma's perceptions of the kitchen and her resulting revulsion in the modes of thought report and free indirect perception. The second sentence, as I said during the discussion, is a description of three actions (eating slowly, nibbling nuts, and making marks with a knife) and is not a direct presentation of consciousness (although the phrase "amuse herself" is marginal). That this sentence is an action description is a very simple point, but neither Auerbach nor Poulet, during their sensitive and intricate analyses of Emma's consciousness, acknowledge it.

Finally, Patrick O'Neill advances the view that there are two types of textual indicator of character. One, direct definition, is diegetic telling; the other, indirect presentation, is mimetic showing that operates by showing characters engaged in action (1994, 49–50). O'Neill then quotes a passage of characterization from Dickens's *Hard Times* as an illustration of direct definition as opposed to presentation of action. The character Bounderby is described as follows: "He was a rich man: banker, merchant, manufacturer, and what not. [Then a description of his appearance.] A man who could never sufficiently vaunt himself a self-made man. A man who was always proclaiming, through that brassy speaking-trumpet of a voice of his, his old ignorance and his old poverty. A man who was the Bully of humility" (1995, 21, quoted in O'Neill 1994, 50). There is a lot of action here for a passage that is supposed to contrast with descriptions of actions. Being a banker, merchant, and manufacturer means habitually acting in certain ways. Vaunting and proclaiming are speech acts. Being a bully means behaving in a bullying way. Presumably O'Neill's distinction is between a description of a single action and a description, like this one, of a series of actions. But the differences should be put in those terms. Although action description shades into characterization, it should still be recognized as action. Just as thought report and the emotions can become invisible, so can action.

8. First-Person Ascription

This section will continue the discussion on intention and motivation by looking at first-person ascription—how we ascribe motives and intentions to our own actions. I will consider the issues raised by third-person ascription—how we ascribe motives and intentions to the actions of others—in the following chapter. The use of the word *ascribe* in the first-person context may sound surprisingly roundabout and indirect: surely we just know directly and immediately what our mental states are? However, as I hope to show, the process can be more problematic than it first appears. The background to the debate about ascription is the objective, third-person conception of the mental that was employed by traditional behaviorist psychology. This approach tried to study the mind as if it consisted simply of observable and measurable phenomena and ignored any notion of consciousness that could be accessed from the first-person point of view of introspection. It therefore reversed our folk-psychology privileging of first-person access in favor of third-person reporting. The following passage considers the two forms of ascription together:

> First, research on introspection and self-knowledge has raised questions about how "direct" our knowledge of our own mental states and of the self is, and so called into question traditional conceptions of first-person knowledge of mentality. Second, explorations of the theory of mind, animal communication and social play behavior have begun to examine and assess the sorts of attribution of mental states that are actually justified in empirical studies, suggesting that third-person knowledge of mental states is not as limited as has been thought. Considered together, this research hints that the contrast between first- and third-person knowledge

of the mental is not as stark as the problem of other minds seems to intimate. (Wilson 1999b, xviii)

Put simply, first-person ascription can be less reliable, and third-person ascription more reliable, than is commonly supposed.

With regard to first-person ascription, we are often wrong about the nature of our mental functioning. Errors of very different sorts occur—from hallucinations right through to inabilities to understand our true motivations. Unconscious motivation is a part of our everyday "commonsense" view of the mind. We would all, I think, recognize the truth of such statements as, "I realize now that it was really frustration with myself that made me so angry with him." A good example of the fallibility of first-person direct access is the feeling of being depressed but not knowing why. You have immediate access to that feeling and no one else has. To that extent it is inaccessible to others and infallible. However, someone who knows you well might know that it is caused by anxiety about something unpleasant coming up. You might then say, "Yes, I suppose it *is* because of that!" Sometimes, we can become intuitively aware that our first-person ascription is not as different from third-person ascription as we usually suppose. Imagine that you are discussing with your spouse or partner whether or not you should do something in the future. They might say, "Well you didn't enjoy the similar thing that you did last month." You reply, "But that was different in some ways and so I think that it won't be like that this time." They retort, "You always say that and I'm never convinced" and you conclude, "Maybe, but I'm fairly sure this time I'll be right," and so on. That sounds like quite a plausible conversation to me. And it is noticeable that there is not much difference between the first- and third-person ascription contained in it. Both are best guesses related to probabilities based on past behavior. In fact, if there is a difference, the third-person ascription sounds if anything rather more confident than the first-person sort. These gaps in our awareness of ourselves can affect our perceptions of our behavior. I recently heard of someone who thought that he had been extremely rude to a colleague when he told her that he could not do something, because he was just going to a job interview. In fact he had been perfectly polite to her, had given her the information that she wanted, and had not mentioned the interview. Even when told this, he was still convinced that he *had* referred to the interview. His mental state was so overwhelming that he was not aware of the behavior that had resulted from it.

Searle has helpfully described at least three ways in which we can be mistaken about our own mental events: self-deception, when the agent has a motive or reason for not admitting to himself or herself that he or she is in a certain mental state (for example, shame at getting angry); misinterpretation (for example, thinking that our feeling for someone amounted to love and later discovering that we were mistaken); and inattention, when we do not notice until later that our states of mind have changed in some way (for example, not noticing for a while that we no longer love someone) (1992, 147–49). In discussing first-person error, many have referred to the gray area between the honest mistakes of Searle's second and third categories and the dishonesty of the first. "Know thyself! If I knew myself I'd run away," said Goethe. Henry David Thoreau thought that it is "as hard to see one's self as to look backwards without turning round." Steven Pinker reminds us, uncomfortably, that sometimes we have "glimpses of our own self-deception. When does a negative remark sting, cut deep, hit a nerve? When some part of us knows it to be true. If every part knew it was true, the remark would not sting; it would be old news. If no part thought it was true, the remark would roll off; we could dismiss it as false" (1997, 423). Antonio Damasio emphasizes that sometimes "we use our minds not to discover facts but to hide them. We use part of the mind as a screen to prevent another part of it from sensing what goes on elsewhere" (2000, 28).

Mistakes about our mental functioning are often associated with Freudian psychoanalysis. However, this is not the end of the story. As *MITECS* indicates, in addition to the "misrepresentations of one's own mental states discovered by Sigmund Freud, other work . . . shows that introspective judgments frequently result from confabulation. People literally invent mental states to explain their own behavior in ways that are expected or acceptable. Daniel Dennett (1991) in effect seeks to generalize this finding by arguing that all introspective reports can be treated as reports of useful fictions. . . . At best, introspection is one tool among many for learning about the mind" (Rosenthal 1999, 420). The reference to fictions is a reminder of how often real-mind discourses turn to the language of narrative to illustrate how the mind works. This is Dennett himself: "Am I saying we have absolutely no privileged access to our conscious experience? No, but I am saying that we tend to think we are much more immune to error than we are. People generally admit, when challenged in this way about their privileged access, that they don't have any special access to the *causes* and *effects* of their conscious experiences. . . . But although people may *say* they are claiming authority only about the isolated contents of their experiences, not their causes and effects, they often overstep their self-imposed restraints" (1991, 68). He makes the important distinction that I referred to earlier between the direct experience of immediate consciousness that only the first person has direct access to and the ascription of reasons for the state of mind and motives for and intentions of the resulting action. In the latter case, the picture is much more blurred. We may know that we feel depressed, but the first-person ascription involved in attributing the reasons for this state of mind is often much less easy. In any case, as Dennett points out, the distinction between the state and the causes of it can be difficult to maintain in practice.

The assumption that direct first-person ascription has a privileged status that is denied to the apparently more indirect third-person ascription is sometimes referred to as *Cartesianism*, following the introspective methodology employed by Descartes in his *Meditations*. (However, it should be noted that this label is often disputed by scholars who claim that it is an unnecessarily reductive view of Descartes' actual arguments.) Many philosophers and psychologists now argue that the sort of privileged first-person access that is implied by the term *Cartesianism* is an illusion and that the sole interpretative device that we have for examining our own internal mental states is a theory of mind that is based on our observation of others. MITECS adopts a balanced view on the question of introspection: "Self-knowledge can arise in many ways. Traditional Cartesian mentalism treated the mind as fully transparent and open in all its significant properties to a faculty of conscious introspection or reflection, which was conceived of by later empiricists as a form of inner perception. Though introspection is now regarded as fallible, incomplete, and theory-laden, it nonetheless remains a major source of self-knowledge" (van Gulick 1999, 736).

If we turn now to the implications of this debate for narrative theory, we see that Monika Fludernik perceptively observes that "to write one's own life requires a sustained Augustinian effort to construct from the random succession of remembered scenes . . . [a] well-structured tale with teleological shape. *Other* people's lives, paradoxically, are knowable and tellable much more easily" (1996, 47). This argument can be intriguingly compared to Daniel Dennett's suggestion that introspections are useful fictions. Dennett illustrates his point with this account of people's behavior in the laboratory. He tells us that "there are circumstances in which people are just wrong about what they are doing and how they are doing it. It is not that they *lie* in the experimental situation, but that they confabulate; they fill in the gaps, guess, speculate, mistake theorizing for observing. . . . To sum up, subjects are unwitting creators of fiction" (1991, 94). Fludernik's description of "a well-structured tale with teleological shape" and Dennett's description of useful fictions both acknowledge the indirect, ascriptive quality of first-person testimony. Although Fludernik is discussing non-fictional narrative, her point is easily applied to third-person novels. This neat reversal of our usual assumptions about the ease with which individuals can explain the workings of their own minds, as opposed to the minds of others, interestingly echoes the philosophical argument that third-person ascriptions of mental states are just as important as first-person ascriptions to our acquisition of the concept of consciousness.

It is, of course, true that narratologists have always acknowledged that characters deceive themselves and that what is contained in the inner speech that is reported in the mode of direct thought is not necessarily to be relied upon as an accurate report of the actual states of affairs in the mental domain of the story-world. But my purpose in reemphasizing the point is to place it in the different context that is provided by the whole argument of this book. To give an idea of the scale of the paradigm shift that is required, have a look at the following three observations by Uri Margolin in which he sets out with characteristic clarity the assumptions on which the traditional narratological account of first- and third-person ascription is based: "Each narrative [individual] identifies himself from inside a center of consciousness in an immediate, non-inferential way which is not grounded on public evidence, especially not bodily criteria" (1995a, 25–26); "A basic convention of literary narrative is that every personalized speaker has direct, immediate access to his own mental states but not to those of his coagents, which he must infer (fallibly!) from their intersubjectively accessible behavior and statements" (2000, 599); and: "In the actual world we can know about another person's decisions . . . regarding himself only through his public claims to this effect" (1995a, 26).

As I have said, while it is true that we have immediate access to some parts of our own current mental world, in other ways we have less access to our minds that other persons do. I may think that I am an easy-going kind of person with a sunny disposition, but everyone else may say that I am grumpy and difficult to live with. So I accept, with difficulty, that there may be a lot of truth in what they say and try to be better behaved. Am I not then identifying myself in an inferential way that is grounded on public evidence? Take Pip in *Great Expectations*. The whole novel is built on the fact that he is fallible about his mental states (for example, his snobbery and feelings of shame toward Joe). Biddy, on the other hand, knows the working of Pip's mind much better than Pip himself does. She and Joe simply wait till Pip knows himself better. With regard to Margolin's third quote, surely we often know about people's decisions from observing their behavior. If you say, "That's not really *knowing*," then what about the possibility of insincere or simply mistaken first-person reports about the motives for our own decisions? The capacity for error in the analysis of our mental states applies particularly to perceptions of our motives for the actions that we take. This is why it is such an important part of the role of the narrator to supplement the self-conscious, and possibly self-serving, flow of inner speech with analyses in thought report that can supply an alternative and more reliable account of the true motivation for characters' actions.

5

The Social Mind

Chapter 4 considered a wide range of mental phenomena within the traditional *internalist* perspective on the mind, although at several points and especially in the sections on emotion, action, and ascription, I referred to the social context within which minds have to be considered. This chapter will now develop the argument further by exploring the implications of an *externalist* view of the mind. It will start with a general overview of the extent to which thought is social, public, and observable. It then pursues this approach in four specific directions: third-person ascription, purposive thought, dialogicality, and situated thought. I also try to show that the social mind is the subject of a good deal of narrative discourse and that an awareness of it is a substantial aid to our understanding of the subject matter of novels.

The terms *internalism* and *externalism* correspond to the subjective first/intersubjective first distinction that was described in chapter 1, section 1. MITECS defines *internalism* (or *individualism*) in the following terms: "Individualists view the distinction between the psychological states *of individuals* and the physical and social environments of those individuals as providing a natural basis for demarcating properly scientific, psychological kinds. Psychology in particular and the cognitive sciences more generally are to be concerned with natural kinds whose instances end at the boundary of the individual" (Wilson 1999a, 397). It then defines *externalism* as follows: "Those rejecting individualism on empirical methodological grounds have appealed to the situated or embedded nature of cognition, seeking more generally to articulate the crucial role that an organism's environment plays in its cognitive processing" (Wilson 1999a, 398). Sperber and Hirschfeld regretfully conclude that too often, however, "these two perspectives are adopted by scholars with different training, very different theoretical commitments, and therefore a limited willingness and ability to interact fruitfully" (1999, cxv). It will be clear, I think, that I belong very firmly to the externalist tendency. Narrative theory tends to adopt an internalist perspective on fictional minds, and so an externalist view may be of value in providing some balance. I am sure, though, that, unlike real-mind theorists, narrative theorists of both persuasions will be willing and able to interact fruitfully.

The key to this chapter, and indeed the whole book, is contained in the final words of Searle's book, *The Rediscovery of the Mind*: "we need to rediscover the social character of the mind" (1992, 248). Searle suggests that the role of society in the study of consciousness is seriously neglected but concedes that "I do not yet know . . . how to analyse the structure of the social element in individual consciousness" (1992, 128). Such refreshing honesty is a reminder to us all that this is not an easy area to explore. What follows in this chapter and the remaining ones is only a first attempt at sketching out some of the issues involved in analyzing the social element in fictional consciousnesses.

1. Public Thought

In Sir Walter Scott's *Rob Roy*, Diana Vernon tells Francis Osbaldistone that she will read his mind. However, she insists that "I do not want your assistance, I am conjuror enough to tell your thoughts without it. You need not open the casement of your bosom; I see through it" (1995, 50). Because the young man's mind is public and accessible to her, she is completely accurate in her descriptions of its workings. This ability to decode other minds without having direct access to them is not confined to fictional characters. It is a vitally important element in the reading process.

The reader is not given any direct access to the mind of one of the most vivid and haunting characters in popular fiction. In fact, the reader never meets her, because she dies before the book begins. But the mind of Rebecca survives in the minds of the other characters in Daphne du Maurier's novel *Rebecca* and makes a deep and lasting impression on most readers of the novel. Edith Bellenden in Scott's *Old Mortality* remarks that "God only can judge the heart—men must estimate intentions by actions" (1975, 332), and we often find that accurate estimates result. A simple description of surface behavior can be as informative as the most direct inside view of a character's consciousness. In the passage from *Emma* that I discussed in section 6 of the previous chapter, Knightley quarrels with Emma over her treatment of Miss Bates. The narrator tells the reader that Emma tries to apologize, but he "had turned away and the horses were in motion" (1996, 309). Direct access to his mind could not make Knightley's anger and disappointment more vivid for the reader.

Wittgenstein famously commented that the "human body is the best picture of the human soul" (1958, 178). The fact that our minds are public and social is known to us all. We say of our friends, family, partners, and colleagues that they know us better than we know ourselves. Others often supply more convincing explanations of our past behavior than we do, and often predict our future behavior better than we do. I mentioned in chapter 3 Ann Banfield's waspish reference to the title of Dorrit Cohn's book, *Transparent Minds*. She was disputing that fictional minds were transparent, even with the aid of direct access to them. I wish to argue here that not only can fictional minds be transparent to readers, there is a strong sense in which real minds can be transparent to other people. Daniel Dennett makes the point that your "body can vigorously betray the secrets *you* are desperately trying to keep—by blushing and trembling or sweating, to mention only the most obvious cases" (1996, 80). The issue of body language is one that recurs frequently in novels. Pip can see, can directly experience, Joe's discomfort while giving him tea in his rooms (Dickens 1965, 241–47). The public nature of thought is as true of pure cognition as it is of emotions such as guilt and embarrassment. In the Hitchcock film *Dial M for Murder*, the villain, played by Ray Milland, is led into a trap in which he will betray himself if, while standing in the hallway trying to work out what has happened to his spare key, he remembers that it is still under the stair carpet. We literally see the villain's mind at work as he carefully thinks through the steps that will lead him to look for the key under the stair carpet and so prove his guilt.

Near the end of his remarkable and beautifully written book *The Feeling of What Happens*, Antonio Damasio discusses the privacy of personal experience and consciousness. He says that he is often asked whether we will eventually be able to gain access to each other's experiences and concludes, "My answer to the question has long been no, and my opinion has not changed" (2000, 305). He goes on to explain the reasons for his opinion, and in the context of current neuroscience, in so far as I can judge, they appear to make perfect sense. However, at the very beginning of his book, Damasio tells a story that in contrast illustrates the apparent accessibility of consciousness to others. He describes how from his office window he sees an old man trying to get to a ferry before it leaves: "He finally reaches the ship. He climbs with difficulty the tall step needed to get on the gangplank and starts on his way down to the deck, afraid of gaining too much momentum on the incline, head moving briskly, left and right, checking his surroundings and seeking reassurance, his whole body seemingly saying, Is this it? Am I in the right place? Where to next? And then the two men on deck help him steady his last step, ease him into the cabin with warm gestures, and he seems to be safely where he should be. My worry is over. The ship departs" (2000, 5). Damasio maintains that consciousness "is an entirely private, first-person phenomenon which occurs as part of the private, first-person process we call mind" (2000, 12). On the other hand, he also points out that consciousness and mind are "closely tied to external behaviors that can be observed by third persons. Both wisdom and the science of the human mind and behavior are based on this incontrovertible correlation between the private and the public—first-person mind on the one hand, and third-person behavior, on the other" (2000, 12–13). So, in a sense, as this passage shows, our minds *can* be perfectly visible to others. As he watched from his window, Damasio knew what was going on in the old man's mind. You may say that he was only inferring belief from the old man's behavior and that this is shown by his use of the word "seemingly." This is true. But, as I asked in the previous chapter, do we always *know* what is going on in our own minds? Supposing someone close to Damasio said to him, "It's clear to me that you were so interested in that old man because he reminded you of your father"; and Damasio had then replied, "Do you think so? That never occurred to me. You may be right!" This conversation does not sound implausible, does it? It is the sort of thing that people regularly say. So the quote shows that, in practice, Damasio is more confident than he appears to think he is about the workings of another mind; and the plausibility of the imaginary conversation shows that it is possible that Damasio may be less confident than he appears to think about the workings of his own mind.

There is a famous scene in the Sherlock Holmes story "The Resident Patient" in which Holmes and Watson are sitting in silence in their study. Then Holmes concludes Watson's line of thought for him. Watson, "suddenly realising how he had echoed the innermost thoughts of my soul" (1981, 423) is gratifyingly thunderstruck. It transpires that Holmes was able to follow Watson's silent thought processes by watching his eye movements and constructing a plausible narrative based on what he had been looking at. You may think that this is a parlor-trick that is suitable only for pulp fiction. So take a look at the character of Lady Deadlock in *Bleak House*, who is given to long and lonely self-communings and who in a different sort of novel might have been the subject of detailed, direct presentations of her consciousness. In such a case, we would probably be presented with her feelings of guilt about her dead lover and her long-lost daughter and so on. However, as she is actually in a very different sort of novel, this is how the narrator describes her in a very early stage in the narrative: "She supposes herself to be an inscrutable Being, quite out of the reach of and ken of ordinary mortals—seeing herself in her glass, where indeed she looks so. Yet, every dim little star revolving round her, from her maid to the manager of the Italian Opera, knows her weaknesses, prejudices, follies, haughtinesses, and caprices; and lives upon as accurate a calculation and as nice a measure of her moral nature, as her dressmaker takes of her physical proportions" (1971, 59). As usual, a balance is required. Her dispositions and many of her states of mind are accessible to others; her secret feelings about her lover and daughter are not. In some ways she *is* as inscrutable as she thinks she is; in many other ways, she is not.

Further balance is provided by the following passage, which amusingly describes the fallibility of third-person ascription based on physical and behavioral clues. The hero of *Epitaph for a Spy* by the great thriller writer Eric Ambler is sitting in a restaurant rehearsing the appearance that he wants to give during a forthcoming confrontation with an adversary:

> No, too clumsy. Perhaps a mocking smile would be best. I experimented with a mocking smile and was in the middle of my fourth attempt when the waiter caught my eye. He hurried over anxiously.
>
> "There is something wrong with the *coq au vin*, Monsieur?" (1984, 54)

It is clear then that a good deal of fictional narrative is based on the fact that thought can be public and available to others as well as private and accessible only to ourselves. As the Proust narrator remarks in *Swann's Way*, "it is only with the passions of others that we are ever really familiar, and what we come to discover about our own can only be learned from them. Upon ourselves they react only indirectly" (1996, 154). Significantly, Sigmund Freud was also interested in the public nature of thought. I say this because it might have been thought that his analysis of the inaccessibility of motives and reasons for action would make such an interest unlikely. But he wrote that "[h]e that has eyes to see and ears to hear may convince himself that no mortal can keep a secret. If his lips are silent, he chatters with his fingertips; betrayal oozes out of him at every pore. And thus the task of making conscious the most hidden recesses of the mind is one which it is quite possible to accomplish" (quoted in Cohn 1999, 51).

With regard to the mental event/state dichotomy, we can draw a distinction between those states of mind that extend over time and that may become very apparent to those who know us well or may be well hidden and the immediate and inner flow of thought that can be private and inaccessible unless revealed, for example, in an uncontrolled reaction to events. Take this example from *Vanity Fair* that I used in chapter 4, section 5: "Away went George, his nerves quivering with excitement at the news so long looked for, so sudden when it came" (1994, 292). There are three different time scales here: The longest, "so long looked for" could well refer to a very public state of mind. Presumably, George Osborne would have revealed his longing for battle to his colleagues and family by his behavior and speech. The middle timescale is "so sudden when it came," and George's feeling of the suddenness of the news may also have been visible to others. The shortest time scale is "his nerves quivering with excitement," and this sounds as though it would also be visible to others. An excited state of mind will usually result in excited behavior. Or take this example: "Her presence used to excruciate Osborne" (1994, 282). What is the origin of this knowledge? Is it possible to know this fact about the storyworld without the privileged and direct access of the omniscient narrator to characters' minds? It is possible for the reader to read this statement as straightforward thought report of George's mind. Equally plausibly, however, it can be read as a description of George's behavior and therefore as information that could be available to other characters in the storyworld. Remember Wittgenstein's question about whether a statement is a report of behavior or of a state of mind. The test for this uncertainty is to imagine whether another character (that is, with no direct access to his mind) could say those words. I would suggest that in this case it is perfectly possible to imagine another character making this statement based on observation of his behavior. The more the distinction between fictional mind *and* action is blurred, the more it can be seen that the real object of study is the mind *in* action.

The inner/outer balance is a very noticeable characteristic of MITECS. Most of us would probably think that a book called an *Encyclopaedia of the Cognitive Sciences* would be concerned primarily with the neuroscience of the brain, with neurons, axons, dendrons, synapses, neurotransmitters, and the rest. Obviously, there is a good deal in the volume on the physical composition of the brain. However, it is perhaps surprising how much of the book is also devoted to the role of social context and the debate about the public/private mind. Brian Cantwell Smith's entry in MITECS on "Situatedness/Embeddedness" describes how the classical view of the mind sees it as individual, rational, abstract, detached, and general, while the new approach sees it as social, embodied, concrete, located, engaged, and specific (1999, 769). The current situation in cognitive science "points to a paradigm shift underway [that] locates human language in the human body and postulates as its theoretic atom the conversational dyad [pair], rather than a monad [individual] with a message to transmit or receive. . . . The shift was foreshadowed by . . . Vygotsky . . . who analysed communicative events as developing simultaneously on an 'inter-' as well as an 'intra-psychic plane'" (Duncan 1999 440). Elsewhere in MITECS, it is suggested that the "complexity of the social environment led Hirschfeld (1996) to propose the existence of specialized knowledge structures dedicated to social group understanding" (Hirschfeld 1999, 581). Hirschfeld also refers to "mechanisms unique to social reasoning" (1999, 581).

The issue of public thought has been raised within possible-worlds theory, although the emphasis is more often on the individual at the expense of the social. For example, Doležel indicates that the "dialectic of social consciousness and private mind provides a flexible model for understanding motivation in the multiperson world: the pressure of the group enforces social factors, but they have to be 'internalized,' appropriated by the individual mind, in order to motivate the person's acting" (1998, 102). Doležel acknowledges the inner/outer balance that is described in this chapter in his reference to "the dialectic between social consciousness and private mind." However, it seems to me that there still remains a perceptible bias toward the private in the language that he uses. The individual consciousness is taken to be primary. It is the norm that is then modified by social factors. The picture of the mind that is painted in this chapter is intended to question and even to suggest a reversal of these priorities.

Narrative theory tends to assume that characters in novels do not know what other characters are thinking and feeling. However, as we have seen, philosophers and psychologists say we *can* know these things. Narrators say we can. Once again, narrative theory appears to be out of step. Obviously, this is a matter of emphasis only. I would guess that everyone would agree that sometimes we have reliable access to our own motives and intentions and sometimes we do not; and sometimes we have reliable access to the motives and intentions of others and sometimes we do not. My point is simply that the paradigm within narrative theory has up until now been one of infallible and direct access to our minds rather than first-person ascription. A good example of this emphasis is the following remark by the philosopher Alain (the pseudonym of Émile Chartier) quoted by Dorrit Cohn: "In short, there is no room for intimacy in history; at best it can bring men to life as we see them in life, always making us move backwards from their actions to their motives. The peculiarity of the novel is its intimacy, an intimacy that cannot be attested, that needs no proof, and that, in reverse of the historical method, makes actions real" (Cohn 1999, 156). This line of thinking seems to suggest that third-person ascription is less "real" than the direct access that narrators give us, that readers of novels do not have to move backward from characters' actions to their motives, and that actions in historical narratives cannot be made "real." I would question all of these assertions.

Dorrit Cohn refers briefly to the importance of conveying character through external description. In commenting on the nineteenth century, she describes how, while "prolonged inside views were largely restricted to first person forms, third person novels dwelt on manifest behavior, with the characters' inner selves revealed only indirectly through spoken language and telling gesture. . . . In most works by Dickens, Turgenev, Fontane and other masters of the novel of manners, character portrayal is far more 'contextual' than 'intrinsic'" (1978, 21–22). Significantly, however, Cohn adds that contextual character portrayal "moves in directions lying outside the central compass of [her] study" (1978, 22). She is explicitly acknowledging that her subject is the private and not the public mind. The public/private distinction is also behind Margolin's division between, on the one hand, the social, interactional, agential public role, the person in social space; and, on the other hand, the mental, the self, consciousness, self-consciousness, will, and emotion (1995b, 379). This is on the face of it a useful and workable distinction. However, whenever I am analyzing fictional minds, I am struck by the difficulties that I experience in practice when trying to keep the social and the individual apart. Pip's feelings about himself are private, but they are based on, determined by, and generally enter into a variety of different relationships with the feelings about him of Joe and Biddy, Miss Havisham, Estella, and the other characters in the *Great Expectations* storyworld. The opportunity exists for narrative theory to develop specialized knowledge structures and mechanisms that are unique to social reasoning and that will allow it to come to a greater understanding of how fictional social groups work and how individual fictional minds function within those social groups. Some possibilities for building this sort of understanding are introduced in section 5 of this chapter and also in chapter 7. In my view, narratology has suffered from the limitation on the study of fictional minds that is implied by Cohn's remark about the compass of her study. The fictional mind does not have to be divided up in this way. The internal/external distinction is an excessively simplistic perspective from which to analyze mental functioning. If we question it, we can study the *whole* mind and also the *social* mind.

2. Third-Person Ascription

This section continues the discussion of ascription that began in the previous chapter but with the emphasis this time on the third person rather than the first person. The attribution to the character by the narrator of motives, dispositions, and states of mind is at the center of the process of constructing fictional minds and is central to the reader process of comprehending texts. Thought report is the chief mode for ascription. This section is closely linked to the previous one: as we have seen, the more public our thought, the easier and more reliable third-person ascription becomes. Empathy is the power of entering into another's personality and imaginatively experiencing their experiences. It is an essential part of the reading process, and this discussion will, I hope, provide some theoretical background to this ability. Consider this statement by Colwyn Trevarthen, in which he compares the relative levels of reliability of first- and third-person ascription: "Conscious monitoring of intersubjective motives is asymmetric; in normal circumstances we are more aware of others' feelings and intentions than of our own inner states" (1999, 416). Even with the benefit of earlier discussions, you may still be so taken aback by this statement that you will wish to read it again in order to check that you did not misread it. It states quite baldly that third-person ascription is the more reliable kind. It does not say that reliability varies: sometimes one kind is more accurate and at other times the other is. It says that "in normal circumstances" the accuracy of our views about the mental states of others exceeds the accuracy of our views about our own mental states. Suddenly, the ability that we have as readers to construct fictional minds out of a minimum of information does not seem quite so extraordinary.

Not everyone develops the ability to ascribe mental states to others. One of the chief symptoms of autism is *mind-blindness*: the inability to recognize that other people have minds. This is a severe and real form of the philosophical doctrine of solipsism, "the view or theory that only the self really exists or can be known. Now also, isolation, self-centeredness, selfishness" (OED). Descartes' famous "Cogito, ergo sum" is the most famous practical demonstration of the theoretical solipsistic methodology. However, solipsism also takes what might be called a practical or operational form. Autism is the most severe variety, but it is also a well-known symptom of the milder Asperger's Syndrome. In addition, there is the very large number of people whose behavior is so selfish that they appear not to believe in the existence of other minds. Driving through London in the rush hour (or at any time, in fact) will illustrate this point quite forcibly.

A number of philosophers have considered the role of behavior in forming what they call the third-person nature of consciousness. According to them, it is a necessary condition of attributing states of consciousness to oneself that one must be prepared to attribute them to others because we cannot learn how to ascribe mental states to ourselves only from our own case: this ability depends on observing other people's behavior. In a familiar example, it is impossible to acquire the use of the phrase "in pain" solely from one's own case. One needs in addition to be acquainted with the pain behavior of others. This means that pain behavior is not merely a sign of pain: it constitutes to a large extent the conditions under which the phrase "in pain" has a use (Priest 1991, 179–80). The emphasis that these philosophers place on the observation and description of the behavior of others, and the subsequent ascription both to ourselves and to others of the mental states that appear to be appropriate to that behavior, has significant implications for the role of the narrator in presenting fictional minds. When the narrator states that a character is depressed, what precisely is it that the narrator is describing? Philosophers suggest that it is both an internal state of mind and external behavior. Remember Wittgenstein's question. They point out that states such as depression and pain are partly felt and partly shown, partly undergone and partly exhibited in behavior. In the words of the philosopher Peter Strawson, "X's depression is something, one and the same thing, which is felt, but not observed, by X, and observed but not felt by others than X" (1959, 109). From this perspective, the distinction that is drawn within narratology between the narrator's external descriptions of behavior and the internal descriptions of mental states is now problematized. In practice it is often very difficult to say whether a particular phrase or sentence in a narrative text is thought report or external description. Once it is understood that the mind extends beyond the skin, the inner/outer distinction becomes more and more difficult to sustain in every case.

The train of thought described earlier is deeply anti-Cartesian because it reverses the Cartesian, first-person view that one takes meaning from one's own case and then extrapolates it to others. Third-person ascriptions are now made conditions for first-person ascriptions. The need for balance is required yet again. It may be that Cartesians are wrong to imply a certain autonomy for the self-ascriptive uses of statements relating to consciousness, but it may also be that behaviorists are wrong to imply a similar autonomy for third-person uses. Neither use is self-sufficient because each type of use depends upon the other (Priest 1991, 181). This balance is characteristic of narrative discourse, which typically contains a balance of direct access to internal states (the fictional equivalent of first-person descriptions) and surface descriptions of characters' behavior (that is, third-person descriptions). The balanced approach is potentially anti-Cartesian because an emphasis on behavior makes it clear that thought is not only private and inaccessible but also public and available as it can be expressed in physical terms. Cartesian dualism, on the other hand, involves the strict division of reality into either the physical or the mental. It is possible that Wittgenstein is the source of much of this anti-Cartesianism as, significantly, the *Philosophical Investigations* is preoccupied as I have said with the difficulty of distinguishing between descriptions of consciousness and of behavior. Searle is quite explicit that his views are also an attack on Cartesianism (1992, 25–26, 149). While a number of thinkers in various disciplines share this public, and therefore social, perspective on thought, the speech category account appears to work within the framework of Cartesian dualism because of its strict division of narrative either into descriptions of the mind or into descriptions of the body.

While arguing against the doctrine of behaviorism, Searle contends that it is a mistake to suppose that we know of the existence of mental phenomena in others only by observing their behavior. The basis of our certainty that dogs are conscious but cars are not is not behavior but rather a certain causal conception of how the world works. Otherwise, the behavior of cars could lead us to think that they are as conscious as dogs. In his view, the behavior of others only makes sense as the expression or manifestation of an underlying mental reality because we can see that the behavior is caused by the mental (1992, 21–22). Referring to the balanced view of the mind with which this chapter is preoccupied, he points out that, where our knowledge of other minds is concerned, behavior by itself is of no interest to us. Rather, Searle maintains, it is the combination of behavior, together with the knowledge of the causal underpinnings of that behavior that forms the basis of our knowledge of other minds (1992, 22). This balance between observation of behavior and awareness of consciousness is as essential to the analysis of presentations of fictional minds as it is to the study of real minds. In the behaviorist narratives of Ernest Hemingway, Raymond Chandler, and Dashiell Hammett in which very little direct access to minds is given, the behavior of the characters only makes sense when it is read as the manifestation of an underlying mental reality. Furthermore, the reader uses a variety of information about a character from which to infer the underlying mental reality that over the course of the novel becomes that character's embedded narrative. The reader is able to construct the continuing consciousness of a character simply from descriptions of behavior, even when no direct access is given to that consciousness. The reader of *Rebecca* knows a good deal about the mind of Rebecca without ever meeting her.

Searle takes a view of the mind that is different from some of the other theorists that I am discussing. He repeatedly draws attention to what he calls the first-person, subjective ontology of minds. He does this in order to emphasize the reality of our immediate consciousness of our own mental states. Searle stresses that it is a mistake to suppose that the ontology of the mental is objective and that the methodology of a science of the mind must concern itself only with objectively observable behavior. In his view, mental phenomena are essentially connected to subjective consciousness and so the ontology of the mental is essentially a first-person ontology. By contrast, it seems to me, fictional minds must always by definition have a third-person ontology. As fictional minds do not exist except by the semiotic operations of reading texts, it is only the reader who can have an awareness of a fictional mind, and that awareness can obviously only be third-person (although it will take account of the first-person testimony of characters as given in the mode of direct thought). A fictional mind can only be constructed by means of third-person ascription. However, I still think that Searle's perspective is valuable in this context because it picks out very clearly an essential first-person element in the readerly process. The empathy of the reader is directed toward and focused on the first-person sensations of the character and so the reader must experience the "objective" storyworld as far as possible from the various subjective viewpoints of the characters who inhabit the storyworld.

In a strikingly perceptive phrase, Searle says (of real minds), "When we study *him* or *her*, what we are studying is the *me* that is him or her" (1992, 20–21). And Searle's point is as true of fictional minds as it is of real minds. When we study Emma, what we are studying is the *me* that is Emma. So, when we are studying the *Emma* storyworld, what we are studying is that world as subjectively experienced by Emma and also as subjectively experienced by Knightley, by Miss Bates, and so on. The fictional text is primarily seen not as the representation of an objective storyworld, but as the interconnection of all of the subjective embedded narratives of all the characters who inhabit that fictional world. When we study the fictional mind of, say, Lydgate in *Middlemarch*, we do not simply study the episodes of his inner speech that are presented in the three speech modes. We study the storyworld of the novel as it is experienced from his subjective point of view. It is by these means that we study the whole of his mind in action. When we study Lydgate in this way, what we are studying is the me that is Lydgate. This point is really a restatement in different terms of Bakhtin's view that the novel should be a polyphony of independent, subjective voices, and not a monological and objective representation of others by a dominant narrator. I pursue this point in section 4 of this chapter.

As is now clear, the primacy of first- or third-person ascription forms a keen debate within the disciplines of philosophy and psychology. On the one hand, some philosophers claim that "in some circumstances some mental states of others can be the objects of direct perception" (Heal 1995, 50). This approach is, as I have said, associated with the later Wittgenstein of the *Philosophical*

Investigations. Stephen L. White refers to the possibility that "our access to the other subjects' agential characteristics may be at least as direct as our access to their objective makeup. . . . If this general approach can be sustained, then the question how we can ascribe mental properties to an objectively characterized other is misleading. From the agential perspective the problem is rather one of acquiring a more objective conception both of one's partner and of oneself" (1999, 734). This view links closely with Wittgenstein's position that meaning is not inner, mysterious, private, and psychological, but outer, evident, public, and behavioral. On the other hand, some theorists such as Searle appear to privilege first-person authority. Pinker remarks that we "mortals can't read other people's minds directly. But we make good guesses from what they say, what we read between the lines, what they show in their face and eyes, and what best explains their behavior. It is our species' most remarkable talent" (1997, 330). Despite his warm words about the remarkable qualities of third-person ascription, he seems to indicate that he gives primacy to first-person knowledge. As stated earlier, Antonio Damasio adopts a similar perspective. He observes that the "study of human consciousness requires both internal and external views" (2000, 82) and that the "solution of the method problem posed by the privacy of consciousness relies on a natural human ability, that of theorizing constantly about the state of mind of others from observations of behaviors, reports of mental states, and counterchecking of their correspondences, given one's own comparable experiences" (2000, 83–84).

Confusingly, what is, in essence, the same debate also takes place in the completely different terminology of *what it's like* and *qualia* that I referred to in the previous chapter. In 1974, the philosopher Thomas Nagel wrote a famous article entitled "What Is It Like to Be a Bat?" (It is the subject of some very amusing literary exercises in *Thinks . . .* [2001, 90–96], the novel by David Lodge about the subject of this book—consciousness, cognitive science, and the novel.) In it, Nagel argued that the "what it's like" quality of a bat's consciousness is not accessible to third-person ascription. We can never know "what it's like" to be a bat. In the same way, we can never know "what it's like" to be someone else. The distinctive quality of qualia as experienced by one individual is inaccessible to others. However, as you might expect, others disagree. In particular, Daniel Dennett is quite blunt: "Nagel claims that no amount of third-person knowledge could tell us what it is like to be a bat, and I flatly deny that claim" (1991, 442). Dennett claims that such knowledge is possible by means of a methodology forbiddingly entitled *heterophenomenology*, which he defines as "a method of phenomenological description that can (in principle) do justice to the most private and ineffable subjective experiences while never abandoning the methodological scruples of science" (1991, 72). Dennett concludes that when "we arrive at heterophenomenological narratives that no critic can find any positive grounds for rejecting, we should accept them—tentatively, pending further discoveries—as accurate accounts of what it is like to be the creature in question" (1991, 443–44).

Yet another debate exists within psychology and philosophy on the nature of third-person ascription with a completely different terminology. It is called the theory-theory/simulation debate. Under the *theory-theory*, "normal adult human beings possess a primitive or 'folk'-psychological theory [that] postulates theoretical entities—in this case, mental states—and contains laws which relates the mental states to one another and to external stimuli (on the input side) and actions (on the output side). When I predict what someone will do, or explain why they have done something, I do so by deploying this theory" (Davies and Stone 1995, 2). No one suggests that what people use is a self-conscious and fully worked theory. All agree that it is used intuitively and non-consciously. Much of the theory-theory has a social origin: we do not just work it out for ourselves independently of others. We acquire it from our family, our friends, our education, and the general social and cultural consensus within which we have been socialized.

According to the alternative account of the *simulation* theory, "human beings are able to predict and explain each others' actions by using the resources of their own minds to simulate the psychological aetiology [causation] of the actions of others. So, instead of being theorizers, we are *simulators*. We are mental simulators, not in the sense that we merely simulate mentation, but in the sense that we understand others by using our own mentation in a process of simulation" (Davies and Stone 1995, 3). Simulation is not imagining me in that situation: it is imagining being the other in that situation. It means pretending to have the same initial desires, beliefs, and other mental states as the other person. We feed these into our inferential cognitive mechanism that then generates further mental states. For example, a practical reasoning mechanism will generate a choice or decision. We then ascribe to the other an occurrence of this state. Predictions of behavior proceed similarly. We run our decision-making system off-line. Like the application of the theory-theory, simulation is a completely social activity in the very obvious sense that it is concerned with attempting to simulate the minds of others.

An example that is often used in the debate concerns a missed plane (Gold-

man 1995, 187). Two people arrive at the airport thirty minutes after the sched-
uled departures of their separate flights. A's flight left on time, but B's flight was
delayed and left only five minutes before. Ninety-six percent of those questioned
said that B would be more upset than A. The question is, How did the respon-
dents arrive at their ascriptions? As I have pointed out on a number of occasions,
real-mind theorists are themselves well aware of the many suggestive parallels
with fictional minds. Robert M. Gordon asks, "Does narrative (including film
narrative) create emotional and motivational effects by the same processes that
create them in real-life situations?" (1999, 766). The missed plane does indeed
sound like a scene from a Hitchcock film.

   Both the theory-theory and the simulation theory can also be applied to first-
person as well as third-person ascription. According to simulation theorists,
we run our decision-making system off-line in order to attempt to predict
how we will react to certain situations in the future. According to theory-
theorists, first-person simulation theory is mistakenly based on two aspects of
the Cartesian theory of introspection (completeness and infallibility) that arise
from the allegedly privileged nature of access to first-person states. However, in
their view, self-knowledge is as much of a theory as the knowledge of others,
and theories can be partial and fallible. Speaking personally from the results
of my own introspections, for what they are worth, the theory-theory of first-
person introspection seems very plausible to me. However, in order to remain
consistent with the logic of my argument, I should stress that my theory might
be partial and fallible!

   A common reaction to this debate is to doubt the validity of the distinction
between theory-theory and simulation and to argue that simulation is simply
the means by which we arrive at a theory. All we can ever have is a theory; what
varies is the way in which we get to that theory, and that is a purely empirical
question. Simulation needs theory and theory needs simulation. Simulation
requires a theoretical basis and theory requires an empirical basis. Together,
they form a coherent account of ascription. This balanced approach illumi-
nates two sides of the activities of the reader of fictional texts. On the one hand,
the reader must have a kind of basic folk theory about how minds work. It is
on this basis that we know that motives and dispositions can be ascribed to
others. On the other hand, readers also simulate in their own minds the specific
dilemmas faced by characters in novels. When reading *Great Expectations*, most
readers will, I would guess, ask themselves, "How would I feel if I were Pip, a
newly made gentleman who found out that I was being supported not by a well-
bred lady but by a convict?" In the jargon of the debate, readers will run their

action planning system off-line in order to simulate the workings of Pip's mind. Pursuing the point further, off-line thinking about mental functioning is central to our understanding of novels. How can the narrative of *Great Expectations* be comprehended except by the kind of train of thought described earlier? Simulation is concerned with seeing the world from another's perspective. This is what the reader has to do for fictional minds. The fictional world cannot be understood except from the point of view of the characters. The plot of *Emma* can be described as Emma experiencing the storyworld in one way, Knightley experiencing the storyworld in another way, Mr. Elton experiencing the story-world in yet another way, and so on. The storyworld is the amalgamation of all these different, individual, subjective, and aspectual storyworlds. The reader has to use both their theory of mind and their ability to simulate the mentation of others to follow all of the different individual narratives and, therefore, the whole narrative.

Much of the theory-theory/simulation debate is concerned with the cognitive development of children. According to Alison Gopnik, the theory-theory position on this issue is that children "develop a succession of theories of the mind that they use to explain their experience and the behavior of themselves and others. Like scientific theories, these intuitive or naïve theories postulate abstract coherent mental entities and laws, and they provide predictions, interpretations, and explanations. The theories change as the children confront counterevidence, gather new data, and perform experiments. One consequence of this view is that the philosophical doctrine of first-person authority is incorrect: our knowledge of our minds is as theoretical as our knowledge of the minds of others" (1999, 840). On the other hand, the simulationists have a different approach: "A second area of developmental research asks whether children ascribe mental states to themselves before they ascribe them to others. Versions of the simulation theory committed to the view that we recognize our own mental states as such and make analogical inferences to others' mental states seem to require an affirmative answer to this question; other versions of the theory seem to require a negative answer. Some experiments suggest a negative answer, but debate continues on this question" (Gordon 1999, 765).

Within the debate, continual reference is made to some empirical false-belief tests that have been given to children. These tests are used because psychologists have found that very young children have difficulty understanding the fact that the beliefs of others can be false. If very young children know that x is the case, they cannot comprehend the possibility that others might mistakenly think that y is the case. Obviously, there is a point in the cognitive development of young children when they come to understand the existence of false beliefs. The purpose of the tests is to find out when this typically happens: "In one experiment, for example, children saw a closed candy box. When they opened it, it turned out that there were pencils inside it, rather than the candy they had been expecting. The children were asked what another person would think was in the box at first, before they opened it. Three year-olds consistently said that the children would think there were pencils in the box. They did not understand that the other person's belief could be false" (Gopnik 1999, 839). So, in a series of well-known tests, children are shown person P putting an object O in place A. After P leaves, O is relocated in place B. So P has a false belief that O is still in place A when in fact it is now in place B. When asked where P will look for O when he comes back, children aged under four will wrongly say B: they are unable to infer a false belief. Children aged over four will typically give the right answer, A, although the jury is out on whether this is because they have developed a theory of mind or whether they have simply gotten better at simulation.

"Infants demonstrate that they perceive persons as essentially different 'objects' from anything nonliving and nonhuman" (Trevarthen 1999, 416). Children have to develop a sense of others. They have to become accustomed to the fact that the world is aspectual: it is perceived under different aspects. Some people will wrongly think that there is candy in the box; others will know that there are pencils. Some people will think that object O is in place A, some in place B. These beliefs exist independently of the actual presence of candy or pencils. To function efficiently, we have to appreciate, if only fleetingly, what the world is like for people who think differently about it from us. In the same way, readers read novels by seeing the storyworld as aspectual: different characters experience the storyworld differently. Pip and Magwich have shockingly disparate experiences of their reunion. Narratives cannot be understood unless the storyworld is understood as a complex, ever-changing intermingling of the individual narratives of the various characters in it. Norman Freeman discusses whether or not "young preschool children can compute an agent's false belief in the context of computing the agent's *action-plan*" (1995, 82). A character's action plan can only be understood in terms of that character's whole embedded narrative.

This empathetic activity can be thought of as a kind of adult play. According to Derek Bolton, play "can be used to experiment with diverse circumstances, emotions, beliefs, capacities, tasks; to try out perspectives and activities different from the child's own. The play is in a space between reality and the imagination.

The experiments are neither in reality nor in thought alone; the simulations are neither on- nor off-line" (1995, 220). This sounds very like the activity of reading novels. The role of perspectives is crucial to both play and reading. In both, we try out different perspectives to see what they are like. We enter the minds of characters necessarily in order to follow the plot. But it is more than that: we do it because it is enjoyable and because it is good for us. In finding out more about the minds of others, we find out more about ourselves.

To summarize, there is a group of interrelated debates within philosophy and psychology about the relative reliability of our knowledge of our own minds and our knowledge of the minds of others. There is a wide range of views and a consensus has not emerged. Of course, all of this may seem to the skeptical reader to be a very elaborate statement of the obvious: sometimes we are wrong about our mental life and sometimes we are right about the mental life of others. But there is more to it than that. I want to emphasize the existence of this debate in order to show that many theorists in the fields relating to real minds do not regard first-person ascription as the norm from which we sometimes accurately depart. They regard third-person ascription as the norm from which first-person ascription is derived. While I am certainly not qualified to add to that debate, I would like to suggest that the ease with which readers are able to employ third-person ascription in order to build up a strong sense of fictional minds at work suggests, at the very least, that it is an extremely powerful tool. However, my main conclusion is that confident and categorical pronouncements about the nature of fictional minds should not be made in ignorance of the rich, insightful, and exciting, but also bewildering, arcane, and difficult debates on the nature of real minds.

3. The Development of Purposive Thought

This section and the next will consider fictional minds in the context of the work of four Russian theorists: Lev Vygotsky and Alexander Luria on psycholinguistics in this section and Mikhail Bakhtin and Valentin Volosinov (possibly a pseudonym for Bakhtin) on discourse analysis in the next. All four share the dominant characteristic of Russian thought following the 1917 revolution: a functional emphasis on the social nature of thought and on the public nature of apparently private mental life. Vygotsky remarked that every thought "fulfils a function, solves a problem" (1986, 218). He felt that, in order to explain the highly complex forms of human consciousness, one must go beyond the individual. One must seek the origins of conscious activity and behavior not in the recesses of the brain or in the depths of the human spirit but in the external processes of social life and in the historical forms and practices of human existence (Luria 1982, 25). For Bakhtin, a single consciousness is a contradiction in terms: consciousness is in essence multiple. He relates this approach more specifically to discourse analysis when he argues that "verbal discourse is a social phenomenon" (1981, 259).

This theme is developed in a satisfying and logical way across a number of different disciplines. Vygotsky made the initial breakthrough in the late 1920s and early 1930s with his theory of the development of inner speech in *ontogenesis* (in this context, the cognitive development of children). Luria then developed this insight by relating it to a large number of different areas in psychology and psycholinguistics. Together, they provide a scientific perspective on the more sociological, political, discursive, and literary treatments of the social basis of thought in the work of Volosinov and Bakhtin. Volosinov draws out some of the philosophical and political implications in his theories of the dialogic nature of the utterance and relates these implications to analyses of various forms of discourse. Bakhtin takes this approach one stage further during his discussions of the texts of Dostoevsky and others. He uses the basic theoretical underpinning provided by the other three in order to redefine the taxonomies of fictional discourse and to raise a number of more general issues relating to the novel. The insights of Bakhtin on, for example, dialogicality and double-voiced discourse benefit from being seen within the psycholinguistic context of Vygotsky and Luria.

In Vygotsky's view, children are, from the very beginning, social beings. Vygotsky argued that children use social speech right from the start, both for communicating with others and for solving problems (Luria 1982, 105). Speech is a problem-solving tool. Luria contends that for the child any mental act begins as a material action such as the manipulation of an object. Later, inner speech creates the possibility of cognitive action such as the formation of concepts. Therefore, volitional acts such as the manipulation of objects are mediated by the cognitive structures formed in inner speech. In this way, and as described in more detail later, mental action is seen as a process that is social in origin and structure (Luria 1982, 106). In Luria's view, language has a third function in addition to its cognitive function (the need to formulate thought) and its communicative function (the communication of information in public speech): its directive function, the role of inner speech in monitoring and controlling our actions. He comments that the word not only reflects reality, it also regulates our behavior (1982, 90).

In their analysis of ontogenesis, Vygotsky and Luria point out that the communicative behavior of the mother, such as labeling and pointing gestures, focuses the child's attention by singling out one particular object from other, equally attractive parts of the environment. The child's attention ceases to obey the rules of natural and patterned reflexes and begins to be subordinated to the speech of the adult. The mother's speech thereby becomes a strong social stimulus that gives rise to a stable and orienting response in the child and that inhibits the child's more elementary and instinctive responses. They argue that the caregiver's speech does not gain these powers immediately. The formation in the child of the directive function that is characteristic of adult inner speech goes through a long and dramatic development (Luria 1982, 90–91). During the next stage of cognitive development, the child transforms the interpsychological activity of the relationship to the mother into his or her own intrapsychological process of self-regulation. This is when the child learns to speak and begins to give verbal commands to him or herself. This speech is external and out loud, but it is still private speech in the sense that its purpose is not communication with others, but regulation of oneself. *Private speech* is the term used for directive speech that is out loud. *Inner speech* is the term used for directive speech that later goes inward and becomes silent. At first, this out loud private speech accompanies the child's activity. At a later stage, it precedes it, thereby enabling the child to plan activity in advance (Luria 1982, 89–90). Private speech becomes an important tool for self-regulation as children use language to plan, guide, and monitor their activities. In the earliest stages of private speech, it cannot be clearly differentiated in either its form or its function from social, communicative speech. The formal and functional differentiations between the regulatory and the communicative roles occur only gradually. However, as the American psycholinguist Juan Ramirez emphasizes, the crucial point is that Vygotsky and Luria established that out loud, private speech is the "overt and observable precursor of covert, inner speech or verbal thinking" (1992, 199).

Vygotsky argues that this private speech disappears at about the age of five when inner speech begins to develop. From this, we can infer that private speech becomes inner speech. This is part of the transition from the collective activity of the child to more individualized behavior. However, the functions of private speech and the later inner speech are the same. Vygotsky stresses that in both cases they do not merely accompany the child's activity, they serve mental orientation and conscious understanding, and thereby help to overcome difficulties (1986, 226–28). Vygotsky states that speech for oneself originates through differentiation from speech with others. Although the child's first speech is speech to others, private speech derives from this early communicative speech. Once this division of function occurs, the structural and functional qualities of private speech become more marked as the child develops. In other words, private speech becomes more and more different from communicative speech as time goes on. At three years old, there is no difference between private and social speech. At seven years old, they are totally dissimilar. As the child grows older, the vocalization of private speech becomes unnecessary. In fact, as thought becomes more complex and as the structural peculiarities of private speech grow, vocalization ultimately becomes impossible. As Vygotsky puts it, speech for oneself cannot find expression in external speech (1986, 229–30).

Luria observes that, when children encounter impediments, they first make some attempt to solve the problem in the practical sphere and then transfer these attempts to the verbal sphere in the form of the cognitive tool of private speech. This speech tends to be used first to describe the setting and state the difficulty and then to begin to plan a possible solution. Observation shows that private speech starts in a very expanded form and then gradually becomes more and more abbreviated, finally turning into whispered speech in which children haltingly describe the difficulty of the situation in which they find themselves. As external, private speech disappears altogether, it is only by watching lip movements that the psychologist can surmise that the speech has turned inward while still retaining all its analytical, planning, and regulative functions (Luria 1982, 104–6). The existence of the independent, volitional act essentially involves the subordination of the older child's behavior, not any longer to the speech of an adult, but to their own inner speech. Luria comments that for a long time inner speech was mistakenly considered simply as speech to oneself that retained the general structure of external speech but with an unclear function (1982, 104). The Russian theorists make it clear that in their view its function is self-regulation. So, private vocal speech, instead of disappearing, goes underground during the later stages of a child's cognitive development and becomes the cognitive tool of inner speech.

To summarize, Vygotsky's substantial contribution to our understanding of the development of thought was threefold. First, he saw that cognitive activity is social as well as individual. He asserted that "higher mental functions appear first on the social, or 'intermental' plane—often in the form of joint adult-child–problem-solving activity—and only then emerge on the intramental individual plane" (Wertsch 1999, 878). Second, he stressed the importance of cultural, mediational tools for cognition. He "formulated intermental and intramental functioning in terms of semiotic mediation" (Wertsch 1999, 879) by developing a "sociohistorical approach to cognitive development that emphasized the way in which development is constructed through social interaction, cultural practices, and the internalization of cognitive tools" (Holyoak 1999, xliii). Finally, Vygotsky realized the particular importance of the tool of language in this process. He "emphasized social interaction though language in the development of children's concepts" (Holyoak 1999, xliii).

Vygotsky's views are intriguingly reminiscent of this famous remark by Wittgenstein: "If a lion could talk, we could not understand him" (1958, 223). The background to this characteristically gnomic remark is Wittgenstein's notion of "forms of life." He argues that "to imagine a language means to imagine a form of life" (1958, 8) and that "the *speaking* of language is part of an activity, or of a form of life" (1958, 11). The concept of a "form of life" is really a restatement in different terms of the Russian emphasis on the social situatedness of consciousness. The thought and language of the individual arise out of, and are necessarily oriented toward, the social group to which they belong. Their thought and language can only be grasped in terms of an understanding of the ways in which that social group functions and the means by which individuals within the culture relate to one another. If we do not understand the form of life of the lion, we will not understand its language. If we do not understand the forms of life that exist in the storyworlds of fictional characters, we will not fully understand their inner language, their use of cognitive tools, or their intermental relations with other characters.

The legacy of Vygotsky's thought is a fruitful one: "His insight that historical, cultural, and institutional contexts condition learning by identifying and extending the child's capacities animates several ecological approaches in psychology" (Sperber and Hirschfeld 1999, cxxiii). His influence on a whole school of psycholinguists such as the American James Wertsch is immeasurable. For example, recent work with young children "suggests that the notion *group* may developmentally precede the notion of self" (Hirschfeld 1999, 580), and such work is deeply influenced by Vygotsky. Vygotsky's influence also has implications for the first- and third-person ascription debate referred to earlier. If the notion of a group developmentally precedes the notion of self, then it seems at least possible that the ability to ascribe mental phenomena to others could precede the highly self-conscious process of ascribing them to oneself.

It is Wertsch's view that the discipline of psychology seems less capable than ever of providing a coherent account of the human mind. In his view, psychologists know a great deal about isolated mental processes and skills but seem incapable of generating an overall picture of mental functioning. Therefore, they have very little to say about what it means to be human in the modern world

(1991, 1). Wertsch holds that one example of an attempt to provide a coherent account can be found in the work of Russian scholars between the revolution of 1917 and the Stalinist purges of the mid 1930s. He suggests that theorists such as Vygotsky and Bakhtin tried to deal with practical issues that extended across disciplinary boundaries. As a result, they combined ideas from a range of what are now considered as quite separate disciplines (Wertsch 1991, 4–5). It is welcome news that the interdisciplinary approach that Wertsch advocates is now being employed by a variety of postclassical narrative theorists.

4. Dialogic Thought

The brevity of this section is not a fair reflection of Bakhtin's importance in the study of the fictional mind. On the contrary, this section is short only because Bakhtin's theories have become well known and well accepted, and the purpose of this book is, as I have said, to introduce some unfamiliar ideas into narrative theory. The previous section concentrated on the psycholinguistic approach of Vygotsky and Luria to the question of inner speech. This section will broaden the perspective and include some of the more general discursive and literary ideas that are contained in the work of Volosinov and Bakhtin.

I will start with Volosinov's notion of *the utterance.* The term is intended to convey the fact that every speech event, both external and inner speech, takes place in a social context, has an actual or potential audience, and, ultimately, has a political meaning. It is an element in the never-ending dialogue between individuals in a social group. Therefore, the technical issues relating to such phenomena as inner speech can only be fully understood within the wider social context. For example, Volosinov argues that it is only by ascertaining the forms of whole utterances and the forms of dialogic speech that light can be shed on the forms of inner speech (1973, 38). The perspective introduced by the use of the term *the utterance* is important because it relates internal consciousness to pragmatics, the study of the various uses of speech in their social and discursive contexts, and therefore by extension also to the study of characters' motives, teleology, and plot. For this reason, it is necessary to examine precisely how the inner utterance is situated within, and is oriented toward, the social group within which it takes place. One interface is Wittgenstein's notion of forms of life. The language and thought of an individual can only be understood by studying the whole form of life of that individual. Another interface is action: the point at which characters' embedded narratives meet in public and social contexts. These perspectives emphasize the dialogic nature of characters' embedded narratives and the nature of the fictional storyworld as a battleground within which the thoughts and actions of individuals contend and clash.

Volosinov's position is that the word is always oriented toward an addressee. In the absence of a real addressee, as in the internal word of inner speech, the presupposed addressee is a normal representative of the speaker's social group. So, each person's inner world and thought has its stabilized social audience that comprises the environment in which reasons, motives, and values are fashioned (Volosinov 1973, 85–86). Volosinov's use of the term *audience* must be understood in quite a wide sense: not literally, as passive recipients of another's word, but more widely as the other participants in the relationships that the character forms in the storyworld. The language used by Volosinov to describe individual consciousness encourages the analyst of the fictional mind to look beyond particular mental events taken in isolation and to examine the whole context of mental action in the storyworld. This is the dialogic relationship between consciousnesses, to use Bakhtin's term.

According to Bakhtin, consciousness never gravitates toward itself but is always found in intense relationship with another consciousness. In this way, every experience, every thought that a character has, is internally dialogic, filled with struggle, and is open to inspiration from outside itself. It is never concentrated simply on itself, but is always accompanied by a continual sideways glance at another individual. He argues that every thought senses itself to be from the very beginning a rejoinder in an unfinished dialogue (1984, 32). His "dialogic imagination," to use the title given to a collection of his essays, is a logical culmination of Vygotsky's and Luria's theories on the origin and function of inner speech and Volosinov's stress on the social situatedness of the utterance. Bakhtin describes his notion of the dialogic or polyphonic novel by noting that the chief characteristic of Dostoevsky's novels is the genuine polyphony that results from a plurality of independent, unmerged, and fully valid voices and consciousnesses. What unfolds in his novels, according to Bakhtin, is not a multitude of characters and fates existing in a single objective world that is illuminated by a single authorial consciousness. (This is the *monologic novel.*) Rather, there are a number of consciousnesses with equal rights and each with its own world combined but not merged in the events of the storyworld (Bakhtin 1984, 6). (This is the *dialogic novel.*) Bakhtin means by his use of the term *voices* not just a mixture of different lexical registers or speech patterns, but also a clash of world-views and ideological positions. For example, he states that a social language is a concrete, sociolinguistic belief system that defines a distinct identity for itself. In what Bakhtin calls an *authentic* novel (a synonym for the dialogic and polyphonic novel), the reader can sense behind each utterance the elemental force of social languages with their internal logic and internal necessity (1981, 356). Bakhtin links this approach to the notion of the utterance by suggesting that, within the arena of every utterance, an intense interaction and struggle between one's own word and the word of another's is waged, a process in which they oppose or dialogically inter-animate each other (1981, 354).

These ideas are of great importance to the embedded narrative approach to fictional minds. They show that Bakhtin conceives of polyphony not simply as a combination of the characteristic speech patterns of the various characters in the storyworld, but as the presentation of the ideological struggle between the various world viewpoints of individuals within a social group. He also sees the narrator as engaged in this struggle and not aloof from it. For example, he comments that the speech of another, once enclosed in a context such as a narrative and no matter how accurately described, is always subject to certain semantic changes. The context that embraces another's word is responsible for its dialogizing background (Bakhtin 1981, 340). It is in this way that narrators are always engaged with, and thereby altering the meaning of, the discourses of their characters. These ideas form the background to Bakhtin's famous notion of *double-voiced discourse*. The complex meanings that Bakhtin attaches to his notions of the word, the utterance, dialogicality, and polyphony all overlap to a considerable extent with the theory of embedded narratives: both the dialogic approach and the embedded narrative approach situate individual consciousness in its social context; use a functional approach toward characters' minds; analyze the whole of a character's mind and not just his or her inner speech; establish through discourse analysis precisely how this is achieved in narratives; and show how the novel can be seen as an interconnection of the embedded narratives, or dialogic consciousnesses, of its various characters.

It is necessary here to refer to an important methodological issue that arises from the monologic/dialogic distinction. In *After Bakhtin*, David Lodge suggests that Bakhtin started with the view that the novel was basically monologic for most of its history and became dialogic with Dostoevsky. However, over time, according to Lodge, he changed his view and came to regard the novel as inherently dialogic from the beginning, seeing the pre-Dostoevskian novel as already a dialogic type of literary discourse. Lodge writes of Bakhtin's first formulation of the notion of the polyphonic novel (in the early monograph *Problems of Dostoevsky's Art*) that "[w]hat then seemed to him to be a unique innovation of Dostoevsky's . . . he later came to think was inherent in the novel as a literary form" (1990, 22). As an example of the latter position, in the essay "Discourse in the Novel" Bakhtin states that there are two distinct lines of development within the history of the novel. The second line, to which belong the greatest representatives of the novel as a genre, incorporates *heteroglossia* (yet another synonym for dialogicality, polyphony, and authenticity) into a novel's composition and frequently resists altogether any unmediated and pure authorial discourse (1981, 375). I would agree with Lodge that Bakhtin never quite managed to reconcile these two accounts (1990, 59). It seems to me that *Problems of Dostoevsky's Poetics* is still, despite his second thoughts, fairly close to his original position: that the dialogic and polyphonic novel began with Dostoevsky. It is written in an intensely prescriptive manner, clearly regarding Dostoevsky's work as intrinsically superior to the work of others because it is dialogic in nature while the others are essentially monologic. However, like others, I am using his work at a very abstract and theoretical level without referring to his views on particular novelists or historical developments except where necessary.

The field of vision is one of the most important aspects of the relationship between the narrator and the characters in a narrative. Bakhtin's position is that the information contained in the discourse should be presented not within the single field of vision of the narrator, but within the various fields of vision of a variety of characters. In a crucially important statement, he contends that these individual fields of vision—this plurality of consciousness centers—which are not reduced to a single ideological denominator, combine in the higher unity of the polyphonic novel (1984, 16). In establishing the importance of the narrator's democratic treatment of the characters' various fields of vision, Bakhtin is emphasizing that the narrator should not have any surplus of vision over and above that which is available to the characters. His point is usually reworded as saying that it is desirable for narrators to use internal focalization rather than zero focalization or omniscient narration. However, I think that the concept of the field of vision can be extended in other, equally interesting ways. Just as Bakhtin's concept of the word can be reworded in terms of embedded narratives, so can the notion of the field of vision. The word of a character does not just mean a regional accent, and the field of vision does not simply mean visual perception. It means each character's knowledge, beliefs, perceptions, memories, habits of thought, intentions, purposes, and plans. It is each character's whole mind in action. It is what determines a character's actions and what is then modified by the consequences of those actions. It is the story of the narrative as it exists in the mind of each character. The narrative can therefore be analyzed in terms of the intersecting, evolving, and conflicting fields of vision that comprise it.

Bakhtin's theories have implications for the study of teleology because they appear to downgrade its importance or at least redefine the term in a way that is very different from its normal use. On the face of it, he seems to be very dismissive of the notions of plot and design. He states that the ordinary pragmatic links at the level of plot—whether objective or psychological—are insufficient because they presuppose that characters have become fixed elements in the narrator's design. Such links bind and combine finalized images of people in the unity of a monologically perceived world. Bakhtin states of Dostoevsky that the ultimate clamps that hold his world together are different because the fundamental event that is revealed in his novels does not lend itself to an ordinary pragmatic interpretation of plot (1984, 7). Bakhtin's point is that, when characters are not objects of authorial discourse but subjects of their own, they are not exhausted by the usual functions of characterization and plot development (1984, 7). There is nothing merely thing-like, no mere matter, no objects, there are solely subjects (Bakhtin 1984, 237). It is difficult to combine subjects into a plot structure without compromising their subjectivity because they would then become simply elements in a narrative framework. This danger can be avoided if the idea of plot includes some notion of the multiplicity of characters' discourses and therefore becomes a more organic and flexible concept than the traditional approach. Part of the competence that is required of the reader is to enter the storyworld of the narrative and thereby take part in the illusion that fictional characters are individuals with as much freedom and autonomy of movement as real people have. At the same time, readers know that the narrative is a semiotic construction and that its ending has been predetermined. So, it is possible to argue that the reader must be able to maintain simultaneously the two irreconcilable elements of freedom and teleology and that this ability is an inescapable and essential component of the ability to read novels. It could be argued that monologic novels are those in which readers will find that design predominates over freedom. In dialogic novels, readers will find that a satisfying balance between the two elements can be maintained. Freedom can be discovered by readers' constructions of characters' embedded narratives; design can be discovered by reading the novel as a combination of those embedded narratives.

To summarize, the work of the four Russian theorists provides part of the theoretical basis for a new approach toward the analysis of presentations of fictional minds in novels. An essential element in this initial theoretical work is the social basis of thought. Another is the purposive and directive nature of consciousness. An occurrence of inner speech is an utterance, a socially situated, pragmatic element in the continuous dialogue that exists between all individuals in a social group because it is an expression of an individual's needs, desires, wishes, and hopes as defined against those of others. It is not possible to have intentions, purposes, and plans without specifying them in terms of the competing intentions and plans of others. The work of Vygotsky and Luria on real minds can be used for this purpose as can the work of Volosinov and Bakhtin on fictional minds in narrative discourses.

5. The Mind Beyond the Skin

You may remember that I first used this strange phrase in chapter 1, section 2. I did so then so that it would reverberate in your mind until the time came to explain its meaning in more detail here. Variants of the phrase have appealed to a number of theorists: "The skin is not that important as a boundary" (B. F. Skinner 1964, 84); "The network is not bounded by the skin but includes all external pathways along which information can travel" (Bateson 1972, 319); "I try to dissolve the boundaries of the skin and present navigation work as a system of interactions among media both inside and outside the individual" (Hutchins 1995, xvii); and "once the hegemony of skin and skull is usurped, we may be able to see ourselves more truly as creatures of the world" (Clark and Chalmers 1998, 18). In *Voices of the Mind* (1991), the American psycholinguist, James Wertsch has extended the work of Vygotsky and Bakhtin by using the notion of *mediated action* to explain how the mind can extend beyond the skin. Mediated action involves thought with the aid of tools. In this section, I will refer initially and very briefly to one tool, language, because this topic has been explored in considerable detail already. After a rather longer discussion of the second tool, physically distributed cognition, I will devote more space to the third and most important for my purposes: socially distributed thought or intermental thinking.

A fundamental assumption of Wertsch's sociocultural approach to mind is that what is to be described and explained is human action. People are viewed as coming into contact with and creating their surroundings as well as themselves through the actions in which they engage (Wertsch 1991, 8). His is an approach to how the mind actually works in practice in the real world. It takes the study of thought out of the laboratory and into the sorts of situations in which actual thought takes place. Wertsch stresses that both Vygotsky and Bakhtin believed that it is social and communicative practices that give rise to mental functioning. He quotes Vygotsky's remark that "the social dimension of consciousness is primary in time and in fact. The individual dimension of consciousness is derivative and secondary" (1991, 13). The sociocultural approach that James Wertsch applies to real minds can be used to analyze fictional minds. Wertsch points out that his approach begins with the assumption that action cannot be separated from the milieu in which it is carried out and that any analysis of it must be linked in some way to specific cultural, historical, and institutional factors (1991, 18). Once a fictional mind is viewed as a subjective narrative that is embedded in the discourse that describes the whole storyworld of the novel, then an analysis of that mind must necessarily link it to the cultural, historical, and institutional aspects of the storyworld. Characters are elements in a fictional structure and have no meaning outside of it. The character of Emma is simply a part of the structure of *Emma*. This can, in a sense, be regarded as the social dimension of fictional consciousness. Of course, the character of Emma is understood by the reader to have private thoughts, but this individual dimension of the character's consciousness is derivative and secondary because Emma's private thoughts acquire meaning only as part of the storyworld of *Emma*.

Wertsch refers to the mind as a kit of mediational tools such as language and he argues that the mind extends beyond the skin in several ways through the notion of mediated action (1991, 14). He emphasizes that mental functioning is shaped or even defined by the mediational means that it employs. Even when individuals think in isolation, it is inherently social because it takes place with the help of mediational tools such as language and also other tools such as computers or number systems. Of these, obviously the shared social process of language is the most important tool (Wertsch 1991, 14–15). The diversity of these tools explains the heterogeneity of verbal thinking and the cognitive pluralism that can be found both across and within different cultures. The tool kit approach allows group and contextual differences in mediated action to be understood in terms of the array of mediational means to which people have access and in terms of their patterns of choice in selecting a particular means for a particular occasion (Wertsch 1991, 93–94). A study of characters' mental functioning necessarily entails a study of the mediational tools, including language in the form of inner speech, that they use to achieve their ends. For example, as I explained in chapter 4, Neumann points out in her analysis of *Pride and Prejudice* that Elizabeth Bennet's mind is presented as highly verbal, intelligent, rational, articulate, and self-conscious. By contrast, Lydia Bennet's mind is visual, unselfconscious, and inarticulate (1986, 384). Put in Wertsch's terms, Lydia's mediational toolkit is very different from and much more limited than Elizabeth's toolkit.

Cognition is the act or process of knowing and acquiring knowledge, and *physically distributed cognition* or *situated cognition* can be defined as follows: "Situated cognition and learning is the study of cognition within its natural context. This perspective emphasizes that individual minds usually operate within environments that structure, direct, and support cognitive processes. [It] argues that the *nature* of cognitive processing is uniquely determined within its context, and that it cannot be studied in isolation without destroying its defining properties. . . . The social environment also influences cognition through the presence of other minds to influence, assist, mislead, demonstrate, question, and raise other perspectives" (Seifert 1999, 767). The psychologist Edwin Hutchins "has demonstrated how the cognitive processes involved in flying a plane do not take place just in the pilot's head but are distributed throughout the cockpit, in the members of the crew, the control panel and the manuals" (Sperber and Hirschfeld 1999, cxxiv). Note how the physically distributed aspects (the cockpit, the control panel, and the manuals) are considered together with the socially distributed aspects (the other members of the crew). Although they can be difficult to separate in complex environments, it should be borne in mind that they are logically distinct.

For the moment then, I will stay with physically distributed cognitive systems: the use of the environment as an aid to cognition. This does not just mean taking the environment as it is in order to aid cognitions, it means in addition creating an environment that acts as efficiently as possible as such an aid. As Hutchins says in *Cognition in the Wild* (1995), "the environments of human thinking are not 'natural' environments. They are artificial through and through. Humans create their cognitive powers by creating the environments in which they exercise those powers" (1995, xvi). Distributed cognitive systems consist in the main of *cognitive artifacts*, which are "physical objects made by humans for the purpose of aiding, enhancing, or improving cognition" (Hutchins 1999, 126). David Herman has taken the notion of cognitive artifacts in an unexpected and thought-provoking direction in "Stories as a Tool for Thinking" (2003) by arguing that narrative itself is a mediational tool and a cognitive artifact. In fact, he goes further, and in arguing that narrative "bridges self and other," he suggests that it is a tool or artifact that aids the socially distributed or situated cognition that I will discuss later. In Herman's words, narrative teaches me "that I do not know my world if I consider myself somehow outside of or beyond that world" (2003, 185).

Daniel Dennett puts situated cognition at the center of human cognition generally by suggesting that the primary source of our intelligence is our "habit of *off-loading* as much as possible of our cognitive tasks into the environment itself—extruding our minds (that is, our mental projects and activities) into the surrounding world, where a host of peripheral devices we construct can store, process, and re-represent our meanings, streamlining, enhancing, and protecting the processes of transformation that *are* our thinking" (1996, 134–5). For example, the labeling of objects and our use of them as landmarks reduce the cognitive load on perception and memory. Discussing such tools as address books, paper and pens, libraries, notebooks, and computers, Dennett asserts that a "human mind is not only not limited to the brain but would be rather severely disabled if these external tools were removed" (1996, 144). As a vivid example of situated cognition, he points out that old people often function much better when they are still in their old home rather than in the new and unfamiliar environment of a nursing home because of the presence of "ultrafamiliar landmarks, triggers for habits, reminders of what to do, where to find the food" and so forth. Dennett's conclusion is that "[t]aking them out of their homes is literally separating them from large parts of their minds" (1996, 138–39). The concept of situated cognition is a lot more than the simple acceptance of the fact that we use tools. It is a recognition of the fact that our minds extend beyond the boundary of our skin and encompass the cognitive tools that we use. Ultimately, our minds are distributed cognitive systems. At the time of my writing these words, the computer that I am using is as much a part of my mind as the neurons, axons, and synapses in my brain. In fact, even when I stop typing, this Word document will remain a part of my mind. Considering how much effort my mind has put into it, how could it not be?

In Balzac's *Eugenie Grandet*, the old miser, Eugenie's father, is a good example of a situated or distributed cognitive system. His house, his estate, his belongings, and his hoard of gold comprise his mind in action. Without them, his mind would shrivel to nothing. In a sense, they *are* him. There are a number of different ways in which the physically distributed quality of fictional minds can be expressed in the discourse. One is the mode of free indirect perception. The use of this mode emphasizes that events in the physical storyworld are aspectual: they are experienced by characters. So physical events do not exist in isolation from characters' perceptions and resulting cognitions, they exist in relation to them. Aspects of the physical world become part of the individual narratives of the characters who are perceiving them. The minds of those characters are extended in this way to include within them the physical phenomena of the storyworld.

Clark and Chalmers draw out an important implication of the concept of situated cognition. They explain that there is a growing body of research in cognitive science in which cognition is "often taken to be continuous with processes in the environment. Thus, in seeing cognition as extended, one is not merely making a terminological decision; it makes a significant difference to the methodology of scientific investigation" (1998, 10). In fact, one can take their point further. The decision whether to consider the mind as something that is bounded by the skin and that makes use of tools or whether to consider the mind as something that extends beyond the skin and that includes tools within its meaning, is not simply a methodological choice. It determines what is considered as a legitimate subject for study. Within narrative theory, regarding fictional minds as extended makes a significant difference to the methodology of analysis of novels. In particular, it materially affects what is considered as an example of presentation of consciousness. I mention in my discussion of the novel *Vile Bodies* in chapter 7 that many of my examples of presentations of fictional minds would not be considered as examples of fictional thought at all within the speech category paradigm.

I will now be concerned with socially rather than physically situated or distributed thought. This notion is a fundamental element in Wertsch's conceptual framework. He states, for example, that the terms *mind* and *mental action* can be used about groups of people as well as individuals (Wertsch 1991, 14). So, it is appropriate to say of groups of people that they think or that they remember. As Wertsch puts it, a dyad (that is, two people working as a system) can carry out such functions as problem solving on an intermental plane (1991, 27). This is *intermental thought*, as opposed to *intramental thought*, which is individual thinking.

Clark and Chalmers, for the bulk of their illuminating essay, discuss the physically distributed cognition of tools such as computers and notebooks to illustrate their case. However, they then ask, "What about socially extended cognition? Could my mental states be partly constituted by the states of other thinkers? We see no reason why not, in principle. In an unusually interdependent couple, it is entirely possible that one partner's beliefs will play the same sort of role for the other as a notebook plays for [a sufferer of memory loss]" (1998, 17). Socially extended cognition seems to me to be a necessary element in the wider notion of generally extended cognition. In fact, I would go further than Clark and Chalmers. They are limiting their example to an unusually interdependent couple because they are asking whether an individual's mental states can be *partly constituted* by another's. However, we could also ask a much less rigorous question such as, Can two or more minds form a cognitive unit of whatever sort, however casual and ephemeral? If we go down that road, then this much more open and inclusive approach will, I think, produce a rich and suggestive body of evidence. The numerous examples of socially extended fictional thought from *Vile Bodies* that are discussed in chapter 7 are simply the start of the research program.

You may remember that I said in chapter 4, section 5 that the work done there on states of mind would gain added significance later when an emphasis on dispositions rather than immediate consciousness would make the idea of the extended mind more palatable. Clark and Chalmers pursue the role of states of mind in the notion of socially extended thought by exploring the concept of an *extended self*: "Does the extended mind imply an extended self? It seems so. Most of us already accept that the self outstrips the boundaries of consciousness; my dispositional beliefs, for example, constitute in some deep sense part of who I am. If so, then these boundaries may also fall beyond the skin. . . . [We are] best regarded as an extended system, a coupling of biological organism and external resources. To consistently resist this conclusion, we would have to shrink the self into a mere bundle of occurrent states, severely threatening its deep psychological continuity" (1998, 18). I take the notion of the extended self another stage further later in pursing the notion of what I call *situated identity*.

What Clark and Chalmers call the *extended mind*, other theorists call *intersubjectivity*, a term that was introduced in chapter 1. Trevarthen defines intersubjectivity as "the process in which mental activity—including conscious awareness, motives and intentions, cognitions, and emotions—is transferred between minds . . . [it] manifests itself as an immediate sympathetic awareness of feelings and conscious, purposeful intelligence in others. . . . On it depends cultural learning, and the creation of a 'social reality' of conventional beliefs, languages, rituals, and technologies" (1999, 415–16). For example, Sperber and Hirschfeld retell James Wertsch's story of how his daughter had lost her shoes and how he helped her to remember where she had left them. Wertsch uses the story to ask, Who remembered in this case? "He didn't since he had no prior information about the shoes' location, nor did his daughter since she was unable to recall their location without his intervention" (1999, cxxiv). For the purpose of finding the shoes, Wertsch and his daughter comprised a single cognitive unit.

The extended mind can usefully be related to the theories explored in the previous two sections. You may remember that Vygotsky and Luria argue that initially the voluntary act is shared by two people as the child first encounters social speech in the form of the command of the adult. The language of the commands of others then develops into commands to the self, first in external speech, then in inner speech (Luria 1982, 89). Therefore, the directive function in speech develops out of the speech of another: the self-commanding speech of the child emerges out of the commands of the caregiver. This is a particularly significant example of intermental thinking because Vygotsky and Luria are arguing that the very first examples of thought in the child are intermental and not as one might have expected intramental thinking. It is easy to see how Volosinov and Bakhtin developed their theories of the utterance and dialogicality from the scientific basis provided by Vygotsky and Luria. Put in Bakhtinian terms, Vygotsky and Luria's argument is that in ontogenesis thought arises out of the child's dialogical relationship with its caregiver. We need to understand the ways in which our knowledge and our skills are constructed by our dealings with others and the technological and cultural webs in which we live, work, think, and communicate. The problem of unraveling what is involved in a child's learning to master a culture and the technology it generates is concerned with interactions. Through interacting we learn how to do things and we realize what needs to be done. Of the various types of representations used in the myriad different problem-solving exercises that we have to negotiate, some are internal and in our heads, some exist out in the world, and some are in the heads of others. What we have to do is to explore the many ways in which these three types of information flow, merge, alter, and interact and to explore how cognition depends on these various relationships. And everything that is said here is as true of fictional minds as it is of actual minds.

Examples of intermental thinking were contained in the discussions in chapter 3, section 4 on the consensus and presupposition subfunctions of thought report. This intermental thinking by groups is often more powerful than individual intramental thought. For example, two people doing a crossword together will, especially if they know each other's minds well, do better that the sum of their individual, separate efforts. The notion of intermental thinking is obviously essential to analyses of fictional presentations of close relationships such as friendship, family ties, and, especially, marriage. These relationships may be regarded as intermental systems in the sense that the reader may have the expectation that the thinking of the characters who make up the relationship will be shared on a regular basis, although it is often the role of the narrator to frustrate that expectation. It could be plausibly argued that a large amount of the subject matter of novels is the formation and breakdown of intermental systems. The importance that we attach to this aspect of fiction is hauntingly and movingly conveyed by this description of a marriage in Pynchon's *The Crying of Lot 49*: "Like all their inabilities to communicate, this too had a virtuous motive" (1996, 30).

The notions of situated cognition, cognitive artifacts, and distributed cognitive systems contribute substantially to our awareness of the importance of culture in influencing the relations between individuals and their world. Sperber and Hirschfeld's view is that cognition "takes place in a social and cultural context. It uses tools provided by culture: words, concepts, beliefs, books, microscopes, and computers" (1999, cxv). In fact, they go on to define culture in cognitive terms. According to what they term an *epidemiological* approach to culture, "cultural facts are not mental facts but distributions of causally linked mental and public facts in a human population. More specifically, chains of interaction—of communication in particular—may distribute similar mental representations and similar public productions (such as behaviors and artefacts) throughout a population. Types of mental representations and public productions that are stabilized through such causal chains are, in fact, what we recognize as cultural" (1999, cxxii).

Edwin Hutchins draws the same conclusion regarding culture as the one drawn earlier regarding Clark and Chalmers's more narrowly conceived notion of extended cognition: how you conceive of an object of study determines what you consider as a legitimate object of that study. If you define the study too narrowly, you may miss important aspects of it. For example, the "ideational definition of culture prevents us from seeing that systems of socially distributed cognition may have interesting cognitive properties of their own. . . . [S]ocial organizational factors often produce group properties that differ considerably from the properties of individuals. Clearly, the same sorts of phenomena occur in the cognitive domain" (Hutchins 1995, xiii). You may be thinking that nobody would disagree with an acknowledgement of the importance of the social aspects of life. But there is more to it than that. The temptation is to regard the individual aspects as primary and the social as secondary, albeit a vitally important additional element. This chapter is asking whether the opposite may be true: the social is primary and the individual is secondary. For example, Hutchins emphasizes that the study of situated or distributed cognition is not simply an optional add-on, studied after the more central mind *within* the skin has been analyzed. In referring to his book on a ship's navigational system, which he considers as an example of a socially and physically distributed cognitive system, Hutchins hopes to show that "human cognition is not just influenced by culture and society, but . . . is in a very fundamental sense a cultural and social process. To do this I will move the boundaries of the cognitive unit of analysis out beyond the skin of the individual person and treat the navigation team as a cognitive and computational system" (1995, xiv). (This is another sighting, by the way, of the "skin" trope that was illustrated at the beginning of this section.) Clark and Chalmers reinforce Hutchins's point: "Once we recognize the crucial role of the environment in constraining the evolution and development of cognition, we see that extended cognition is a core cognitive process, not an add-on extra" (1998, 12). This argument can be related to narrative theory. For example, in *Heterocosmica*, Doležel starts his discussion of storyworlds with a chapter on single-person storyworlds before going on to consider multiperson storyworlds in a later chapter. In the light of the earlier discussion, a suggestion that the order of chapters should have been reversed may seem quite plausible.

Uri Margolin has done valuable pioneering work on group narratives and he has drawn attention to a number of significant aspects of the relationships between individuals and cultures. For example, his work on groups has shown how misunderstandings or radically different understandings of the same data by people from different groups, usually referred to as "culture clash" or "different ways of viewing the world," can profitably be redescribed in terms of dissonant cognitive categories and modes of reasoning. It is at this point, in his view, that the individual and social dimensions of cognition begin to shade into each other. But it is important not to limit unnecessarily the scope of this insight. I am arguing that it is not just at the point of culture clash that the individual and social dimensions of cognition begin to shade into each other, but that the shading process begins from the very start of our lives and that we are to a large extent constituted by this process.

While criticizing the neglect of action by the disciplines of linguistics and psychology, Wertsch argues that the role of mediational tools such as language can only be properly understood if they are considered as part of the concept of action. These tools have no magical power in and of themselves. There is a widespread tendency in several disciplines to focus on language and other sign systems in isolation from their mediational potential. In his view, this means that sign systems have become abstracted from human action (1991, 119). In order to put fictional action in the sociocultural setting that Wertsch advocates, I will summarize his typology of action and illustrate it with examples, all in thought report, from "The History of the Nun" by Aphra Behn. Wertsch's five types of action (in part derived from the work of Jürgen Habermas) are these:

(a) *Teleological action.* A person attains an end or brings about the occurrence of a desired state by choosing the means that have the promise of being successful in a given situation and applying them in a suitable manner. The central concept is that of a decision among alternative courses of action, based upon an interpretation of the situation, in order to realize an end (Wertsch 1991, 9–10). The teleological implications of embedded narratives are explored in chapter 6, section 3. Example: "Isabella . . . thought it time to retrieve the flying lover, and therefore told Katteriena she would the next day entertain at the low gate, as she was wont to do" (1994, 162).

(b) *Dramaturgical action.* A person evokes in their public audience a certain image or impression of themselves by purposefully disclosing their subjectivity. Each agent can monitor public access to the system of their own intentions, thoughts, attitudes, desires, feelings, and so on. Thus, the presentation of the self does not signify spontaneous, expressive behavior, it stylizes the expression of their experience with a view to the audience. A person typically carries out this impression management with strategic goals—as in type a—in mind (Wertsch 1991, 10). A character's management of other characters' impressions of them is an important element in the way in which his or her mind works in action. Impression management is one of the points at which different characters' embedded narratives enmesh: those of the manager and those of the managed. It is possible to see this type, along with the others, as specific aspects of type a, in that they are all means to attain an end. Example: "Yet still she dissembled with a force beyond what the most cunning practitioner could have shown, and carried herself before people as if no pressures had lain upon her heart" (1994, 161).

(c) *Normatively regulated action.* This refers not, as a and b do, to the behavior of solitary individuals, but to members of a social group who orient their action to common values or the norms that obtain within a social group. The individual may comply with or may violate a particular norm or generalized expectation of behavior (Wertsch 1991, 11). This is a very clear statement of the social situatedness of action, and it is also a very precise statement of the plots of a large number of novels in which protagonists initially comply with and then violate the social norms of the storyworld. Example: "The rest of the nuns began to ask Henault of news . . . and he, . . . to conceal the present affair, endeavoured to assume all the gaiety he could" (1994, 165).

(d) *Communicative action.* This is the interaction of at least two persons. The actors seek to reach an understanding about the present situation and future plans in order to coordinate their actions by way of agreement (Wertsch 1991, 11, following Habermas 1984, 86). This is a restatement within a different context of the notion of intermental thinking. It is significant that there is very little difference in practice between the two terms *intermental action* and *intermental thinking.* Example: "they both resolved to get up what was possible for their support" (1994, 169).

(e) *Mediated action.* This type can be seen as a more sophisticated restatement of type a. Like type a it is goal-directed, but it does not assume that the appropriate focus of analysis is the solitary individual or that there is a neat separation between means and ends. It takes account of the fact that human action typically employs mediational means such as tools and language that shape the action in essential ways (Wertsch 1991, 12). Characters make use of a wide range of mediational tools in effecting their actions, one of which is the use of the tool of inner speech in mental action. Example: "This was the debate. She brings reason on both sides; against the first, she sets the shame of a violated vow" (1994, 166).

It is noticeable that most of these examples can be used to illustrate more than one type of action. This suggests that, although Wertsch refers to them as alternative types of action, it may be more accurate to describe them as, potentially, different perspectives on the same action. Wertsch relates all of them to situated and intermental thinking by pointing out that both individual actions and the actions of small groups are components in the life, not just of that individual or group, but also of the whole social system. Intermental actions and the social interactions that make them possible are defined and structured by the broader social and cultural system (Wertsch 1991, 47). In the same way, the actions of fictional individuals and groups can only be understood by reference to the whole social and cultural system that comprises the storyworld of the novel.

Van Dijk has supplied a philosophical perspective on this issue. He refers to communicative or intermental action as interactions between several agents that include all forms of cooperative social behavior such as the use of language (1976, 296). The simplest examples are those cases where two agents together accomplish the same action while having the same intention. More complex are the cases where the intended actions are the same but where the purpose is different, and so the action is done for different reasons. Alternatively, the purposes may coincide, but the actions are different. For example, the joint action may be preparing dinner, but each agent fulfils different tasks within the overall action. Some actions can be carried out by either one or more agents, while others, such as marrying or fighting, must have at least two agents (van Dijk 1976, 298). Fictional actions can be analyzed in the same way. Interaction is obviously relevant to the construction of plot in narrative fiction. When characters undertake joint actions, their embedded narratives overlap during the extent of their joint purpose before diverging again.

I will conclude this section by introducing the concept of *situated identity*. In the thriller *Giotto's Hand* by Iain Pears, the narrator tells us of the hero-detective: "For the last ten days, it seemed, everybody he'd met had been telling him to make up his mind. He'd never really thought of himself as being so feeble, but majority opinion seemed against him" (2000, 257). So, which is it? Is he as decisive as he thinks, or is he as indecisive as everyone else seems to think? Which is more reliable, his own first-person ascription of the attribute of decisiveness or the third-person ascription to him of indecisiveness? An aspect of his identity is under consideration, but how is it to be determined? Where is his identity situated, in his own views about himself or in the views of others?

So far in this section I have discussed the ideas of real-mind theorists on mediational tools, physically distributed cognition, socially situated thought, intermental thinking, and situated action. However, I would like to end by making a very strong claim derived from these conceptual tools that I shall call *situated identity*. This idea will underpin much of the discussion in the next two chapters. If you want to find out about an aspect of someone's mind, say whether or not they are selfish, who do you ask? Certainly not just them, because you know that you cannot be sure that you will get a complete answer. Selfish people are not likely to admit to being selfish. Also, unselfish people may be so laceratingly self-critical that they might admit to being selfish when everyone else would disagree. (There seems to be a kind of benign Cretan liar type of paradox at work there.) We are all reluctant to take somebody's word for the workings of their own mind, and this seems to me to be a tacit admission that there is a strong sense in which our mind is distributed among those other people who have an image of us in their minds. How else can we say that someone is selfish when there is no representation of selfishness in their mind? This image is in the minds of others, but we are attributing it to this particular mind. Surely then, our identity is distributed among the minds of others. The concept of situated identity is also clearly related to the question of action. In a sense we are not so much what we say we are, but what we do. Action is public and so is a fairly reliable, though not infallible, basis on which other individuals can judge the workings of our minds. (Of course, there is still room for a good deal of doubt: an apparently hostile act might result from hostility but might also be a result of shyness.) During the bulk of *Great Expectations*, Pip is noticeably lacking in self-awareness. Only a small part of his whole identity is contained within the workings of his own mind. His identity is distributed among all the various Pips that exist in the minds of Biddy, Joe, Estella, Miss Havisham, and so on and that are based on their judgments of his actions.

Conclusion

I would ask you now, having read this chapter and the previous one, to flick back to chapter 3 for a moment. If the debates described there do not now seem a long way away, and rather beside the point, then these two chapters will have failed in their purpose. All that I have read in the real-mind discourses of philosophy, psychology, psycholinguistics, and cognitive science has convinced me that we can come to a fuller and deeper understanding of the construction of fictional minds only by making extensive use of them. Clifford Geertz stresses that thinking is "primarily an overt act conducted in terms of the objective materials of the common culture, and only secondarily a private matter. In the sense both of directive reasoning and the formulation of sentiment, as well as the integration of these into motives, man's mental processes indeed take place at the scholar's desk or the football field, in the studio or lorry-driver's seat" (1993, 83). Now that chapters 4 and 5 have placed fictional thinking at the scholar's desk, the football field, in the studio, and lorry driver's seat, the next two chapters will consider in more detail the precise means by which we can study this thinking.

6

The Fictional Mind

1. Summary

As I explained at the beginning, chapters 2 and 3 both focused on existing narratological approaches toward fictional minds. Chapters 4 and 5 considered the implications of real-mind discourses for fictional minds and laid the theoretical basis for a new approach for this area of narrative theory. This chapter and the next chapter will now outline the new approach. This one will describe it in general terms by, in part, recapitulating some of the findings of the previous four chapters, and chapter 7 will develop it further in three specific directions. Next though, it may be a good idea at this pivotal point in the book to see some of the ideas discussed so far in action. I will analyze two very small pieces of narrative discourse in order to summarize the current position.

The first passage is from *Emma*: the narrator is describing Emma's feelings about Frank Churchill:

(a) Not that Emma was gay and thoughtless from any real felicity; it was rather because she felt less happy than she had expected.
(b) She laughed
(c) Because she was disappointed;
(d) and though she liked him for his attentions, and thought them all, whether in friendship, admiration, or playfulness, extremely judicious, they were not winning back her heart.
(e) She still intended him for her friend (1996, 304).

The second passage was discussed in chapter 3, section 2, but I will repeat it here. It is from *Tom Jones*: "These Meditations were entirely employed on Mr. *Allworthy*'s Fortune; for, first, he exercised much Thought in calculating, as well as he could, the exact Value of the Whole; which calculations he often saw Occasion to alter in his own Favour: And secondly, and chiefly, he pleased himself with intended Alterations in the House and Gardens, and in projecting many other Schemes, as well for the Improvement of the Estate as of the Grandeur of the Place" (1995, 72).

The speech category approach is not very informative about the presentations of Emma's and Blifil's minds in these short extracts. But it is clear that there are minds in action here. So, how do we reconstruct those minds? And how do we describe that reconstruction? I suggest six observations (four here, two later in section 3) that a reader might want to make on these passages that do not fit comfortably within classical narratology, together with some initial indications of how the theory that is currently in existence in other fields can be brought together into a newly expanded, postclassical narratology of the fictional mind. The discourses on real minds of cognitive science, psycholinguistics, psychology, and the philosophy of mind are parallel discourses to narratology in the sense that they consist of vastly different pictures of the mind from the one that tends to emerge from narrative theory. However, I do not see these disciplines as being in conflict with narratology. For example, the speech category account is certainly not wrong, it is simply one method of analysis among others. The drawbacks that were discussed in chapter 3 will arise only if it is considered to be the only perspective on minds in narrative discourse.

1. *Both passages are presentations of mental functioning and of dispositions to behave in certain ways.*
Emma is deciding on her future relations with Churchill on the basis of her feelings about him, and Blifil is planning how to make as much money as possible out of Squire Allworthy. In saying this, I am talking about how their minds are working and what their thinking is for. This is a functional approach toward consciousness. In the paradigm of the mind that emerges from the discourses of cognitive science, psychology, and the philosophy of mind, thought is seen primarily as a mode of action in which mental language is not privileged. The background to Emma's and Blifil's states of mind is their dispositions to behave in certain ways. Blifil has an avaricious disposition, while Emma's is controlling and manipulative in her pleasure in matchmaking, her attempts to exercise power over others, and her avoidance of worthwhile relationships. She is disposed for these reasons to be pleased by Churchill's flirtatious attentions. The language of dispositions comes more naturally to philosophers than to narratologists. It is odd that the discourse of narrative theory leaves so completely out of account a class of phenomena that are so central to another discourse on the mind. The mode of thought report is much better suited to the characteristic interests of psychology and philosophy than the other two modes

of direct thought and free indirect thought. For example, dispositions are most easily presented in thought report.

2. *The passages consist of thought report of a dense, complex layering of a wide variety of states of mind that comprise a causal network of reasons and motives for actions.*

Both extracts illustrate the purposive, regulative role of mental functioning in planning, directing, and monitoring our actions and contain the expressions of short- and long-term intentions, plans, goals, motives, and reasons for action. Blifil is exercising his mind on planning what to do with Allworthy's fortune. Emma's mental functioning relates more to the management of her relationships with others. The narrator of *Emma* presents the causal network of reasons and motives behind this management with great skill and sensitivity. I will analyze this presentation of the causal network in some detail now because it is an example of the kind of standard thought report of states of mind that has been neglected by narratology but that contains a good deal of information about fictional mental functioning. This information becomes clearly visible within the paradigm that I am advocating. The following discussion refers to the passage from *Emma*.

In part a, in just twenty-three words, the narrator refers to four states of mind: gay and thoughtless; felicity; being less happy; and an expectation of happiness. The two present states (gay and thoughtless, and being less happy) are compared to the two others. One of these is counterfactual (felicity), and the other refers to the past (expectation of happiness). The fact that she is gay and thoughtless is given a counterfactual or negative explanation as it is not due to the non-existent state of felicity. Then, the degree of her current state of happiness is defined by reference to the past as it is less than her expectation had been. In addition, a causal relationship is established between the two present states. She is gay and thoughtless because her current level of happiness is less than she had, in the past, expected. On the face of it, this is a paradox, although the meaning emerges in part d.

The name *indicative description* may be given to descriptions of actions that appear to indicate an accompanying state of mind. This term is explained further in chapter 7, section 2. "She laughed" (b) is indicative description because it relates to behavior, laughter, that generally indicates an amused state of mind. However, it is an important function of the device of indicative description that it can be an inaccurate indicator of actual states of mind. The laughter may result from a bitter or sardonic state of mind. In this case, the laughter is quite complex. It appears to be real laughter but with an ambivalent, rather bittersweet quality that suits the paradoxical nature of her thought processes.

The state of mind in part c, disappointment, again has a causal function: it is given as a reason or explanation for the action of laughing and is another apparent paradox. The use of the feeling of disappointment here reinforces the issue of the inaccurate expectations that were described in part a.

It is possible to identify six more explicit states of mind in the twenty-seven words in part d, together with one implicit state, making a total of twelve in two short sentences. The explicit states are liking for Churchill generally; in particular, liking for his friendship; for his admiration; or for his playfulness; belief that his behavior is judicious; and the feeling or belief that her heart is not being won back. The state of mind that is implied by all of these, but not explicitly stated, is the feeling of relief that her heart is not being won back. The causal relationships between these states are complex. The liking for him is caused by the belief in the judiciousness of his behavior. This pair of states is in turn caused by the three possible or hypothetical explanations for his behavior: admiration, feeling of friendship, and feeling of playfulness. (Of course, Emma is mistaken, and the primary motive for his behavior is the desire to create a smokescreen that will conceal his secret engagement to Jane Fairfax.) However, the use of the word "though" balances all of these states against the belief that her heart is not being won back. This is the explanation for the disappointed expectations conveyed by parts a, b, and c. Finally, the state of relief (that her heart is not being won back) that is implied by the whole sentence is the belated explanation for the two apparent paradoxes.

Part e is the statement of an intention to act in a particular way toward Churchill in the future. The function of the previous two sentences has been to present the causal network of states of mind that explains this intention.

3. *The narrators refer to Blifil's and Emma's actions and behavior as well as to their consciousness.*

The description of Emma's mind includes action (laughter), behavior (which is gay and thoughtless), and an intention to act (that is, to treat Churchill as a friend). The acts that Blifil performs to further his interests are key ingredients in his narrative. In fact, the quoted passage is in effect a list of actions and intentions to act, for example, calculations of the size of the fortune, intentions to alter the house, and projections for many other schemes. The relationship between action and consciousness is explored by the philosophy of action, which is concerned with the difference between, on the one hand, willed actions and, on the other hand, mere doings, happenings, and events. It analyzes the mechanism of action: the intricate relationships between the various mental operations such as intentions, purposes, motives, and goals and the resulting physical behavior. It follows from such a perspective that narratological examinations of fictional action need not involve just the study of physical actions on the story level, it should also entail the systematic analysis of presentations of mental action in the discourse. The psychologist Jon Elster discusses the role of the emotions in mental functioning and, specifically, whether or not emotions such as anger can properly be regarded as "action tendencies" (1999, 60–61, 281–83). Emma's pride and Blifil's avarice might be examples of such action tendencies. Irrespective of the outcome of the debate on real minds, this notion is one of the ways in which texts can be interrogated to find out how narrators and readers link together presentations of immediate mental events such as explicitly labeled or implicitly suggested emotions, dispositions, and descriptions of physical behavior into causal chains by means of such concepts as motives, intentions, and reasons for action.

4. *Both passages are clear examples of the socially situated and dialogic nature of consciousness.*

Emma's and Blifil's thoughts are inescapably part of their social context. In particular, the two minds are seen as active, social, and public dialogues with others. Blifil's plans for the future include anticipations of, and therefore calculations about, the minds of others and are about such social issues as class and money. Emma's dialogue is discussed later. Mikhail Bakhtin explored with great sensitivity the inherently dialogic nature of the inner utterance. He showed that our thought consists to a great extent of responses to and anticipations of the thought of others. It is conditioned by the culture in which we live and is, therefore, in an important sense, a social and public dialogue with others. His theories of the social nature of consciousness reveal that there are ways in which inner speech is not really inner at all. It is a voice that is part of the continuing dialogue that we have with other individuals in the culture within which we live. Our thought is in many ways social, public, overt, and observable. A postclassical perspective on the construction of fictional minds should be concerned with this complex relationship between the inaccessibility to others of a character's thought and the extent to which the same thought is publicly available to others in the storyworld.

This relationship is very clearly shown when a character is anticipating, speculating on, reconstructing, misunderstanding, evaluating, reacting to, and acting upon the thought of another. Emma's thoughts are in a fundamentally misconceived dialogue with what she imagines to be Churchill's thoughts. As

Proust's narrator remarks, "our social personality is a creation of the thoughts of other people" (1996, 20). Emma, with Churchill's assistance, has created a social personality for him that exists in a complex and interesting relationship with the rest of his mind. For example, he enjoys the game playing and the dissembling that is involved in his flirtation with Emma. To begin the process of considering Churchill's behavior in terms of the concept of mediated action, his "attentions" can be rewardingly analyzed in terms of Wertsch's five types of socially situated action (1991, 9–12). His action is teleological in that it is geared to the realization of a desired end; it is dramaturgical because it involves impression management of an audience; it is normatively regulated as it works within the social and moral norms that obtain within the social group; it is communicative as Churchill is trying to give Emma a misleading perception of his situation; and, finally, it is mediated because the ends referred to earlier are mediated through his use of the tools of language and behavior.

2. The Continuing-Consciousness Frame

In chapter 2, section 4 I discussed the relationship between cognitive science and narrative theory. My purpose was to build on the large amount of highly original and thought-provoking work that has been done recently on the application of cognitive science techniques to a wide range of issues relating to narrative comprehension. I am thinking particularly of such scholars as David Herman (1997, 2002, 2003b), Manfred Jahn (1997, 1999a), Mark Turner (1991), Gilles Fauconnier (1997), Monika Fludernik (1996), and Catherine Emmott (1997). This section will attempt to relate some cognitive science notions to the specific area of reader comprehension of fictional minds. This is a companion section to the following one on embedded narratives. Here I am arguing that we are able to read a character's mind as an embedded narrative by applying what I call the *continuing-consciousness frame.*

Cognitive science can be applied to the construction of fictional minds by helping narrative theory to analyze the cues that enable readers to create the effect of characters' mental functioning. Readers use a wide range of cognitive frames and scripts in order to interpret texts. Specifically, the embedded narrative approach can plausibly be restated in terms of recent applications of frame theory to narrative because a key frame is the ascription of consciousness to narrative agents. The reader uses existing or prestored knowledge of other minds in the actual world in order to process the emergent knowledge that is supplied by fictional-mind presentations. The work that we put into constructing other real minds prepares us as readers for the work of constructing fictional minds. Because fictional beings are necessarily incomplete, frames, scripts, and preference rules are required to supply the defaults that fill the gaps in the storyworld and provide the presuppositions that enable the reader to construct continually conscious minds from the text. For example, Herman has suggested that "current research indicates that we would do well to ask, not just about story structure as such, but about the patterned, nonrandom ways in which readers and listeners tend to impute structure to certain strings of events presented in discourse" (1999a, 8). The processing strategies that are used by readers to infer characters' inner lives are a central way in which structure is imputed to strings of events. The reader collects together all of the isolated references to a specific proper name in a particular text and constructs a consciousness that continues in the spaces between the various mentions of that character. The reader strategy is to join up the dots. As readers we strongly prefer to read a text for maximum cognitive payoff. We always try to get as much information as we can from a text. This much is well known. But, in particular, the reading process is very creative in constructing coherent and continuous fictional consciousnesses from what is often a bare minimum of information. We frequently finish novels with a strong sense of the individual personality of a particular character. However, if we were to take the trouble to count up the specific references to that character in the text, we might be surprised at how little there is in the text on which we have based our vivid impressions. So the question is, How can we talk more informatively about this process of the reader *bringing something to* the novel?

The processing of fictional minds, and in particular the applications of the various frames and subframes relating to thought, action, context, causation, and so on are bidirectional and interactive in that the information flows are both top-up and bottom-down. A character frame is established on meeting them or hearing of them for the first time (this is top-down). It is then fed by specific information about the character from the text (this is bottom-up). The reader then sets up some initial hypotheses (top-down) that are modified by further information (bottom-up) and so further refined and so on. Minds are mapped from the source domain (the real mind of the reader and in particular their knowledge of other minds) to the target domain of the storyworld within which the reader perceives the fictional minds to function.

An example that is used by the cognitive scientists Roger Schank and Robert Abelson illustrates very clearly how the application of the continuing-consciousness frame works. They maintain in *Scripts, Plans, Goals, and Understanding* (1977) that there has been "increasing recognition that context is of overwhelming importance in the interpretation of text. Implicit real-world knowledge is very often applied by the understander, and this knowledge can be very highly structured. The appropriate ingredients for extracting the meaning of a sentence, therefore, are often nowhere to be found within the sentence" (1977, 9). They then illustrate this point with the following example: "The policeman held up his hand and stopped the car." Their conclusion is that "[s]omehow in understanding this sentence we effortlessly create a driver who steps on a brake in response to seeing the policeman's hand. None of the intermediate links are mentioned in [the] sentence" (1977, 9).

However, it seems to me that we can go further than Schank and Abelson do in revealing the basis of our understanding of the sentence, which is that the reader has to use the available information to try to create the consciousnesses of both the policeman and the driver. This inferential process might perhaps proceed along the following lines: the policeman perceived the car; the policeman came to the belief that he should stop the car; the policeman decided to stop the car; the policeman then undertook the action of holding up his hand; the driver perceived the policeman holding up his hand; the driver understood the meaning of this sign; the driver came to the belief that he should comply with the sign; the driver decided to put on the brakes; and the driver then undertook the action of putting on the brakes. Somehow, to extend Schank's and Abelson's conclusion, in understanding this sentence, we effortlessly create the supposed mental functioning of the policeman and the driver. Comprehension is simply not possible unless we have available to us hypothetical versions of the minds of the actors that appear to account for the events described. (We may be wrong of course, but that is another issue.) We do not just create the driver, we create the driver's mind and the policeman's mind. Narrative is in essence the presentation of fictional mental functioning.

Of course, it is not necessary to make these steps explicit in such laborious detail during actual reading conditions. Because the process is usually automatic, as Schank and Abelson say, frames and scripts "let you leave out the boring details when you are talking or writing, and fill them in when you are listening or reading" (1977, 41). The task of the analyst who wishes to add back in the boring details is to "break down a sentence into its minimal meaning units" (1977, 16). In chapter 7 I will be attempting to break down a number of the sentences in *Vile Bodies* into some of the minimal meaning units that relate to the maintenance of characters' consciousnesses. I will explain this process, which I refer to as *decoding* action statements into consciousness statements, more fully then. Schank and Abelson explain that their approach "is oriented towards handling actions by goal-oriented humans. Problems in representing inner affective life . . . are issues still to be dealt with as well. We are not ready to handle novels, in other words" (1977, 167–68). I believe that there are ways of bridging the gap between the two discourses of cognitive science and narrative fiction and that if not cognitive scientists, then at the very least narratologists using the techniques of cognitive science, *are* ready to handle novels. However, if cognitive science terminology is to be integrated successfully into narrative theory, it will be necessary first to deepen and enlarge our understanding of the central role that fictional minds play in the functioning of narrative. Manfred Jahn (1997) successfully integrates the cognitive science terminology of frames and slots into Franz Stanzel's three narrative situations (1984), but the other frames that can be applied during the reading process should not be forgotten.

As the policeman example showed, the attempt to isolate the basic elements of fictional-mind construction is similar to the need to make as explicit as possible every step of an artificial intelligence (AI) program. Computers are completely literal machines that do only what they are explicitly asked to do and are not able to use any initiative. If there is a gap, they do not fill it. This is why AI programs look so odd to readers who use a good deal of initiative and creativity in joining up the dots without conscious thought. The decoding of action statements into consciousness statements is almost like writing an AI program on how to read a narrative. When all the immensely sophisticated work that the reader does in constructing mental processes from surface descriptions is made as explicit as possible, the results necessarily look very strange. As Steven Pinker remarks, "[r]obot design is a kind of consciousness-raising. We tend to be blasé about our mental lives" (1997, 18). To the real reader, the implied reader, and the model reader should now perhaps be added "the robot reader"!

The continuing-consciousness frame that is required for constructing fictional minds from narrative is interestingly similar to Daniel Dennett's concept of the *intentional stance*, which he claims is required for the construction of real minds and which he defines as "the strategy of interpreting the behavior of an entity (person, animal, artifact, whatever) by treating it *as if* it were a rational agent who governed its 'choice' of 'action' by a 'consideration' of its 'beliefs' and 'desires.' . . . The intentional stance is the attitude or perspective we routinely adopt towards one another" (1996, 27). The working hypothesis that visibly coherent behavior is caused by a directing consciousness in the actual world is used by extension in the application of the continuing-consciousness frame to the storyworld. Both are a way of relating the present event or action to past regularities and patterns of events and to expectations regarding future patterns.

Much has been written about the influence of past and future on the present

workings of real minds. John McCrone discusses the point that, "being dynamic, the brain could bring the full weight of a lifetime's experience to bear
on each moment as it was being lived" (1999, 268). The past is brought to
bear on the present in order to produce the future. As I said earlier, Daniel
Dennett points out that the task of a mind is to "produce future." This line
of thought brings us again to a functional perspective on goal-directed action. The psychologist Philip Johnson-Laird "has argued that the planning and
control of intentional action requires a self model that explicitly represents
one's goals, abilities, options, and current state" (van Gulick 1999, 736). It is
significant that Schank and Abelson in a brief digression on fictional minds
continue the functional approach toward goal-oriented activity that is characteristic of their approach to real minds. They observe that "in stories with
a lot of contextual information about the main character . . . there are many
expectations about likely events [that] are based on detailed knowledge of the
genesis and nature of particular goals" (1977, 102). Schank and Abelson also
refer to the "personal scripts" (1977, 62) of the actors in a narrative, and it is
these scripts that determine which aspects of the storyworld are perceived by
those actors. Yet another perspective on this past-present-future relationship
is provided by the *homeostasis/homeodynamics* distinction that is used in neuroscience. *Homeostasis* describes those aspects of the brain that maintain it
in a steady state and ensure continuity between the past, present, and future.
Homeodynamics describes those aspects of the brain that allow it to cope with
change. The reader understands fictional minds as containing both homeo-
static and homeodynamic features that allow the minds to maintain stasis and
cope with changes to the environment. Cues regarding these features are also
important for readers when following the changes and also the regularities and
uniformities in characters' embedded narratives. As with Damasio's notions of
the core self and the autobiographical self (chapter 4, section 5), characters have
to remain stable entities (apart from perhaps certain fantasy, science fiction, and
postmodern narratives), but they also have to change in order to stay interesting.

The remainder of this section reflects the fact that a number of narrative
theorists have referred to aspects of the continuing-consciousness frame from
within their own theoretical frameworks. Paul Ricoeur remarked that narrative
is "the operation that draws a configuration out of a simple succession" (1984,
65). What I am considering are ideas that suggest that the key to the resulting
configuration is the continuing consciousnesses of the characters in the narrative. As I have said, Monika Fludernik puts experientiality at the center of the
perspective on narrative that she describes in *Towards a "Natural" Narratology*.

Also, Mieke Bal explains the difference between the two editions of her book *Narratology* (1985, 1997) in terms of a new and growing emphasis on subjectivity: "This attention paid to subjectivity is, indeed, the basic tenet of the theory presented in this book" (1997, 11). E. M. Forster drew a famous distinction in *Aspects of the Novel* between a story and a plot. Forster's terminology is now rather confusing, and his point is perhaps best stated in Ricoeur's terms as the distinction between a succession of events (Forster's "story") and a narrative (Forster's "plot"). Forster stated that he "defined a story as a narrative of events arranged in their time sequence. A plot is also a narrative of events, the emphasis falling on causality. 'The king died and then the queen died' is a story. 'The king died and then the queen died of grief' is a plot. The time sequence is preserved, but the sense of causality overshadows it" (2000, 87). Forster relates the issue of causality very clearly to the presentation of characters' minds. The cause of the second event, the queen's death, is a state of mind: the queen's grief. The argument of this book is that the paradigms for the causal links that create a narrative are events and states in characters' minds. However, it is possible that Forster overestimates the importance of the explicit reference to the Queen's state of consciousness. The difference between the explicit "of grief" version and the implicit non-specific version is perhaps not as great as Forster appears to suggest. I am sure that most readers, if given the "story" version, would provide the appropriate fictional-mind construction for themselves and turn it into a "plot." They would *assume* that the Queen had died of grief because the King had died. This is precisely the sort of gap that readers are adept at filling.

Ruth Ronen, Catherine Emmott, Menakem Perry, and, of course, Marie-Laure Ryan are among the narrative theorists who have added substantially to our knowledge of how readers create storyworlds generally and also the characters that inhabit them. With regard to the physical aspects of storyworlds, Ronen mentions as examples of the uses made by readers of basic real-world knowledge the fact that we know without having to be told explicitly by the text that the lawn on which Mrs. Ramsay sits in *To the Lighthouse* is outside the house and not inside it and also that the Sistine Chapel referred to in that novel is in Rome and not in Florence (1988, 499). With regard to characters in storyworlds, Ronen defines her concept of *definitization* as "that stage or process in which it is textually indicated that a name or a description denotes a single, concrete, and well-individuated (i.e. distinct from others) object" (1988, 506). She points out that this can be done with a very small number of attributes, possibly even a single one. As I have said, readers are very resourceful. From the point of view of the reader accessing a storyworld, the existence of well-individuated characters is as much a part of the elementary reality of the storyworld as the fact that lawns are found outside houses and the Sistine Chapel is in Rome. The elementary reality of the storyworld is not simply a matter of physical facts, it comprises in addition the virtual mental subworlds of the characters in the storyworld.

Catherine Emmott in *Narrative Comprehension* (1997) describes the process of the construction of fictional minds in the following terms: "For every reference that is made in the text to a particular character, whether by a noun or a pronoun, the reader needs to access the mental representation. . . . The proper noun 'Lady Chatterley' therefore refers technically to a mental representation made up from all previous mentions of Lady Chatterley plus information in the accompanying text plus inferences. This makes sense because it means that reference is to a representation of a character with whom we can empathize rather than just a word or words in the text" (1997, 201–2). Elsewhere she states that "'entity representations,' cognitive stores which hold information about characters (and locations and objects), can explain the significance of events and enable readers to empathize with the participants. Conversely, readers must respond to events by updating their knowledge and opinions of the characters. Often, the text does not make these links explicit, but readers cannot really understand and appreciate a narrative without supplementing the text in this way" (1997, 106). Emmott refers explicitly here to a number of the points that I am making: the scattered quality of fictional characters and the need to link the various mentions of them in the text into a single entity; the importance of empathy; the use of real-world knowledge to fill gaps; the past-present-future links that form minds and so on. What I wish to do here is to supplement her line of reasoning and to make more explicit and specific precisely what information and which links are used by the reader to construct fictional people. Emmott is very informative indeed on the precise strategies by which readers place characters in a physical context. Her contextual frame theory contains a number of conceptual tools such as binding, priming, and so on that can be used to great effect within the continuing-consciousness paradigm. The fact that a character is currently in or out of a particular physical context crucially affects their perceptual viewpoint and state of mind at that time. What I wish to stress is that the reader processes this knowledge from the subjective point of view of that character and, by a process of empathy, vicariously experiences the particular physical context of the storyworld as the character does. It is only by these means that the reader can plausibly interpret the character's subsequent behavior. This process is understood better when we make explicit the centrality of fictional minds.

In trying to follow characters' mental functioning, readers must make a series of inferences. As Menakem Perry points out, most of the information that a reader derives from the text is "not explicitly written in it; rather it is the reader himself who supplies it by the mere fact of choosing frames. This is not limited merely to subtle information such as complex causal connections or the secret motives of characters, but involves even elementary components of the 'reality' to which the text refers. . . . Most of what the reader infers from the text, it will be discovered, is the reader's own gap-filling" (1979, 45). He also stresses that this is a continuous and evolving process: "The reader of a text does not wait until the end before beginning to understand it, before embarking upon its semantic integration. . . . Of course, inferences in the initial stages are necessarily tentative" (1979, 46). What Ronen, Emmott, and Perry have in common is a desire to stress that the impressive storyworld-creating abilities of readers are not limited to sophisticated and subtle understandings of the deep meanings of texts but are concerned with apparently basic and simple-sounding issues such as knowing that lawns occur outside houses. This is what Perry refers to as "elementary components" of the actual world. This understanding of the importance of readers' cognitive skills in being able to understand texts on even the most elementary level marks a huge advance in our knowledge of narrative comprehension. However, there is the danger that theorists, in order to stress the magnitude of the task facing the reader in comprehending a text, may tend to emphasize the more obviously elementary components of reality at the expense of issues such as complex causal connections and secret motivations. Yet, complex causal motivations and secret motivations are also elementary components of storyworlds. For example, Perry is concerned with the hypotheses and frames with which the reader constructs the storyworld of William Faulkner's short story "A Rose for Emily." But what Perry does not make explicit is that the hypotheses and frames that he describes nearly all relate to fictional mental functioning in general and to the construction of Emily's mind in particular (1979, 351–54).

In her article, "The Modal Structure of Narrative Universes" (1985), Marie-Laure Ryan describes "an 'algorithm' for the cognitive processing of narrative discourse" (1985, 750–51) in this way: "A program with this ability to form hypotheses, chain events backwards, reconstrue game-plans, and revise its representation of past states or events would fulfill one of the most ambitious projects of textual semiotics: it would capture—as Stanley Fish . . . puts it—'the temporal flow of the reading process' and the 'successive responses of the reader' as he goes through the text" (1985, 753–54). What is of particular interest here is her use of the term *game-plans*. This is an explicit recognition that cognitive frames are crucially related to the mental functioning of characters: their goals, desires, plans for achieving them, and so on. The psychologist Alan Parkin points out that the reader has a goal when addressing a text: to achieve a representation of the text that is coherent at both the local and global level, at the level of both microstructure and macrostructure (2000, 240). It is the representations by readers of the mental functioning of characters that ties together the microstructural level of specific mental events and particular actions with the macrostructural level of long-term plans and goals. The next section will address the relationship between microstructural and macrostructural issues in more detail.

3. Embedded Narratives

The embedded narrative approach has underpinned many of the arguments advanced so far throughout this book, so this section will summarize some of the points made to date, link the concept to the continuing-consciousness frame, pick out a few of the issues raised by Marie-Laure Ryan's original work on it, and develop some of its teleological implications. The relationship between the continuing-consciousness frame and the notion of embedded narratives is this: the former is the means by which we are able to construct fictional minds; the latter is the result of that construction. Embedded narratives are the product of the application of the continuing-consciousness frame to the discourse. The term *embedded narratives* is intended to convey the point that the reader has a wide range of information available with which to make and then revise judgments about characters' minds. The three subframes of the continuing-consciousness frame that are described in chapter 7 are just some of the ways in which this wide range of information is obtained. First though, I wish to continue the discussion started in section 1 of this chapter on the Blifil and Emma passages. You will remember that I made four comments on the two passages. Here is one more.

   5. *These pictures of the minds of Blifil and Emma that are contained in the two passages form part of their embedded narratives.*
A key mediational tool for the study of fictional minds can be found within the story-analysis side of narratology. It is Marie-Laure Ryan's notion of embedded narratives, which I am extending by applying it to discourse analysis and using it to mean the whole of a character's mind in action: the total perceptual and cognitive viewpoint; ideological worldview; memories of the past; and the set of beliefs, desires, intentions, motives, and plans for the future of each character in

the story as presented in the discourse. It is a narrative because it is the story of the novel as seen from the limited, aspectual point of view of a single character. Both passages may be called narratives because we see the storyworlds of *Emma* and *Tom Jones* from the limited cognitive and ethical viewpoints of Emma and Blifil. The results of this analysis can in turn be enmeshed into analyses of the other minds in the storyworld with their own embedded narratives, their own motives, intentions, and plans. The embedded narrative approach can relate states of mind to the other presentations of Blifil's consciousness in the discourse as well as to his behavior and actions. The *Emma* passage is related to the subsequent development of Emma's embedded narrative because the final sentence expresses an intention regarding future action. In this way, a complete picture of an aspectual, subjectively experienced storyworld results. The storyworld is aspectual in the sense that its characters can only ever experience it from a particular perceptual and cognitive aspect at any one time. As Searle explains, "[w]henever we perceive anything or think about anything, we always do it under some aspects and not others" (1992, 156–57).

There is a link between the activity of reconstructing Emma's fictional mind in particular and the activity of understanding the larger narrative within which it is located. This link is the relationship between different minds. There is an important sense in which the *Emma* passage is about two minds rather than one: it is about Churchill's mind as well as Emma's. The two minds are in some sort of relationship, but what sort of relationship is this? How can it be successfully theorized? In addition to the "actual" embedded narratives of characters' minds, the overlapping and intertwining of narratives referred to earlier results in the creation of what might be called doubly embedded narratives. That is, embedded within Emma's narrative is a virtual version of Churchill's. In making assumptions about the reasons for his behavior, she is reconstructing, incorrectly, an aspect of his mind within her own. The whole passage is based on a complete misunderstanding of his actual embedded narrative. This doubly embedded quality of embedded narratives is a restatement in different terms of the dialogic nature of consciousness. In aspectual terms, Emma sees a particular aspect of Churchill that causes her to misread his whole narrative. When she hears of his true position, she is forced to reconstruct it from the beginning and thereby see him under a different aspect. I will discuss doubly embedded narratives in more detail in chapter 7, section 4.

To summarize the conclusions up to this point, the embedded narrative approach draws attention to the fact that narrative is, in essence, the presentation of fictional mental functioning. It highlights the following aspects of fictional minds, many of which have been discussed in earlier chapters:

- the future (goals) and the past (memory) relate to the present (immediate consciousness, emotions, and dispositions);
- the mind is an information-processing device that adapts to its environment by dealing with surprises;
- much of our mental functioning is public and social in nature;
- we make stories of our lives;
- a good deal of our mental functioning is counterfactual in nature;
- there is a network of causal mental events behind our actions, and many of the action descriptions in narrative discourse make the existence of this network clear;
- ascription has an important role to play in assessing the nature of this network, and it takes the form of first-person as well as third-person ascription;
- the use of the word *embedded* stresses the situatedness of our mental functioning;
- the storyworld is aspectual: it is seen from the points of view of the characters in it and it is, in a sense, the amalgamation of the various subworlds of the characters' minds; and
- it is an open concept that stresses the wide variety of information, both public and private, that is available for the process of constructing fictional minds.

I think that the embedded narrative approach is valuable for a number of reasons: it is a detailed precise approach to the whole of a particular fictional mind that avoids the fragmentation of previous approaches; it views characters' minds not just in terms of the presentation of passive, private inner speech in the modes of direct or free indirect thought, but in terms of the narrator's positive role in presenting characters' social mental functioning, particularly in the mode of thought report; and it highlights the role of the reader, the process by which the reader constructs the plot by means of a series of provisional conjectures and hypotheses about the embedded narratives of characters.

The term *embedded narrative* is in a sense simply a label for an approach that has always been used by literary critics in practice but that has not yet been sufficiently theorized. As I said in chapter 2, the material that is covered by the term has been categorized separately within narrative theory under a number of different headings: consciousness representation, focalization, characterization, and so on. The usefulness of the embedded narrative label is that it encourages a detailed, precise, functional, and inclusive approach toward the whole of a fictional mind. It clarifies the process by which the reader constructs a series of encounters with a particular fictional mind into something that is coherent and continuous. Currently, there is a hole in literary theory between the analysis of consciousness, characterization, and focalization. Oddly, as I hope to have shown, a good deal of fictional discourse is situated precisely within this analytical gap.

It may appear that I am stretching the term *narrative* too far and overextending its scope to the point where it ceases to be useful. However, I would argue that the use of the phrase has great value because it focuses attention on the teleological value of the information that texts provide on fictional minds. Characters are obviously different from real people in that they exist only within a narrative structure. The detail on fictional minds provided in texts gains significance within that structure, and the use of the word *narrative* is intended to draw attention to this point. It is noticeable that there is now a growing interest within a number of real-mind disciplines in the role of narrative in thought. This trend strengthens an identification of the two concepts.

Manfred Jahn draws attention to "the spreading insight that a person's perceptions are already informed by internal narrative 'scripts'" (1999b, 18). Daniel Dennett refers to the self as a "center of narrative gravity" (for example, 1991, 410, 418). Using a variety of metaphors, theorists from various disciplines have suggested that life plans are scripted on fairy-tale patterns and that in a sense we are all novelists. For example: "*Story* is a basic principle of Mind. Most of our experience, our knowledge, and our thinking is organized as stories" (Turner 1996, v). Geoffrey White considers the issue from an anthropological point of view: "The relevance of prototype schemas for emotional understanding follows from the wider salience of narrative as an organizing principle in ethnopsychological thought generally. . . . Among the many types of narrative used to represent and communicate social experience, 'life stories' appear to be an especially salient genre across cultures." He notes, however, that there is "some evidence that Euro-American cultures tend to 'package' experience in the form of individualized life stories more than many non-Western cultures that do not value or elaborate individual self-narrative" (1999, 287). Like so many of the comparisons made within anthropology regarding the differences between Western culture and other cultures, this line of inquiry makes it easy to understand why the novel has developed into an important art form that is identified with the West.

As I have said, the term *embedded narratives* expresses Bakhtin's vision of the novel as a polyphony of independent voices and his view that readers should regard characters not as objects but as subjects. Wertsch comments that Bakhtin followed the collectivist orientation of Russian culture and assumed that meaning was always based on group life (1991, 68). Readers experience the subjectivity of characters' embedded narratives and realize that the events in the storyworld are aspectual. The same object or event will be experienced under a different aspect by another character or by the same character at a different time. Much of the sense of the situated and contextual nature of consciousness is conveyed by Volosinov's notion of the utterance and, in particular, Bakhtin's concept of voice. In fact, the notion of voice has a good deal in common with the concept of embedded narratives. Both are the concrete expression of the ideological viewpoint and total world-view of fictional characters. However, I prefer the term *embedded narrative* to the term *voice* for two reasons: First, it is more complete as it conveys, at least to me, more of a sense of the action and behavior of characters in addition to their cognitive, ideological, and perceptual viewpoint. Secondly, it is more accurate as it conveys, again at least to me, a clearer sense of a discursive construct, an element in narrative discourse. Because of this, it invites analysis of the means by which the narrator constructs and the reader reads a particular fictional character. By contrast, the notion of voice invites the analyst to see the fictional mind as more of a given.

Some approaches to the role of narrative in thought adopt a functionalist perspective on the issue. This is a particularly interesting example: "embodied agents can inventively exploit facts about their physical circumstances to avoid explicit representation and reasoning. . . . [M]ost human activity, rather than implementing preconceptualized plans, consists of incessant, creative improvisational mobilization and appropriation of the vast array of resources that environments regularly make available. Not only do people rarely 'figure it all out in advance' . . . their stories should be understood not as veridical reports of how activity comes to be, but as after-the-fact reconstructions whose role is to retrospectively render activity intelligible (and perhaps accountable)" (Smith 1999, 770). These insights relate closely to the discussion on first-person ascription in chapter 4, section 8. The reports that people give of their thought processes are not necessarily reliable. We tend to create narratives for ourselves in order to make intelligible what has happened to us. Antonio Damasio reminds us that the narrative mind has a use not just for the past, but also for the future: "The changes which occur in the autobiographical self over an individual lifetime are not due only to the remodeling of the lived past that takes place consciously and unconsciously, but also to the laying down and remodeling of the anticipated future" (2000, 224). Damasio's last point there interestingly echoes Dennett's argument that the purpose of the mind is to "produce future." Brian McHale has drawn attention to the need for a functional approach within literary theory in a way that reinforces the remarks by real-mind theorists that I quoted in the section on functionalism in chapter 4: "A functionalism would not organize taxonomies, but would explain teleologies; it would not define what, abstractly, sentences *are*, but rather would give an account of what sentences *do*, what, in particular contexts, they are *there for*" (1983, 44). I hope that this study will go a little way toward fulfilling McHale's program within the specific field of fictional minds.

Marie-Laure Ryan defines her concept of *embedded narratives* as "any story-like representation produced in the mind of a character and reproduced in the mind of the reader" (1986, 320). I have considerably extended the meaning of the term by placing it in the context of the parallel discourses described in this study and, therefore, by using it to refer to all aspects of the fictional mind. Ryan explains that for a discourse to evoke a storyworld, it must bring a universe to life and convey to the reader the sense that at the center of this universe there resides an actual or real world, a realm of factual states or events. This world is understood by the reader to be inhabited by intelligent beings who produce a variety of mental representations such as beliefs, wishes, projections, intents, obligations, dreams, and fantasies. Taken together, these mental constructs constitute the private domain of characters (Ryan 1986, 320). It is Ryan's view that the study of embedded narratives is "most rewarding in genres with the most canonical plot structures, such as folk tales, spy stories, soap operas, tragedies, and comedies of errors." But, she ventures, the concept "can also find useful applications in the modern novel, possibly the least canonical of all narrative genres" (1986, 326). This seems to me to be an unnecessarily tentative view of the value of the approach. I have tried in this study to demonstrate that a more fluid and flexible use of the notion can be of great value in analyzing all novels, including subtle and difficult modern novels such as *The Crying of Lot 49*.

Ryan presents an astonishingly complex analysis of a single-paragraph Aesop fable using the embedded narrative technique, and Fludernik comments very generously on this aspect of Ryan's work as follows: "An interesting proposal that significantly develops the analysis of plotting is Marie-Laure Ryan's essay . . . [that] stresses characters' intentions and plans as well as their wishes and hopes, and the effect of these on possible plot development. Incorporating these several layers of fictional virtualities, the model provides for a more complex account of narrative in process than traditional plot analysis allows. Yet even Ryan's account uses a simple text, a fairy tale, as its object of analysis—a move that . . . puts in doubt a possible application to the novel" (1996, 56). In an endnote to her comment, Fludernik qualifies it somewhat to concede that in fact "applicability to the novel is hindered for reasons of textual length—it is not (in principle) rejected. Marie-Laure Ryan's approach would be highly useful in the analysis of individual scenes of chapters of a novel" (1996, 384). As I have suggested, it is inappropriate to talk simply in terms of simple texts, genre novels, and analyses of single scenes in novels. A necessarily simplified version of the notion of embedded narratives can be applied to the teleological structures of the whole range of complete novels. When Ryan's quasi-scientific and technical method is applied in this way, it gains in breadth, insight, flexibility, and heuristic power what it may lose in scientific rigor and completeness.

It may be worth stressing again here the point that I made in chapter 1, section 5 regarding the range of novels that I have in mind. Because my interest is in consciousness, you may have been tempted to think that I regard as my paradigm the "consciousness novel" or the "stream of consciousness novel." This is not the case. I am concerned with the role of consciousness in all novels. Here is an illustration. In *Text Worlds* (1999), Paul Werth discusses a well-known interior monologue novel, William Faulkner's *The Sound and the Fury*. As Werth points out, "we can regard the character frames of Benji, Quentin and Jason as both building up representations of their inner worlds, and also as providing vantage points from which commonly experienced events are viewed. . . . We can regard them, then, as three separate text worlds, representing a set of overlapping circumstances. . . . Our privilege as readers is to be able to experience separate 'realities' vicariously" (1999, 333). It seems to me that his term *text worlds* can, in this context at least, be regarded as a synonym for the term *embedded narratives*. Both emphasize the centrality of fictional minds to the reading process. However, there is a danger that the force of this insight will be reduced if it is thought that it should be applied only to stream of consciousness novels. Werth makes the point about the texts worlds of Benji's, Quentin's, and Jason's minds that "Faulkner presents the three worlds 'raw,' as it were: there is no narrative envelope within which the three stories unfold; they are simply presented one after the other" (1999, 333). This is true. But it should be emphasized that the constructions of fictional minds as text worlds occurs in *all* narratives and not just those (stream of consciousness) narratives in which the worlds happen to be presented "raw" and apparently unmediated. The minds of Emma, Lydgate, and Blifil, which are all "processed" and highly mediated, are just as much text worlds as the minds of Benji, Quentin, and Jason.

This is my final comment on the Blifil and Emma passages with which I began this chapter:

6. *Both passages have a teleological significance.*

The Austen passage has a significant teleological purpose within the functioning of Emma's embedded narrative. The superficiality and self-deception that it conveys will cause the collision between Emma's and Knightley's embedded narratives and those of others such as Churchill that will ultimately determine the teleological shape of the narrative. The concepts of motive and intention have a pivotal role in this line of inquiry because they link the mass of consciousness that is contained in embedded narratives with its visible and overt expression in behavior and action. This is the point at which characters publicly engage with, and conflict with, each other throughout the events that make up the story. I refer to teleology here because readers read the plot of a novel as the combination of the concrete expressions of the embedded narratives of all of its various characters: the thoughts they think and the actions they take. The teleological approach to the presentation of mind in narrative fiction forms a conceptual framework within which texts can be analyzed to show how particular examples of access to characters' minds contribute to the presentation of the plot-forming process. Within the discourse, the contents of characters' minds in the story are presented directly when the narrator needs to provide explicit explanations for their embedded narrative that are required in addition to descriptions of their behavior. Obviously, the narrator cannot give the reader continued and total direct access to the minds of all the characters. Readers infer their continued mental processes from all of the available evidence. From this steady flow of information, the reader constructs the initial hypotheses and undertakes the complex sets of modifications that reading involves. The reader then aggregates each character's embedded narrative from the discourse to form that reader's story. Readers read plots as the interaction of characters' embedded narratives.

I referred earlier to Emma's need to reconstruct Churchill's embedded narrative once she hears of his secret engagement. From the point of view of the reader, there is a parallel process of construction and reconstruction. The reader is presented with a narrative for Churchill (as the available flirt) that is refracted, in the main, through the prism of Emma's perception of him.

However, the reader is forced in the light of the revelation at the end of the book to reconstruct Churchill's "actual" embedded narrative (as the secretly engaged, resourceful manipulator) and to abandon the earlier narrative that he had successfully presented to Emma and also to the reader. This reading process requires the reader in effect to recreate the whole storyworld of the novel. Fictional minds are semiotic constructs that form part of an overall narrative pattern. They are elements in a plot as well as centers of consciousness. A slightly different approach is taken by Fludernik: "Actants in my model are not defined, primarily, by their involvement in a plot but, simply, by their fictional existence. . . . [T]heir acting necessarily revolves around their consciousness, their mental center of self-awareness, intellection, perception and emotionality" (1996, 26). But surely fictional characters exist to be in a plot. Both aspects are essential. The notion of embedded narratives appears to me to be an exciting and rewarding way out of this narratological dualism. The study of a character's embedded narrative is a study of their consciousness and, simultaneously, a study of the context of that consciousness. It is the study of fictional thinking and acting together with, and in conflict with, other consciousnesses and is, therefore, the study of the plot. When a fictional consciousness is viewed as the storyworld as experienced from a particular viewpoint, it becomes difficult to drive the kind of wedge that Fludernik envisages between the different aspects of that consciousness.

Direct presentations of a character's consciousness in any of the three modes are used by the narrator to give access to that embedded narrative when the narrator needs to do so in order to provide any explanation that is necessary in addition to descriptions of that character's actions. The narrator will give inside views of an embedded narrative when it appears that other evidence relating to that fictional mind is insufficient for the reader to follow its workings. Ryan observes that a study of fairy tales shows that unrealized embedded narratives tend to be fully expressed by the narrator in order to rescue them from oblivion. On the other hand, actualized embedded narratives are likely to remain implicit because there would then be duplication when the events of the storyworld were retold (Ryan 1986, 328). A detailed examination of a number of novels would establish whether Ryan's suggestion is generally true of complex fiction. In a famous paralipsis (withholding of information) in *Emma*, the narrator decides not to give access to a character's successfully realized embedded narrative, though for reasons different from those suggested by Ryan. During Frank Churchill's brief conversation with Jane Fairfax in chapter 43, the reader is deliberately and pointedly not given any access to his thoughts, because the narrator does not wish to reveal their secret engagement. When Jane Fairfax speaks, Frank Churchill "made no answer, merely looked, and bowed in submission" (1996, 308). The narrator can conceal the true situation only by not giving the reader access to their thoughts. Instead, the narrator uses surface description and misleading indicative behavior such as the description of his speech to her as "grave." By the end of the narrative, the reader knows that this was misleading because the grave behavior was not indicative of a grave state of mind at all but was intended to conceal his playful and conspiratorial thoughts. Obviously, the teleological shape of the narrative would have been very different if the narrator had informed the reader at that point of the true nature of his embedded narrative.

Although direct access is frequently given to Emma's mind in chapter 43, there are only two occasions on which other minds (Miss Bates's and Mr. Knightley's) are directly viewed. However, these two occasions are significant because they come at crucial points in the development of Emma's education, or in other terms, in the modifications to her embedded narrative that will be necessary for the conclusion of the plot to be reached. The first is Miss Bates's reaction to Emma's insult: "her meaning . . . burst on her" (1996, 306); and the second is Knightley's mistaken view of Emma's feelings during the quarrel that they have about the insult: "He had misinterpreted" her feelings (1996, 310). The first shows the divergence of another character's embedded narrative from Emma's own, and the conflict that arises from her blind and selfish pursuit of her goals. The second is the logical consequence of this divergence. Within Knightley's embedded narrative, Emma is spoiled and self-centered and is not at that moment capable of remorse for hurting Miss Bates. As their narratives conflict, Knightley fails to read the signs of her change of heart. Because of this, the reconciliation of their narratives is postponed for convenient and teleological reasons until the end of the narrative. Considered in functional terms, other minds are dipped into in order to illuminate Emma's dilemmas.

It is possible to construct a greatly simplified teleological model for the information that is used by the reader during this process, which summarizes the material explained in the previous chapters as follows:

desires and beliefs $\rightarrow$ intentions and motives $\rightarrow$ inner speech and self-regulation $\rightarrow$ decisions $\rightarrow$ action and behavior $\rightarrow$ long term plans and goals $\rightarrow$ embedded narratives $\rightarrow$ character $\rightarrow$ plot

This is simply an initial attempt at a model that will necessarily be modified as more work is done along the lines suggested by this book.

Several examples of what might be called *teleological consciousness* can be found in *The Crying of Lot 49*. I mean by this phrase the use of thought report by the narrator to link the character's consciousness to the teleological shape of the narrative, often by presenting it in a heavily schematic fashion. Examples include "So began, for Oedipa, the languid, sinister blooming of The Tristero" (1996, 36); "Trystero. The word hung in the air as an act ended and all lights were for a moment cut; hung in the dark to puzzle Oedipa Maas, but not yet to exert the power over her it was to" (1996, 51); "She could, at this stage of things, recognize signals like that, as an epileptic is said to" (1996, 66); and "She glanced down the corridor of Cohen's rooms in the rain and saw, for the very first time, how far it might be possible to get lost in this" (1996, 66). These examples can be read along a scale of character consciousness. They start with the narrator addressing the reader regarding the plot over the head of the character as it were and end with the character herself becoming aware of the shape of the narrative in which she is acting. This is shown most clearly in the following example when in the climax to the novel Oedipa addresses herself alone. She methodically lists the four possible explanations for the situation in which she finds herself and thereby summarizes the plot of the narrative: "Either you have stumbled indeed, without the aid of LSD or other indole alkaloids, on to a secret richness and concealed density of dream. . . . Or you are hallucinating it. Or a plot has been mounted against you. . . . Or you are fantasying some such plot. . . . Those, now that she was looking at them, she saw to be the alternatives. Those symmetrical four" (1996, 117–18).

Finally, in commenting on the interpretive activity of readers while constructing embedded narratives, Ryan introduces an interesting perspective by relating it to our roles in real life. She comments that in a dramatic performance the spectator reads the plot into the gestures and utterances that are observed on the stage in an attempt to rationalize the behavior of the characters. She then suggests that the same interpretive activity is performed on data in real life: "Just as we read a plot into a play, we may form a story out of private experiences or out of personally recorded observations" (Ryan 1991, 265). As the various theorists quoted earlier told us, we construct a story out of our own life. We have to form stories in order to make our lives coherent. It is by these stories that we live. Our lives are narratives that are embedded in the social context within which we function. Specifically, there is the context of other narratives. Our lives do not just consist of the single embedded narrative that we construct for ourselves. In addition, we are burdened, or blessed, with the knowledge that alternative embedded narratives exist for all of us within the embedded narratives of all of those who know us.

4. The Storyworld

In chapter 2, section 2 I briefly considered the application of possible-worlds theory to narratology. The purpose of this section is to apply the notion of fictional storyworlds more specifically to the issue of fictional minds.

The aspectual nature of the storyworld

Doležel contends that it is "worlds with persons or, better, persons within worlds that generate stories" (1998, 33). Chapter 5 tried to show that our minds are social and that the norm for mental functioning is multiperson worlds. This means that it is the relationships between persons that generate stories. Stories are generated by the conflicts between persons, and the conflicts are caused by the fact that the storyworld is aspectual. Each character sees the storyworld under a different aspect or from a different point of view. If they did not, there would be no conflicts and no stories. Crucially, fictional minds, once created and then re-created with each new hypothesis, are themselves aspectual. They exist, or are seen from a certain aspect, within the minds of the other characters in the novel. The same goes for physical events, apart from marginal examples such as narrator-supplied information on background events in historical novels. It is for this reason that it would perhaps be better in general to refer to storyworld events as *experiences*.

Although the point developed earlier is a simple one, I think that a good deal of narrative theory is structured in such a way that one can easily lose sight of it. Doležel asserts that the factual domain of the fictional world is split into these two subdomains: "fully authenticated, by authoritative narrative, and collectively authenticated, by consensual fictional persons' accounts. As to the virtual domain, the domain of possibles that remain nonauthentic, it divides into private domains, the beliefs, visions, illusions, and errors of individual fictional persons" (1998, 151). This is completely true, but is there not also a sense in which *all* fictional mental life is virtual? From the point of view of an individual mind, the distinction between beliefs that are shared by others and those that are not shared by others may not be apparent to the individual, or at least not to begin with. Both sorts will simply be beliefs. As for beliefs that have been certified as true by the narrator, and those that have not, the earlier point is even more apt. The character can never know which is which. Both sorts, narrator-certified and non-narrator-certified, will always be simply beliefs for that character. This is not a trivial point. The aesthetic appeal of a plot is a function of the richness and variety of the various aspects under which the storyworld is perceived by the characters in that world. In Marie-Laure

Ryan's terms, this is the domain of the virtual. All of those aspects are virtual and subjective in the sense that they form a part of a character's belief system, including those that are made "real" and "objective" by the statements of the narrator and those that are shared with other characters.

I said at the beginning of the discussion of fictional-worlds theory in chapter 2, section 2 that the theory arose out of the philosophical concept of possible worlds and that this notion had developed as a tool to consider various technical issues in philosophy. One of those technical issues is relevant to the discussion here. It is the distinction drawn by the philosopher Gottlob Frege between sense and reference. Put very crudely, the *reference* of an object or entity is the "objective" meaning of it that holds true under all circumstances and in all possible worlds. Names are rigid designators (to use Saul Kripke's phrase) that express the reference of a sentence. *Sense* relates to the various "subjective" descriptions of an object or entity that can affect the truth or falsity of a sentence in various ways when they are substituted for its name. For example, the name "Jocasta" is a rigid designator that expresses the reference to that person. Various descriptions of or senses for the entity "Jocasta" include "The Queen of Thebes" and "the mother of Oedipus." So, it is true to say that "Oedipus wished to marry Jocasta"; it may or may not be true to say that "Oedipus wished to marry the Queen of Thebes" (he would have to know that she was the Queen of Thebes, and he may not care whether she is or not); it is obviously false to say that "Oedipus wished to marry the mother of Oedipus." Again, very crudely, the same distinction can be expressed by using the technical philosophical terms, *extension* (corresponding to reference) and *intension* (corresponding to sense).

My purpose in mentioning this abstruse argument here is to point out that Doležel makes use of the sense/reference and intension/extension distinctions in *Heterocosmica* to refer to the aspectuality of the fictional world. He explains that a fictional world can be "structured intensionally in many different ways by different intensional functions. In this thesis, a feature of Frege's 'sense' is reflected: a variety of senses can be associated with one and the same referent, the various senses 'illuminating' the referent's different aspects" (1998, 141). Put very simply, the subjective side of both pairs (sense and intensionality) account for the aspectual nature of the storyworld reality. Different characters experience the objective reference or extension of the storyworld under a variety of different subjective intensional senses or aspects. The tragedy of the narrative of *Oedipus Rex* derives from the fact that Oedipus wished to marry Jocasta but was horrorstruck when he found that he had married his mother.

Encyclopedias

Doležel refers to the cognitive element in the role of the reader as an *encyclopedia*: "Encyclopedia as shared communal knowledge varies with cultures, social groups, historical epochs, and for these reasons relativizes the recovery of implicit meaning" (1998, 177). This is the real-world encyclopedia or store of knowledge that readers possess and that they bring to texts in order to comprehend them. Knowing that lawns occur outside houses and that the Sistine Chapel is in Rome are examples of elements in a reader's actual-world encyclopedia. However, Doležel then goes on to explain that, in order to "reconstruct and interpret a fictional world, the reader has to reorient his cognitive stance to agree with the world's encyclopedia. In other words, knowledge of the fictional encyclopedia is absolutely necessary for the reader to comprehend a fictional world" (1998, 181). The reader's real-world encyclopedia has to be modified in order to create the storyworld. My actual-world encyclopedia contains the fact that Baker Street is in the center of London. My storyworld encyclopedia contains the "fact" that Sherlock Homes lives in Baker Street. Doležel calls this the *fictional encyclopedia*: "Knowledge about a possible world constructed by a fictional text constitutes a fictional encyclopedia" (1998, 177).

However, this is only part of the story. The fictional encyclopedia is the totality of possible knowledge about a storyworld. In addition, characters each have their own fictional encyclopedias that are much smaller than the total one. Not all of the characters in the Conan Doyle stories will know that Sherlock Holmes lives in Baker Street. We can refer to these as *internal encyclopedias*: the encyclopedias that all fictional characters possess about their storyworld and that are different from the reader's storyworld encyclopedia. As Doležel points out, "[c]ognitive relations—the knowledge and beliefs of each person about the other members of the agential constellation—play a major role in the agents' decision making, plans and strategies" (1998, 101). The cognitive relationship between a character and the storyworld (that is, how much the character knows about the storyworld) and the cognitive relationship between the reader and the storyworld are both key elements in the narrative process. Doležel explores several of the implications arising from characters' cognitive relations.

> The modal system of knowledge, ignorance and belief imposes epistemic order on the fictional world. . . . The person of the fictional world is an epistemic "monad," perceiving himself or herself, other persons and the entire world from a definite and distinct vantage point. The person's practical reasoning and, consequently, his or her acting and interacting

are to a high degree determined by this epistemic perspective, by what the agent knows, is ignorant of, and believes to be the case in the world. . . . Epistemic modalities release their story-generating energy because of uneven distribution of knowledge among the fictional persons. The epistemic imbalance produces the basic epistemic narrative, the story with a secret (mystery story).(1998, 126)

There are several significant insights in this passage. The list in Doležel's second sentence is particularly useful: "himself," so first-person knowledge of inner states is not necessarily more reliable than third-person knowledge (see chapter 5); "other persons," hence the importance of the concept of doubly embedded narratives (see chapter 7); "the entire world," hence the importance of internal encyclopedias; Doležel's reference to practical reasoning and interaction shows the importance of aspectuality to the social and purposive nature of fictional mental functioning; and finally, he usefully relates epistemic aspectuality to the teleology of plot (see the previous section).

However, it seems to me to be a mistake to limit these insights to particular kinds of narrative. In the remark quoted earlier, Doležel refers to the mystery story. He later comments that "[e]pistemic quest can also be perceived at the core of the *Bildungsroman*" (1998, 127). But it is important to recognize that it is not just in mystery stories and the Bildungsroman that epistemic imbalance is a significant generator of plot. It is true of all narratives. Is there a novel that you know of in which every character knows what every other character knows? Given the aspectuality of fictional worlds, that state of affairs must be impossible. This necessary imbalance is as true, and as teleologically significant, of Henry James as it is of, say, the thriller writer Patricia Highsmith.

Marie-Laure Ryan also makes the same point about the aspectual nature of the storyworld and, in particular, the epistemic imbalance between characters and readers. She observes that "the reader's representation of the actual world of a fictional universe is much more accurate (though usually more limited) than the representation of the characters who must base their knowledge on their own empirical experience" (1985, 721). A part of this process is the need to reorient one's cognitive stance in order to agree with all the characters' encyclopedias. It is not possible to follow the plot otherwise. You can try an experiment yourself in order to test the validity of this argument. Choose a novel—any novel!—and briefly summarize the plot in your mind. Then see whether any elements of your summary are not dependent on the sort of cognitive and emotional empathy that I am discussing. My guess is that there will be very few.

Gaps

I referred in chapter 2 to the various gaps that arise between both the story and the discourse on the one hand and on the other hand the storyworld. Even the most detailed story and the most exhaustive discourse can only ever be a very partial and limited description of the whole storyworld. There are gaps in the information provided in the story because behind that story there exists the theoretical postulate of a storyworld that contains the missing information. The story is necessarily incomplete because it can never list every possible fact about the storyworld. It is the function of the discourse to assist the reader to fill in those gaps in the story that appear to the reader to be significant. To do this readers need strategies for dealing with the necessary incompleteness of fictional beings. These strategies are contained in the frames, scripts, and so on that are necessary for comprehension of a text. As Ruth Ronen indicates, the "reliance on a frame of reference can explain how a text, characterized by a paucity of information about its world, rhetorically overcomes the incompleteness of its constituent objects" (1988, 512). The aspectual nature of perception that I discussed earlier can be related to the role of the reader as much as to the activities of characters. Fictional people are perceived by the reader under a particular aspect, which is the explicit description in the discourse; and what is not made explicit under that particular aspect is indeterminate. It is then part of the competence of the reader to fill in the gaps by creating more aspects under which the character may be implicitly or hypothetically perceived.

However, we have to be careful to ensure that the language that we use about the incompleteness of possible worlds accurately fits the specific case of fictional minds. For example, the first sentence of Ruth Ronen's "Completing the Incompleteness of Fictional Entities" (the title itself is revealing) is this: "Fictional entities are inherently incomplete because it is impossible to construct a fictional object by specifying its characteristics and relations in every detail" (1988, 497). But is it possible to specify in every detail the characteristics and relations of *real* minds? Ronan's answer is that in "reality, as opposed to fiction, gaps are filled by reference to a complete, fully detailed and, at least in principle, available object" (1988, 497). So, Ronen appears to be arguing, it is possible to arrive at a complete and fully detailed description of a real mind. Even with the "in principle" caveat, this seems a strange way to talk about real minds. It is possible that Ronen and the other possible-worlds theorists are thinking about such features of fictional worlds and real worlds as eye color and the number of children that Lady Macbeth had. These are issues that are easy to decide. Take other examples: The town where Emma lives may or may not be based on the real town of Epsom in Surrey. Emma may or may not be five feet six inches. Her eyes may or may not be blue. These things are indeterminate in the *Emma* storyworld. On the other hand, they are easily determined in the actual world. We tend to know, or can easily find out, where we are. We can see the height and the eye color of ourselves and of others. However, minds both real and fictional seem to me to be somewhat different. I have tried to show that we should feel a little uncomfortable with the assertion that we can easily determine facts about our own minds and other minds. I might think that I am generous and he is selfish. It would not be any surprise though to hear that the other person feels the exact opposite. Who is to say who is right? In this respect, it seems to me that the relative determinacies and indeterminacies of real minds and of fictional minds are in many significant respects quite similar.

I said just then that we can determine simple facts in the actual world. But is this necessarily true? While it is true that we do not know Emma's neck measurements, we do not know Jane Austen's either (let us assume for the sake of argument). The difference, possible-worlds theorists will say, is that the latter is in principle knowable, while the former is not. The difference is a theoretical one: the Emma gap in our knowledge is ontological because the neck size does not exist; the Jane Austen gap is epistemological because it did exist once, but we do not now know what it was. While this is true, the fact remains that they are both still gaps, and in practice (if not in theory), they amount to the same thing. Our attention is also often drawn to the question of the finiteness of fictional beings. They are different from real people because they end when the novel ends. They do not continue to exist as we do. Well, that may be true of people who are alive, but what about people who are now dead? Also, less dramatically, surely we regularly experience others as finite beings in the sense that we lose touch with people and do not see them again. Obviously they are still alive somewhere, so again it is a question of practice as opposed to theory, but I am talking about our *experience* of others.

The reader can cope with the gaps in the continuing consciousnesses of fictional minds because in the real world we experience gaps in other, real minds too. From an aspectual point of view, another mind is sometimes present to us (when we are with that person) and sometimes absent. Our real-world cognitive frame enables us to construct a continuing consciousness for the absent person unless we suffer from an abnormal condition such as autism that causes "mind-blindness." So, is too much made of the incompleteness of fictional worlds? I do not mean that they are not incomplete. They are. What I mean is that in practice real individuals also find the actual world incomplete. We only ever know a fraction of what is going on around us. Obviously, the difference is that it is *theoretically* possible for us to find out simple facts, and so it is an epistemological not an ontological issue. But, in *practice*, what is the difference? Readers who access fictional worlds and people who live in the actual world both have to make inferences and construct hypotheses on the basis of limited information. This is especially true in the case of other minds, where talk of facts seems inappropriate. The reader thinks, Is a certain character well intentioned? An individual thinks, Is this acquaintance of mine well intentioned? Theoretical completeness is not going to help very much in the latter case. Gaps are a part of fictional individuals, and so the reader has to construct continuing consciousnesses, but is the same not true to a certain extent of the real people that we know? As I just said, we are with them some of the time but they are absent at other times. Do not real absences equate to fictional gaps? When we see them again we generally attempt to reconstruct what they have been doing since we last saw them in order to work out roughly how they are feeling now. We reconstruct their narrative. You will remember that the point of the false-belief tests for children that are used in the theory/simulation debate (chapter 5, section 2) is to test how children can construct continuing consciousnesses following the absence or "gap" of the person in the test. This process is surely very similar to the activities of readers. We bring to the reading process our real-world knowledge of how to fill gaps and construct narratives for actual people.

Finally, the emphasis in the thought of the social theorists that was discussed in chapter 5 is on environment and context. This is another way in which parallels can be drawn between our construction of real people and readers' constructions of fictional people. The point is often made, quite rightly, that characters are only elements in a story or plot: they have no existence outside of that context. Real people are obviously different, but are they that different? We too exist only in a social context. It is rare for individuals to find themselves in the single-person worlds that Doležel describes. Our minds are reconstructed (rightly or, we may often feel, completely wrongly and unfairly!) within the minds of others, and this process forms the social context within which we function. I must emphasize that I am not denying that fictional people are different from real people. I am simply saying that, in describing the undeniable differences, we must not give an unrealistic picture of how real minds work, and we must also acknowledge the equally undeniable similarities between real minds and fictional minds.

The limits of storyworlds

As described in section 2 of this chapter, the continuing-consciousness cognitive frame has a default value or slot: the reader assumes that the character's consciousness will continue between mentions of them in the text unless informed otherwise, say, because of exceptional circumstances such as amnesia, a coma, or a death and return to life or some such magical event. I am not concerned in this book with the range of values that arise from confounded expectations (for example, as in science fiction, fantasy, or postmodernist narratives). My study relates to the sorts of fictional minds that are contained in all kinds of narratives. Exceptional consciousnesses could perhaps be the subject of a further study. This brings me to a concern that I have regarding the limits of storyworlds.

Possible-worlds theorists emphasize the independence and autonomy of possible worlds from the actual world. It can sometimes seem as though there is no limit to the extent of storyworlds. Doležel maintains that "[t]extual poeisis . . . constructs fictional realms whose properties, structures, and modes of existence are, in principle, independent of the properties, structures, and existential mode of actuality" (1998, 23). Being independent from the real world means that they are not constrained by the actual structure of the real world. Hence, highly imaginative literatures such as science fiction, fantasy, utopias, postmodernist texts, and so on are possible.

However, from my perspective, a very important limit to the extent of storyworlds suggests itself. This is the need to describe fictional minds engaging in mental functioning. To read narrative coherently, the reader must posit the existence of continuing consciousnesses that can embody the various causal networks behind the actions of the characters in the narrative. This will surely be as necessary of the inhabitants of Pluto in a science fiction story as it is of the people being described in a grittily realistic "faction" narrative. There are certain sorts of magical minds that are conceivable: those capable of ESP, mind reading, telekinesis, and so on. But if one looks at the fundamentals of cause and effect, mental events causing actions, and so on, these differences begin to look rather superficial. Of course, the causal connections will often be very different, and these differences will form the interest of the narrative. But the differences are small in the context of the powerful operation of the basic frame. It is never a good idea to underestimate the ingenuity of narrative theorists where challenges regarding the nature of narrative are concerned. Nevertheless, I will suggest this test: Is it possible to think of a narrative for which the continuing-consciousness frame is inapplicable? My weasely caveat here is to concede that it might be possible to construct some sort of tortured example of a science fiction or postmodern narrative, but a pretty poor specimen of narrative it might well be. In practice, even fictional realms are very much tied to the properties of the actual world. Fictional minds, even on Pluto, have to operate very much like actual minds.

(In fact, David Herman has suggested as a possible exception to my suggested rule a very compelling narrative. It is Christopher Nolan's film *Memento*, in which the events are focalized through the main character who suffers from short-term memory loss. To make matters more confusing, his story is told backward. However, it seems to me that it is precisely the viewer's ability to use the continuing-consciousness frame in order to construct, eventually and with difficulty, an embedded narrative for this character that imposes coherence on what would otherwise be an incomprehensible experience.)

A helpful perspective on the issue of the limits of storyworlds comes from an unexpected source. In *mitecs*, Sperber and Hirschfeld suggest that religious representations work well when "a balance between counterintuitive and intuitive qualities is reached. A supernatural being with too few unexpected qualities is not attention demanding and thus not memorable. One with too many unexpected qualities is too information rich to be memorable" (1999, cxxi). This point applies equally well to science and fantasy fiction. In both cases there has to be in place a sufficient number of appropriate consciousness frames and subframes for the narrative to be comprehensible. As F. E. Sparshott noticed, "either the place and the participants are conceived on the model of familiar types, in which case the element of fantasy becomes scarcely more than decoration, or the story becomes thin and schematic, because we cannot tell what sort of background to provide for what we are explicitly told" (1967, 5, quoted in Pavel 1986, 60).

Thomas Pavel lists a number of the elements that he suggests are indispensable to the sort of background that he has in mind. He writes that

every period, no matter how diverse and sophisticated its functional arrangements, seems to have at its command a certain number of indispensable elements. . . . Birth, love, death, success and failure, authority and its loss, revolution and war, production and distribution of goods, social status and morality, the sacred and the profane, comic themes of inadequacy and isolation, compensatory fantasies, and so much more, are always present, from early myths and folktales to contemporary literature. Changes of taste or shifts of interest seem to affect the inventory only marginally. Since we need an alien space in which to deploy the energy of the imagination, there have always been and always will be distant fictional worlds—but we may also use close fictional worlds for mimetic purposes, in order to gather relevant information or just for the pleasure of recognition. (1986, 147–48)

Pavel's list of indispensable elements seems to me to be completely convincing. However, I think it would be a good idea to extend the point. I do not think that it is just the inventory of themes that stays pretty much the same; it is also the basic cognitive frames relating to fundamental fictional world construction. It seems to me that these frames impose a basic uniformity on fictional worlds that is necessary in order for us to be able to access them. Despite the dazzling variety and imaginativeness of fictional worlds, they all, even science fiction worlds, have to be "conceived on the model of familiar types" for us to enter them. If we cannot use real world frames to reconstruct them, they will remain unintelligible. Ryan's principle of minimal departure, which I referred to in chapter 2, section 2, comes into play here. The departures required for fictional minds are not as radical as their surface variety would suggest. Distant fictional worlds are, I think, closer to us than they may at first appear.

On a more general point, Pavel's final sentence seems to me to be indicative of a rather worrying gulf between possible-worlds theorists and other readers. Literary critics and general readers read novels "to gather relevant information" (the social history side of literary criticism) and also "for the pleasure of recognition" (the feeling that the fictional minds behave just like real minds). But the word "just" is revealing. It seems to trivialize a large amount of people's reactions to novels. What is the interest in reading, say, *Emma*? Is it not for the many, detailed, and complex correspondences and other relationships between the *Emma* world and the real world? The gathering of information and the pleasure of recognition, if these two phrases are interpreted widely enough, are at the heart of the reading process. I am sure that possible-worlds theorists would not deny this, but it does not appear that it is often said explicitly. To say this is certainly not to subscribe to a naïvely mimetic or realist view of fiction. Readers gather information about and gain the pleasure of recognition from fictional minds in distant fictional worlds, just as much as they do from close ones.

Conclusion

As I write this, news has just been announced that a large group of novelists has been asked to vote on the greatest novel of all time and that the winner is Cervantes's *Don Quixote*. It is often said that all novels derive from this, the first great novel. As the poll shows, many think even now that it is still the greatest novel. It is, therefore, very satisfying to see that it is particularly well suited to an embedded narrative analysis. The point of the novel is that the narrative that Don Quixote constructs for himself is regularly in conflict with the narratives of the other characters in the storyworld in a variety of different ways. He sees giants where they see windmills. At every point in the novel, he constructs the reality of the storyworld differently from others because he aspectually interprets every event in a way that ensures that it coheres with his embedded narrative.

7

The Fictional Mind in Action

1. Background

This chapter will expand on the basic conceptual framework for the analysis of fictional minds that was described in the previous chapter and develop it in some of the ways that were suggested by the explorations of the whole mind in chapter 4 and, in particular, the social mind in chapter 5. I will explore three major subframes of the main consciousness frame: the relationship between thought and action (section 2), intermental or group or shared thinking (section 3), and what I am calling *doubly embedded narratives*, the representations of characters' minds that are contained within the minds of other characters (section 4). All three utilize fundamental aspects of our real-world knowledge of the mental functioning both of ourselves and of others. These subframes are certainly not the only ones, but I have chosen them because they show the mind beyond the skin in action. They contain a number of areas of interest that, although the terminology is now becoming rather cumbersome, one might label *sub-subframes*. Within the thought and action subframe, I discuss the decoding of action statements, the thought-action continuum, indicative description, causation, and local and teleological motivation; and within the group-thinking subframe I discuss norm establishment and maintenance, group conflict, and intramental assent and dissent. The unfamiliar terms are explained later. These discussions will be illustrated mainly by examples from Evelyn Waugh's *Vile Bodies*. The novel, written in 1930, is about a group of "Bright Young People" who attend an endless round of parties in London. The main character is Adam, whose fiancée, Nina, calls off their engagement because she meets someone else with more money. The novel ends with a shocking change of tone. Global war is announced, and we last see Adam wandering around a desolate battlefield.

The rest of this section is taken up with a few introductory remarks that may be of assistance to you when reading the rest of the chapter.

Behaviorist narrative

In chapters 4 and 5 I referred occasionally to the concept of *behaviorism* in psychology and philosophy, particularly when discussing third-person ascription. Behaviorism is a psychological method that uses the objective observation of other people as the basis for theories and conclusions, and so is highly reliant on the reliability of ascriptions of mental states to others. The concept of *behaviorist narrative* is derived from this basic sense of the term, and in this chapter I will be using examples from a particular behaviorist narrative, *Vile Bodies*. I chose it because of the apparently unpromising nature of its presentations of consciousness. The reader strategy of joining up the dots is particularly important in the case of this sort of narrative where the reading process has to be very creative in constructing fictional minds from less information than is available in other types of narrative. The *Dictionary of Narratology* defines *behaviorist narrative* as an "objective narrative; a narrative characterized by external focalization and thus limited to the conveyance of the characters' behavior (words and actions but not thoughts and feelings), their appearance, and the setting against which they come to the fore ('The Killers'). In this type of narrative, the narrator tells less than one or several characters know and abstains from direct commentary and interpretation" (Prince 1987, 10). It is well known that "pure" behaviorist narrative is difficult if not impossible to find. There are even different views on the extent to which Hemingway's self-conscious experiments in this mode, such as the short stories "The Killers" and "Hills Like White Elephants," are purely behaviorist. This is an argument that I would prefer to avoid. I will simply suggest that behaviorism in narrative is a tendency toward the features described by Prince and that *Vile Bodies* is an illustration of that tendency. (All the page references in the examples are to the 1996 Penguin edition.)

My guess is that most readers of the novel would say that they were struck by how little direct access is given to characters' minds. What little there is tends to consist of a few words of thought report discreetly inserted into accounts of the happenings in the storyworld:

(1) he told her that she looked like a fashion drawing without the clothes.

Nina was rather pleased about that. (68)

In fact, this is the only direct access that is given to Nina's mind, which is significant as she is an important character in the novel. We see a little of Adam's inner life but very little of the other characters', and this lack of access creates a faintly disturbing impression. In fact, the novel has become associated with its famous chapter 11, that, apart from "Adam rang up Nina" and "Later

Nina rang up Adam," consists in its entirety of forty-three very short episodes of untagged speech.

I am not questioning the general validity of the *behaviorist* label. Neither, in view of the narrative's distinctive features of pure dialogue, attenuated characterization, and minimal motivation, am I questioning the application of the label to *Vile Bodies*. My point is merely that behaviorist narratives contain a good deal more information about fictional minds than has generally been appreciated. Specifically, I hope to show that this particular discourse is saturated with meanings that are closely related to the inner lives of characters. A character's name is a space or a vacuum into which readers feel compelled to pour meaning: characteristics, dispositions, states of mind, causations. Readers take even the most apparently uninformative references to characters as cues to construct attributes. However, much of this process can only be theorized by defamiliarizing, labeling, and so making visible some of the hitherto neglected devices that enable readers to understand how fictional minds function within the context of their storyworlds.

Inner speech, direct thought, and free indirect thought

I will say a little about inner speech and the speech categories at this point before discussing the three subframes. There is very little evidence in the novel of the presence in characters' minds of inner speech. One reason for this is that the use of direct thought necessarily entails inner speech, and there is very little direct thought in the novel. What little there is consists of just a few rather inconsequential and uninformative words such as these: "'More trouble for Simon' thought Adam" (76); "'Has he given all to his daughters?' thought Adam" (118); and "('What indeed?' thought Adam)" (165). Of course, the two other modes of thought report and free indirect thought can also be used to represent inner speech. In the case of the relatively small number of episodes of free indirect thought, some appear to represent inner speech and some do not. I quote a large number of episodes of thought report, and almost all of them appear to me to describe states of mind such as desires, emotions, dispositions, beliefs, and attitudes rather than inner speech.

The following discussion of free indirect thought anticipates some of my main argument, but it is placed here because of the intense interest in this particular speech category. There are two aspects to the use of free indirect thought in *Vile Bodies* that are concerned with the mind beyond the skin. First, the following grammatical form occurs on no less than nine occasions:

(2) (a) It was awful when Mrs Ape was like this. (8)
    (b) It was so difficult. (40)
    (c) It had been an awkward moment. (85)
    (d) It would be awkward. (113)
    (e) It seemed odd. (119)
    (f) It was all like one of those cabinet meetings. (87)
    (g) It was clearly going to be a bad crossing. (7)
    (h) It seemed odd that a man so bulky could be so elusive. (98)
    (i) It was clearly suitable that he should marry before he was thirty.
       (108)

Although it is not apparent from this heavily truncated presentation, these sentences, with the exception of examples 2g and 2h, occur in the context of some form of social awkwardness. The character has internalized the social norms that he or she perceives to be appropriate to the occasion and is embarrassed by the danger that they might be transgressed. The intimate link between social norm and individual consciousness is particularly well illustrated by example 2i, a sentence of free indirect thought that occurs in a passage of thought report of Edward Throbbing's mind. It takes place two paragraphs after this description of the social context in which the character is thinking:

(3) It was generally understood that now Edward Throbbing was back these two would become engaged to be married. (108)

This episode of consensus thought report is a statement of reinforcement of the social norm of marriage that is unmistakably echoed in the free indirect thought in example 2i. It is clear that the norms of the social consensus have been very efficiently internalized and that Throbbing's mental functioning has been severely constrained by the public context within which it occurs.

Second, the text contains some examples of intermental free indirect thought. I will start with some marginal cases, and go onto some more definite examples. The second sentence in the following example could be a comment by the narrator:

(4) A profusion of men in plus-fours were having "quick ones" before the start. There was no nonsense about not smoking. (141)

It could, however, also be a free indirect rendering of the collective consciousnesses of the users of the bar. In the next example, a long list of various features of the physical context, clearly focalized through a group of people, is followed by this statement:

(5) There was nothing for it but to go back to the bar. (148)

Again, it is possible to interpret this statement as a narratorial judgment on the situation but equally possible to regard it as the collective decision of the group expressed in free indirect thought. The following three examples are made less ambiguous by the use of expressive devices:

(6) (No one had warned them that there was a motor race on; their hotel bill *was* a shock.) (133)

(7) and at last they all went to bed, very tired, but fairly contented, and oh, how they were bitten by bugs all that night. (132)

(8) The angels crowded together disconsolately. It was awful when Mrs Ape was like this. My, how they would pinch Chastity. (8)

The expressive emphasis on the italicized "*was*" allows example 6 to be plausibly interpreted as free indirect thought rather than thought report. The same goes for "oh how" in example 7, which is perhaps indeterminate between thought and speech. In example 8 the collective action (crowding) and the collective feeling or sensation (being disconsolate) is followed first by a free indirect presentation of their awareness of the reason (Mrs Ape's behavior) for the action and the accompanying state of mind (see example 2a), and second by a free indirect presentation of their intention to act in response by pinching Chastity. Free indirect perception (or internal focalization) also has a group form: "But there was no sign of Miss Runcible" (152).

The final example is particularly interesting for the skillful way in which the narrator alternates between collective thought report in examples 9a and 9c, collective free indirect speech in 9b, and collective free indirect thought in example 9d:

(9) (a) Their flashes and bangs had rather a disquieting effect on the party, causing a feeling of tension, because everybody looked negligent (b) and said what a bore the papers were, and how *too* like Archie to let the photographers come, (c) but most of them, as a matter of fact, wanted dreadfully to be photographed and the others were frozen with unaffected terror that they might be taken unawares (d) and then their mamas would know where they had been when they said they were at the Bicesters' dance, and then there would be a row again, which was so *exhausting*, if nothing else. (45)

Contextual thought report

Almost all of the direct access with which I am concerned for the rest of this chapter consists of *contextual thought report*. I am using this term for the short, unobtrusive sentences, phrases, or even single words that describe an aspect of a character's mind and that are often combined with descriptions of action or context. This device often refers to intentions to act or motives for action and is, therefore, purposive and explanatory in nature. In discussing a story from *The Decameron*, Wayne C. Booth refers to its use as "frequent—though by modern standards certainly shallow—inside views" of characters' thoughts (1987, 12). Most of the following examples illustrate the complexity of the relationships between contextual thought report, action, and context. The three are often inextricably linked, and so it can be a very artificial operation to lift contextual thought report out of the sentence that contains it. This inseparability is an illustration of the centrality of consciousness to narrative that Monika Fludernik has stressed so persuasively. Specifically, many of the following examples contain a reference to the social and physical context within which the mental functioning takes place, although a number have been cut for reasons of space. The following sentence uses twenty-two words to describe not just mental states, but also several facts about the physical environment: how the group are positioned, the fact that they have a book in front of them, and the movement of Mrs Ape:

(10) Their heads were close together and they were so deeply engrossed in the story that they did not hear Mrs Ape's entry. (80)

Sometimes the reference to the context accompanies the action or consciousness description:

(11) Adam sat in the back of the car with Miles, who was clearly put out about his friend's lack of cordiality. (138)

At other times, the context is contained within the description:

(12) They went down the hill feeling buoyant and detached. (145)

Contextual thought report plays an important role in the process of characterization. The term *characterization* can imply the presence of long and ponderous passages in Victorian novels that appear to tell the reader everything there is to know about a character. But one should not lose sight of the characterization illustrated in example 13, which occurs when Adam tells Lottie, his landlady, that he now has money:

(13) "Have you now" said Lottie indifferently. She lived on the assumption that everyone she knew always had several thousand pounds. (64)

In only fourteen words, the reader has learned a good deal about Lottie.

2. Thought and Action
The decoding of action

The first subframe of the continuing-consciousness frame that I wish to discuss is the relationship between thought and action. Constructions of fictional minds are inextricably bound up with presentations of action. Direct access to inner speech and states of mind is only a small part of the process of building up the sense of a mind in action. This centrality of consciousness to narrative can be demonstrated by asking readers to retell the plot of a novel. My guess is that most would not be content to respond by saying: X did A, Y did B, Z did C. They would be much more likely to describe characters' actions in terms of mental functioning such as: X decided to do A, Y wanted to do B, Z regretted doing C. Deciding, wanting, and regretting are the mental events and states that provide the causal network behind the physical events, and they are just as much a part of the storyworld as the physical environment, events, and happenings. *Vile Bodies* contains very few action descriptions that simply describe only the surface of physical behavior. The mental event that necessarily accompanies the action is often made part of the action description or is added in an adverb, rather than left implicit. Take this simple statement:

(14) The three statesmen hid themselves. (86)

This is a description of an action, but it goes further in identifying the accompanying mental processes than a statement such as "They stood behind the curtain," that leaves more work for the reader to do in deciding why they are standing there. It can be decoded in consciousness terms as follows: the three agreed that it was in their interest to conceal themselves from someone, realized that it was possible for them to do so, and decided together to take the action of hiding. In this way, the reader as part of the process of understanding narratives has to translate passages of action description into mind description in the manner of a "psychological" novel. As I said in chapter 4, it is significant that philosophers often discuss action in terms of how onlookers to an action would reasonably interpret it. This perspective is very similar to the role of the reader in considering the motives behind and the reasons for a character's actions.

When we explain an action by giving the reason for it, we often redescribe the action by placing it in its context. The descriptions of the physical context and the causal network behind the fictional behavior are sometimes identical:

(15) People had crowded into the Underground station for shelter from the rain. (29)

In just twelve words, the narrator describes the action, the physical context in detail (the rain, the station, and the crowd), and the fact that this context is the reason for the action of sheltering. However, many narrative statements require a good deal more decoding than examples 14 and 15. For example, some convey information about more than one consciousness:

(16) Here an atmosphere of greater geniality prevailed. (141)

Decoded, this might mean that the consciousnesses of the individuals in the group are open and welcoming and are enjoying the atmosphere. It might also mean that the consciousness of anyone coming in would feel welcome and at home. Narratorial statements such as examples 16 and 17 might seem a long way from a study of the presentation of consciousness:

(17) You see, that was the kind of party Archie Schwert's party was. (43)

But as with example 16, when example 17 is decoded, we find that that it is precisely about consciousness. It is saying that within the storyworld of the narrative this is what the fictional minds of the group of characters that comprised the party thought, felt, perceived, experienced when they were present in the social and physical context of the party. Mental functioning is always present however oblique the explicit reference to it.

The distinction between action and non-action is frequently not clear, illustrating the point that it is the mental process, not the physical movement, that is the significant issue:

(18) This time no-one troubled to pick them up. (15)

The absence of action, such as not picking something up, can be as much of an action as a physical movement, particularly when the nature of the intention is specified, as in this case. When non-action is deliberate, it is an action.

(19) They were very late for the film Nina wanted to see, and that set them back again. They didn't speak for a long time. (76)

Not speaking is a non-action that amounts in a context such as this to a very significant action.

The thought-action continuum

Talk of decoding action statements into consciousness statements can, however, be misleading if it gives the impression that, notwithstanding the intimate and complex connections between the two, thought and action are easily separable. They are not, and many of the statements in fictional narratives inhabit the large gray area between the two. I shall refer to this phenomenon as the *thought-action continuum*, and it is one of the key senses in which the mind extends beyond the skin. Wittgenstein's question ("Is this a report about his behavior or his state of mind?" [1958, 179]) is particularly relevant here.

(20) Adam undressed very quickly and got into bed; Nina more slowly arranging her clothes on the chair and fingering the ornaments on the chimney piece with less than her usual self-possession. At last she put out the light. (68)

This passage, with the exception of the phrase "with less than her usual self-possession," consists of what might be called *significant action*: the reader is provided with enough contextual information to appreciate the significance of Adam acting very quickly and Nina acting more slowly. The reader can speculate with assurance about what mental events accompany these two actions because he or she knows that they are about to go to bed together for the first time: Adam is eager and Nina is nervous. However, the phrase "with less than her usual self-possession" is in the gray area between thought and action. Wittgenstein's question is appropriate because the words appear to be a description both of Nina's behavior and of her state of mind.

I will illustrate the thought-action continuum with a study of the speech tag adverbs in *Vile Bodies*. Prince defines words such as these as *attributive discourse*: "The discourse accompanying a character's (direct) discourse and specifying the act of the speaker or thinker . . . and (sometimes) indicating various dimensions or features of the act, the character, the setting in which they appear etc" (1987, 7). The purpose of this discussion is to apply a cognitive perspective to the question, What precisely is being attributed? The adverbs listed are descriptions of actions in the sense that they describe the manner in which speech acts are performed, but they can also be regarded as contextual thought report as they provide important information about the functioning of characters' minds. The descriptions can be placed at various points along the thought-action continuum (and readers might well disagree with the suggested placings). In some cases, at the thought end of the spectrum, a state of mind is directly and obviously indicated. Subject to the context showing that the indication is ironic and therefore misleading, these cases seem straightforward:

Triumph: "said Lottie triumphantly" (34)
Desperation: "said Jane's father desperately" (49), "he shouted desperately" (139)
Anger or annoyance: "said the stranger crossly" (86), "said the Colonel crossly" (179), "said the Colonel crossly" (126), "said the Prime Minister sharply" (112)
Bitterness: "said Father Rothschild bitterly" (87)
Anxiety: "asked the barmaid anxiously" (142)
Thoughtfulness: "repeated Mr Benfleet thoughtfully" (27)
Gentleness: "said Father Rothschild gently" (111), "said Adam gently" (164)

In other cases, perhaps in the middle of the spectrum, one might say that a state of mind is indirectly indicated:

Wish to give encouragement: "said Adam encouragingly" (72)
Absentmindedness: "said the Colonel dreamily" (184), "said Mr Henderson mechanically" (16)
Various negative feelings: "said Miss Runcible severely" (146), "said the drunk Major distantly" (151), "he said rather stiffly" (163), "repeated Miss Runcible firmly" (146)
Lack of concern: "said Mr Isaacs airily" (123)

However, at the action end of the spectrum, there are some very interesting examples in which the adverb appears to relate primarily to the manner of speaking:

"said the General hospitably" (188)
"said Miss Runcible rather faintly" (131)
"said the Matron archly" (156)
"he hinted darkly" (20)
"she asked plaintively" (79)
"said Adam in no particular manner" (27)

These examples appear to contain a larger element of narratorial judgment and seem to require more work from the reader, than the others. In particular, although the real-world knowledge that we bring to texts tells us generally what they mean as action descriptions (we *kind-of* know what an "arch" tone of voice sounds like), their significance in terms of the character's consciousness can be unclear when taken out of context. As a consequence, the accompanying state of mind is not obvious and has to be inferred from the surrounding narrative. These cases also raise issues related to focalization and free indirect perception. Other characters will be listening to the General and Miss Runcible and will be understood by the reader as perceiving the various tones of voices as "arch," "dark," and so on. These adverbs need not simply be reports of the speaking characters' minds, they can also be read as reports of the listening characters' minds.

Indicative description

Readers use the preference rule system in reading actions. That is, they prefer to use the default of the indicated mental state unless other evidence that is contained in the context indicates otherwise. I am giving the name *indicative description* to a description of an action that appears to indicate an accompanying state of mind. As I have said, it is not easy to distinguish between such descriptions and thought report, as in chapter 29 of *Emma*, "everybody had a burst of admiration on first arriving" (1996, 303). To apply Wittgenstein's question again, Is this a report of their behavior or their state of mind? The word "admiration" could refer to their thought processes or to their behavior. In a sense, it is describing a public event, but there is a private side. The phrase "a burst of admiration" could mean that they felt genuinely admiring or that they were only behaving in an admiring way, possibly insincerely out of politeness. Later, Mr Weston is referred to as "cheerful." This is another indicative description that may conceal a different state of mind from that indicated. Although we are not told explicitly, we can guess from the context of the Box Hill picnic that the cheerful behavior may be accompanied by a rather stressed state of mind. It is possible to apply what might be called the *opposite thought test* to an action description of this sort. This means asking whether the state of mind that appears to be implied by the action is in fact present in the storyworld. The character might be thinking the opposite of what is implied by the description of the action. In the case of polite behavior, it is clearly possible for the character to be having anything other than polite thoughts. In *Emma* the politeness of the actions of all the characters but Emma toward Miss Bates does not necessarily entail less impatient feelings toward her garrulousness. It is often for the reader to decide. Indicative descriptions only *indicate* and do not conclusively establish the state of mind that would normally be associated with the behavior. The use of misleading indicative description is characteristic of heavily ironic novelists such as Jane Austen and Evelyn Waugh.

Indicative descriptions tend to occur in the middle of the thought-action continuum. They can be identified when the answer to Wittgenstein's question is unclear. Take this example:

(21) Unsteadily, but with renewed hope, the passengers had disembarked.
(19)

In the case of "with renewed hope" and "had disembarked," the answer to Wittgenstein's question is straightforward: the former is contextual thought report that refers to a state of mind and the latter is behavior. But what about "unsteadily"? I would suggest that the answer to the question is not obvious. On the one hand, it is a description of the manner in which the action of disembarking is performed; on the other hand, it appears to indicate that the action is accompanied by a sensation or feeling of unsteadiness.

(22) then rose . . . the despairing voices of Mrs Ape's angels, in frequently broken unison, singing, singing, wildly, desperately, as though their hearts would break in the effort and their minds lose their reason. (12–13)

Here, the description of the action of unison singing is followed by indicative description: the two adverbs "wildly" and "desperately" describe a quality in the sound but also appear to indicate the accompanying state of mind of wild desperation. However, it is by no means certain that this state of mind does exist within the reality of the fictional storyworld. The uncertainty is reinforced by the explicitly modal nature ("as though") of the next indicative description. It seems too far-fetched to suppose that the angels really are suffering broken hearts and lost reason. It is perhaps best understood as a comment by the narrator on the general states of mind or dispositions of the angels, which has a validity beyond their mental state at that particular time.

The ironic possibilities of misleading indicative description are extensive:

(23) the Café Royal was crowded and overflowing. Everyone was being thoroughly cross, but only the most sarcastic and overbearing were given tables, and only the gross and outrageous were given food. (150)

Starting with the physical context, four groups are described: "everyone," the "sarcastic and overbearing," the "gross and outrageous," and the staff who are putting up with this behavior. This last group is understood, like the car driver in the Schank and Abelson example (chapter 6, section 2). "Cross" is usually used to refer to a state of mind, but everyone "being" cross sounds more like a description of behavior with an element of calculation about it. This suspicion is confirmed by the rest of the sentence, where the mental states present in those getting tables and then food are not necessarily the ones indicated. Their states of mind are probably related more to a cold-blooded decision to use this sort of behavior in order to get what they want. This difference results in misleading indicative description.

A good deal of twentieth-century narration is characterized by a reluctance to make the decoding of action too explicit and a disinclination to use too much indicative description or contextual thought report. Wayne Booth mentions that in the manuscript of *Stephen Hero*, James Joyce's early version of *A Portrait of the Artist as a Young Man*, Joyce originally wrote that Stephen put his spoon through the bottom of his eggshell angrily and then deleted the word "angrily" (1987, 97).

Causation

One of the most important functions of contextual thought report is to present explanations for behavior, reasons for action, the causal networks that are present behind apparently simple action descriptions. Explicit motivations are also provided by what I shall call *cue-reason* words such as "for," "caused," "so," and "to." In example 15, the word "for" cues the reader to read the clause following it as an explicit and sufficient reason for the action. In example 24, the physical context is again given as the reason for the behavior:

(24) It was this last movement that caused the most havoc among the passengers. (11)

(25) So they all had another drink. (36)

(26) Then they went away to interview some more drivers. (133)

Implied or indirect motivation is even more interesting. In this case, everyone is relieved that a punishingly boring film has finished:

(27) When the reel came to an end everyone stirred luxuriously. (178)

The use of "when" instead of the cue-reason word "because" leaves the motivation for the action teasingly implicit.

(28) There was a hush all over the course, and the refreshment tent began to empty quickly. (141)

The first part of the sentence can be decoded as a deliberate non-action that is caused by the race being about to start. The next action is also caused by the same reason, but it is very different because here there is a clear intention. The cue-reason phrase "to see the race" is understood.

(29) Outside this ring clustered a group of predatory little boys with autograph albums and leaking fountain pens. (135)

The use of the word "clustered" and the narratorial comment of "predatory," together with the circumstantial evidence of the autograph albums and the pens all imply that this is not a random group and that they are gathered together for a common purpose. However, the information regarding the purpose is given by implication. It is not spelled out that they are waiting to collect autographs. But, because the purpose is so clear to the reader, it is easy to overlook the fact that it is merely implied and never explicitly stated.

The causal networks surrounding actions can be subject to regressive questioning. For example in the case of example 15 one can ask, "Yes, but why did they shelter?" "Because they did not want to get wet." "Why not?" "Because it is uncomfortable." And so on. These motivations tend to get larger and larger, but the chain is not infinite because it tends to end in a fairly unanswerable motive such as "I want to be happy." Even when the motivation for an action appears to be explicitly provided, the reader often still has to fill in the implicit chains in the reasoning. The characters in *Vile Bodies* are vague, sketchy, and attenuated because the cues for the reader tend to be short-term, specific, and localized. When, for example, a character is described as saying something "thoughtfully," this does not necessarily imply that the reader should read that person as a thoughtful character: the word may be significant only for the effects to be obtained in that particular scene. There is a good deal of what might be called *local motivation* of this sort, explanations and reasons for actions that are specific to the particular context. There is almost none of the *extended* or *teleological motivation* that readers require in order to build up a full, detailed, and coherent sense of character. This absence means that there is more for the reader to do. It is not possible to be too dogmatic about this issue as one reader may find contextual clues to be localized while another may be more resourceful in using them to build up a coherent account of a character. Having said that, the following sentence is clearly an unusual example of teleological motivation as opposed to local motivation:

(30) It hurt Adam deeply to think much about Nina. (156)

This simple statement derives much of its power and impact from the fact that there is no other description of such deep feeling in the novel.

Strong vivid characterization and clear teleological shape rely on big and important motivations such as love or money that can propel a whole narrative. Weak, hazy characterization tends to be associated, it seems, with local and specific motivation. It is a notable characteristic of *Vile Bodies* that these larger motivations are almost never made explicit. This gives the narrative its highly distinctive quality of aimless and restless desperation.

3. Intermental Thought

This section will consider the second subframe of the continuing-consciousness frame: intermental or joint, shared, or communal thought as opposed to intra-mental, or individual thinking. You may remember that James Wertsch's explanation in chapter 5, section 5 that "the notion of mental function can properly be applied to social as well as individual forms of activity" (1991, 27), and that "the terms *mind* and *mental action* can appropriately be predicated of dyads [that is, pairs] and larger groups as well as of individuals" (1991, 14). Unsurprisingly, given his work on the formation of the social mind, Lev Vygotsky noticed a vivid example of fictional intermental thinking in Tolstoy's *Anna Karenina*. He commented that good examples of the condensation and reduction of external speech are found in the novels of Tolstoy, who demonstrated that for people living in close psychological contact communication by abbreviated speech is common (1986, 236–38). He was referring in particular to the famous scene in which Kitty and Levin write out only the initial letters of the words that they wish to say, and the other understands perfectly.

I will refer briefly to the work of two theorists on fictional groups before explaining how intermental thinking works in practice in *Vile Bodies*. Pioneering research has been done by Lubomir Doležel and Uri Margolin on the notion of groups within the possible-worlds paradigm. In *Heterocosmica*, Doležel is very informative about the dynamics of what he calls *multiperson worlds*: "The vast majority of stories . . . are generated in multiperson worlds" (1998, 96); "The semantics of narrative is, at its core, the semantics of interaction" (1998, 97); and "The agential constellation is not only a precondition of interacting but also its scope (space)" (1998, 98). He explains that the "existence of groups and social organization gives rise to collective consciousness. Its cognitive form is socially based knowledge" (1998, 101). This knowledge includes "language, cultural archetypes, racial and ethnic beliefs, religious creeds, ideologies, and scientific knowledge" (1998, 101). Doležel also makes this important distinction between informally coordinated groups and formal organizations: "Informal coordination prevails in communities, groups whose collective acting is 'a function of individual actions' . . . its structure and modes correspond to those defined for interaction between persons. . . . In contrast, formal organization motivates social acting in institutions, which impose a number of supraindividual constraints: explicitly formulated regulations, well-defined power hierarchy, charted division of labour, specific role distribution, and, last but not least, reinforcing social representations (legitimizing ideologies, identifying emblems, and so on)" (1998, 111). Uri Margolin sets out in two articles ("Telling Our Story: on 'We' Literary Narratives," and "Telling in the Plural: from Grammar to Ideology") a typically rigorous and comprehensive account of the portrayal of large organizations or cultures in a wide range of fictions. He calls these fictions *"we" narratives* in order to stress that they are first-person rather than third-person narratives. This is the sort of organization that Doležel and Margolin have in mind: "A mammoth organization like this—it embodies too much experience. It possesses in fact a sort of group mind" (Dick 1999, 45).

As my interest in groups in narrative is very different from Doležel's and Margolin's, I should start by making the differences explicit: I am more interested in "they" (third-person plural) narratives than in "we" (first-person plural) narratives; I am also more interested in informal small groups than in formal large organizations; I will be exploring a very fluid and flexible notion of a group as any aggregate of characters, including a pair and even including people who may not be particularly close, but who are, for however short a period, thinking intermentally; and I am as interested in the negative group dynamics of conflict and fragmentation as in the positive dynamics of group solidarity and joint identification.

The extent of the difference in approach can be gauged from the fact that Margolin feels that the case of a character speaking about some group of which she or he is a member is "ubiquitous, trivial and of no significance for our purposes" (1996b, 123). He is here describing exactly the sort of area that I think *is* worth investigating. Within my perspective, the role of groups in narrative is not marginal. In fact, it is central, given that most novels are about the conflicts between individuals and the social groups to which they belong. Both Doležel and Margolin have prioritized large organizations, but some very interesting work can be done in the middle of the individual/collective continuum where individuals relate to each other in pairs or other small groups. Margolin states in the opening paragraph of "Telling in the Plural" that "groups or collective agents are optional elements in literary narratives, and when they do occur, they usually occupy a background or secondary role" (2000, 592). This is not the case within the informal, small group perspective that I am adopting.

In Margolin's view, the "tension between individual and collective levels of description reaches its climax in the representation of mental activity or experientiality . . . since mental activity is essentially and inalienably individual" (2000, 604). I hope that it is clear by now that this remark comes from an intellectual tradition that is very different from the intersubjective, externalist perspective that informed chapters 4, 5, and 6. An inevitable consequence of this internalist, subjective first approach is that the difficulties involved in the concept of joint thinking are heavily overestimated. The examples of intermental thought in *Vile Bodies* that are contained in this chapter do not seem to me to be at all problematic. What could be simpler than "They decided to go"? Also, I am not sure that I accept the firm distinction that is implied here between joint action and joint thought (that is, the former is easier to represent in discourse than the latter). In practice, descriptions of the two in fictional narratives are likely to amount to the same thing. Joint action requires at least a measure of joint thinking, and joint thinking will often result in joint action. Margolin states that the "general feeling of 'we-ness' or 'us' . . . can in principle be described from the outside in the third person plural, especially in literature. . . . But a more effective, immediate and convincing manner of expressing this reflexive dimension is to let its possessors speak for themselves" (1996b, 128). The very different tradition that I referred to earlier is again evident here. Within the social mind paradigm, it is not at all clear why it is only "in principle" that groups can be described in the third person. Why cannot a group be described perfectly adequately by the usual kind of omniscient narrator using the third-person ascription that was explained in chapter 5, section 2? It is like saying that any individual character can in principle be described by a third-person narrator, but it is more effective, immediate, and convincing to let the character speak for him or herself in the first person.

Margolin emphasizes the importance of the individual member's sense of a group (for example, 1996b, 128), whereas my focus of interest is equally related to the sense of a group that can be possessed by outsiders or even another group. Outsiders looking at a bureaucracy tend to see it in monolithic terms and regard the people who work in it as robotic adherents to a single and inflexible bureaucratic line. However, working within a bureaucracy as I do, I see that life inside one is really fragmented, diffuse, and incoherent. I am sure that this is true of many other large organizations. I am also particularly interested in the conflicts between individuals in groups that Margolin illuminatingly discusses in a passage on intragroup conflict (2000, 609). Evelyn Waugh's *Men at Arms* is in part about the conflicting feelings of the protagonist toward his regiment. They include affection, a feeling of belonging, and so on, but also exasperation, disgust, and eventually a feeling of falling out of love with it. Obviously, the other soldiers in the story have equally ambivalent feelings toward the regiment and toward each other. Margolin refers to the fact that a number of individual actions carried out simultaneously do not necessarily constitute group action because the participants may be acting independently of each other (2000, 594). This is true. However, I would like to explore the cases that are marginal from this perspective because I would like to see how far the concept of intermental action can be pushed. This would mean, for example, asking what it is about a particular social or physical context that might cause individuals to undertake simultaneous individual actions, and whether the answer to that question shows that there is a gray area between group actions and connected individual actions.

With this context in mind, I now wish to consider more systematically the second subframe of shared or group thinking. I say "more systematically" because I have already been implicitly discussing this device in some detail in the previous sections. I am sure that you will have noticed that a large number of the examples of thought and action given earlier—examples 3 to 10, 12, 14 to 19, and 21 to 29—were examples of intermental thinking. A Bakhtinian emphasis on the shared, social, and dialogic nature of mental functioning is after all clearly suitable to a novel that is explicitly concerned with

(31) all that succession and repetition of massed humanity. . . . Those vile bodies. (104)

Communicative action

One of the terms in James Wertsch's fivefold typology of situated action that I discussed in chapter 5, section 5 was communicative action. This notion is closely linked to the concept of intermental thinking. I argued in the previous section that fictional thought and action descriptions form a continuum and this argument works particularly well in the case of intermental action and thought. As Clark and Chalmers suggest, if their argument is "taken seriously, certain forms of social activity might be reconceived as less akin to communication and action, and as more akin to thought" (1998, 18). In other words, action descriptions can within the situated thought paradigm be easily and informatively reconceived as consciousness descriptions. For these reasons, I am not going to make a hard and fast distinction between intermental thinking and communicative action. However, although communicative action clearly requires intermental functioning, and core or paradigmatic intermental thinking is joint or cooperative decision making, I have widened my use of the term to include joint states of mind and other interesting marginal cases such as what might be called conflicted or competitive actions (such as quarrelling). Intermental thinking and communicative action can both be linked to the embedded narrative approach by being regarded as joint or merged embedded narratives.

This is a core example of group decision making:

(32) When they reached the pits they decided they were hungry. It seemed too far to climb up to the dining tent, so they ate as much of the mechanic's lunch as Miss Runcible's cigarette had spared. (147)

This is paradigmatic functional intermental thinking because it involves an initial shared decision, a joint perception (of distance), a shared judgment (regarding the distance), and, finally, a group decision to act. The cue-reason word "so" makes explicit the communal motivation for the communicative action.

(33) Outside his door, two very limp detective sergeants had deserted their posts. (12)

Contained within this description of a joint action of desertion is the joint decision to take that action. "Deserted" makes the mental processes much clearer than a simple description of mere physical movement. The shared feelings or emotions (for example, sensations of tiredness and feelings of resentment) that presumably caused the decision to leave are not made explicit but can be inferred from the context. In the next case, the adverbs used in the description emphasize that this is very conscious communicative action and that the individuals are clearly aware that it is a joint enterprise:

(34) Then they all pinched her all over, but precisely and judiciously, so as not to disturb her wings or halo. (79)

The following passages move away from core functional intermental decision making in various ways. For example, some intermental thinking is counterfactual:

(35) The gatecrashers wondered whether it would not have been better to have stayed at home. (85)

(36) The race was not due to start until noon, but any indecision which they may have felt about the employment of the next few hours was settled for them by the local police. (136)

Example 36 describes a counterfactual intermental state of mind. The group might have experienced, but did not in fact experience, the state of mind of indecision. The reason why the indecision did not occur is then given.

Here are illustrations of conflicted communicative action:

(37) He and Nina were lunching at Espinoza's and quarrelling half-heartedly. (91)

and competitive communicative action:

(38) (a) The others were jostling one another with their luggage, (b) trying to attract the Customs officers (c) and longing for a cup of tea. (19)

These actions clearly differ from the cooperative actions described in examples 32 to 34. In example 38, the joint mental event of the attempt to attract attention makes it clear that the passengers have all taken the decision deliberately to jostle one another in order to gain an advantage. Competitive action is intermental in the sense that the individuals are united in recognizing the need to engage in this action. It is also worth noting that the same considerations regarding Wittgenstein's question, the thought-action continuum, and the nature of action apply just as much to joint action as to single agent action. Example 38a is a description of bodily movement, but can it be called an action as it is presumably unintentional? Example 38c is thought report of a state of mind. But what is example 38b? It is Wittgenstein's question again: Is it a report of behavior or of a state of mind? It is important to note also that example 38b has a causal function: it is the reason for the jostling, and it is the intention to get off the boat quickly. The potential complexity of competitive intermental thought is clearly demonstrated in a game of chess. For a good chess player, the attempt to construct the probable thought processes of the opponent can stretch to a very large number of moves ahead.

Descriptions of the shared perceptions and states of mind that cause and emerge from joint actions such as emotions, feelings, and sensations are very common:

(39) It was not a really good evening. The long drive . . . chilled and depressed them, dissipating the gaiety which had flickered rather spasmodically over Ginger's dinner. (103)

This is a description of the thoughts and feelings of a group in very abstract terms. The word "evening" in the first sentence functions as a metonymy for "the group of people spending the evening together." The passage describes shared emotions and feelings such as the sensation of being chilled, the state of mind of being depressed, and the previous state of mind of gaiety. Although this sort of thinking is different from functional decision making, it is the product of a shared group dynamic. The individuals are experiencing the same states of mind because of the common situation in which they find themselves. See also examples 12, 16, 17, and 46. Group verbal action is common: "All teams were confident of victory, they said" (133).

Not all groups are intermental. It may be that individuals simply happen to share beliefs or feelings that have not been worked out together or caused by the same group dynamic. In example 40 it is not clear whether there is intermental agreement between Chastity and Divine Discontent or whether they intramentally happen to think the same thing:

(40) At intervals letters arrived from Buenos Aires in which Chastity and Divine Discontent spoke rather critically of Latin American entertainment. (92)

(41) (Many doctors, thus diverted, spent an enjoyable day without apparent prejudice to their patients.) (137)

Example 41 refers to two groups, but as discrete individuals and not as intermental groups. Although the reason for the doctors' and patients' states of mind happens to be the same, they are not cooperatively shared.

Relationship with intramental thinking

In a sense, intermental thinking is simply the aggregate of the individual, intramental consciousnesses that make up the group. On the other hand, intermental thinking is often more than the sum of its parts, and this difference can sometimes be quantified. My partner and I actively cooperate on the answers to a weekly quiz (every Saturday in the *Guardian* newspaper) and regularly get scores of six to eight out of ten, compared to a probable aggregate of individual scores of about two or three. The intermental dividend is clearly substantial. The power of intermental thought is clearly related to the concept of synergy, which specifies that a combined effect is greater than the sum of the parts and that increased effectiveness and achievements are produced by combined action and cooperation.

In example 42, an intramental state of mind, being moved, is put in an intermental context because all the other listeners are moved as well:

(42) The American who, like all the listeners, had been profoundly moved by the ex-King's recitation. (33)

Sometimes, an individual description becomes intermental with the introduction of others such as, in this case, co-conspirators:

(43) Father Rothschild was conspiring with Mr Outrage and Lord Metroland. (82)

The narrator chooses a form of words that gives the weight to Father Rothschild rather than saying, "The three were conspiring," thereby cueing the reader to surmise that he is the most enthusiastic conspirator. Intermental thought report is sometimes necessarily approximate. In an example such as "They all fell back in amazement," it seems likely that some individuals would be more amazed than others. It may be necessary in some cases of intermental thought to develop a division between the core and the periphery, which would indicate that some individuals had the specified mental states to a greater degree than others. On a related point, groups are sometimes specified with a leader:

(44) The old brigade, led by Mrs Blackwater, threw themselves with relish into an orgy of litigation. (92)

A strange kind of leadership occurs when Adam works as a gossip columnist:

(45) arguing that people did not really mind *whom* they read about provided that a kind of vicarious inquisitiveness into the lives of others was satisfied, Adam began to invent people. (94)

The activities of Adam's creations then begin to respond to the public's reception of them as real people. Symbiotically, the fictional creations then influence readers' actual behavior, which in turn modifies their actions and so on. Adam's mind is in a Bakhtinian dialogue with what he anticipates, correctly, the public mind to be. His wholly fictitious narratives take on a life of their own and achieve a kind of reality within the storyworld that is based on the dialogic relationship between Adam's intramental thought processes and the public's intermental mind.

In one scene, three characters are described as

(46) maintaining a moody silence. (150)

This phrase implies three separate conscious decisions to remain silent, and the resulting non-action maintains the group dynamic. "Moody" indicates the shared reason for the silence. The next three passages contain very complex interrelationships between intermental and intramental thinking. Example 47 occurs before and example 48 after Adam and Nina make love for the first time:

> (47) (a) But this raised a question in both their minds (b) that had been unobtrusively agitating them throughout the journey. (c) Neither said anymore on the subject, (d) but there was a distinct air of constraint (e) in the Daimler from Pulborough onwards. (67)

An intermental event is described in example 47a, but example 47b makes it clear that it is based on previously existing or latent states of mind (of uncertainty and apprehension regarding the possibility that they might be making love that night). "Unobtrusive" refers to the fact that their state of mind had not made itself obvious in their behavior. Example 47c is non-action that arises from a conscious intermental decision not to do anything. Example 47d can be decoded as Adam is experiencing a feeling of constraint; Nina is experiencing the same feeling; and an observer could tell from their external behavior that they were experiencing that feeling. Example 47e is the physical context.

> (48) (a) They treated each other quite differently (b) after their night's experiences. (c) Adam was inclined to be egotistical and despondent; (d) Nina was rather grown up and disillusioned and distinctly cross. (76)

The action in example 48a is intermental in the sense that their thoughts and actions have changed as a unit. The reason for the changes given in example 48b consists of a joint experience. However, in examples 48c and 48d, their reactions are intramentally different. "Despondent" is clearly a state of mind. "Egotistical" is slightly different because it has more of the quality of a behavior description and also a judgment by the narrator. "Inclined to be" puts these mental states in the context of Adam's whole personality. As regards Nina's reactions, Wittgenstein's question is unanswerable.

> (49) (a) Adam and Miles and Archie Schwert (b) did not talk much. (c) The effects of their drinks had now entered on that secondary stage, vividly described in temperance handbooks, when the momentary illusion of well-being and exhilaration gives place to melancholy, indigestion and moral decay. (d) Adam tried to concentrate his thoughts upon his sudden wealth, but they seemed unable to adhere to this high pinnacle, and as often as he impelled them up, slithered back helplessly to his present physical discomfort. (149)

The listing of the individuals in example 49a seems significant, paving the way for the progression in this passage from intermental to intramental thought and the eventual disintegration of the group later in the narrative. Example 49b is significant action: it soon becomes clear why they did not feel like talking. Example 49c is group thought report that describes a typical process of consciousness as it applies in this case to these three individuals. Example 49d is intramental thought report that is standard in most novels but comparatively rare in this one. Adam's thought processes are preoccupied, as this discussion has been, with the importance of physical context.

The thriller writer Donna Leon is very good at conveying the intimate ebb and flow of the intermental unit of a marriage that is not explored in *Vile Bodies*. For example, "She laughed at the joke: contempt for Freud and all his works and pomps was part of the intellectual glue that held them together" (1997, 235); "He stood at the door and watched her turn a page. The radar of long marriage caused her to turn to him" (1996, 128); and "As if she had read his thoughts, she answered" (1996, 98).

Group norms

The foundation for a good deal of the work done in this chapter has been laid by possible-worlds theorists and social thought analysts, and this is particularly true of group norms. As Doležel remarks, "[s]ocial representations and collective emotions are essential for group cohesion, splitting the world into 'us' and 'them' and, consequently, motivating interacting between groups" (1998, 101). Doležel also discusses the role of power in interpersonal relationships in *Heterocosmica* (1998, 103–4). Thomas Pavel's excellent book *Fictional Worlds* (1986) has a chapter on social conventions and their role in regulating the behavior of groups. Vygotsky, Bakhtin, and the other thinkers that I examined in chapter 5 show that we are constituted by our social relationships and, in particular, by the acquisition and use of the shared cultural resource of language. Intersubjectivity is a part of us. A particularly important function of intermental thinking and communicative action is the formation and maintenance of group norms and conventions, such as in this case:

(50) the sort of people who liked that sort of thing went there continually and said how awful it was. (71)

Here is one of the few examples in the novel of beneficial intermental action in which the norms are shared:

(51) Soon they were all at it, singing like blazes, and it is undoubtedly true that they felt the better for it. (16)

The language used by the narrator in example 50 to describe this consensus creates a noticeable distance between the values of the Bright Young People and the values of the implied author and therefore, implicitly, the implied reader. This effect is even more apparent in this passage when Lady Circumference sees

> (52) a great concourse of pious and honourable people . . . people of decent and temperate life, uncultured, unaffected, unembarrassed, unassuming, unambitious people, that fine phalanx of the passing order. (106–7)

It appears for most of the narrative that the novel does not contain an implied moral norm (that is, one established by the implied author) against which the implied reader is invited to judge the norms of the various sets such as the Bright Young People and other, older sets. However, the strength of the language used in this important passage, albeit focalized by free indirect perception through Lady Circumference, appears to suggest that it should be read as more than just the perception of one character. It reveals a bedrock of "norm-alness" or "norm-ality" against which the artificiality, cruelty, and futility of the lives of the Bright Young People are clearly revealed. The implied author appears to intend these judgments to form the moral center of the novel.

> (53) (a) There were about a dozen people left at the party; (b) that hard kernel of gaiety that never breaks. . . . (c) "Of course there's always the Ritz" said Archie. . . . But he said it in the tone of voice that made all the others say, (d) no, the Ritz was too, too boring at that time of night. . . .
> (e) Soon someone would say those fatal words, "Well, I think it's time for me to go to bed . . ." (f) and the party would be over. (46)

This passage begins with narrative description in example 53a. Example 53b is a subtly worded comment or judgment by the narrator on the minds of the whole group. Superficially, they are gay but all the other words apart from "gaiety" convey a sense of their aimlessness and desperation. This is the consensus in action. The action in example 53c can be decoded as follows: he intended that his action would have an effect on their minds that would be the opposite to the surface meaning of the words and cause them to come to the same decision regarding an intention to act as he has (that is, to go elsewhere). Example 53d is intermental free indirect speech, similar to the group free indirect thought that I referred to in an earlier section. Example 53e is a statement by the narrator that one of the group will come to an intramental decision to leave and so destroy the intermental consensus. Example 53f describes the consequences of example 53e. Social norms are always liable to be transgressed by individuals, and the fatal words are a potentially norm-breaking intramental action. Such dissent is characteristic of many aspects of the relationship between intermental and intramental thinking.

Dissenting action can be comically inadvertent:

(54) Then Mrs Melrose Ape stood up to speak. A hush fell in the gilt ballroom beginning at the back and spreading among the chairs until only Mrs Blackwater's voice was heard exquisitely articulating some details of Lady Metroland's past. (84)

But, in example 55, the same act, breaking a socially agreed silence, quite deliberately defies the consensus:

(55) But suddenly on that silence vibrant with self-accusation, broke the organ voice of England, the hunting cry of the *ancien regime* . . . "what a damned impudent woman" she said. (85)

Sometimes, inter-group conflict will require adroit social management by others:

(56) it is only a very confident hostess who will invite both these sets together at the same time. (81)

Obviously, intramental dissent can also take place among the norm-reinforcement of core, collaborative intermental decision making:

(57) After further discussion the conclusion was reached that angels were nurses, and that became the official ruling of the household. But the second footman was of the opinion that they were just 'young persons.' (79)

The final aspect of intermental thinking to which I wish to draw attention is the group conflict that can arise when the social norms established by two or more groups are incompatible:

(58) They stopped for dinner at another hotel, where everyone giggled at Miss Runcible's trousers. (129)

(59) Two little American cars had failed to start; their team worked desperately at them amid derisive comments from the crowd (142)

These examples may seem rather trivial, but the next is representative of the social fissures that are such a marked feature of the novel:

(60) The real aristocracy . . . had done nothing about [coming in fancy dress]. They had come on from a dance and stood in a little group by themselves, aloof, amused but not amusing (44)

In describing the self-conscious conflict and hostility between the small group (the aristocrats) and the larger group (the rest of the party), the passage is an interesting example of how focalization can change in just four words: "amused but not amusing." "Amused" describes the consciousness of the aristocrats:

"we are amused in a superior sort of way at the rest of the party." "Amusing" describes the state of mind of the rest of the party: "they are very superior but we do not find them amusing."

On occasions the reader can experience a bewilderingly complex mélange of different intermental groups, which also contains very marked group conflict and hostility:

> (61) (a) From the window [the angels] could see the guests arriving for the party. (b) In spite of the rain quite a large crowd had collected . . . (c) to criticize the cloaks with appreciative "oohs" and "ahs" or contemptuous sniffs. . . . (d) The Bright Young People came popping all together. . . . (e) Some "gatecrashers" who had made the mistake of coming in Victorian fancy dress (f) were detected and repulsed. (g) They hurried home to change for a second assault. (h) No one wanted to miss Mrs Ape's debut.
> (i) But the angels were rather uneasy. (78)

Example 61a consists of intermental free indirect perception: the angels are watching the other groups. In example 61b, the crowd is a second group of whom we are told the circumstances under which they took the decision to come. Example 61c is communicative action, and the adjectives used to describe it are indicative of the accompanying states of mind. The contempt of one group for another is an obvious manifestation of group conflict. Example 61d describes the action of a third group. Example 61e consists of a fourth group and their action of coming in Victorian dress. However, the fact that they come wrongly dressed makes it clear that there is a fifth group, understood but norm-regulating, who had decided that it was the wrong dress. The norm-regulating group, still unnamed, takes the action in example 61f of detecting and repulsing the gatecrashers. In example 61g, the gatecrashers then take the decision to follow another course of action with the intention of evading the norm regulators. In example 61h, the reason given for the course of action in example 61g gives information about the state of mind (anticipation, excitement, and so on) of all the groups so far referred to. Finally, in example 61i, the focus is narrowed again, and we are back with a very specific piece of intermental thought report related to the first group mentioned.

4. Doubly Embedded Narratives

In this section I am extending the concept of embedded narratives by linking it to the notion of situated identity that I discussed in chapter 5, section 5 in order to develop the third subframe. This is the doubly embedded narrative: a character's mind as contained within another character's mind. The claim that I make by using the term *situated identity* is that a fictional character's identity consists, not just of his or her own embedded narrative, but of all the doubly embedded narratives of which he or she is the subject. Here is an example of a doubly embedded narrative: "The mind of the young Lord of Glenvarloch was filled with anticipation, not the most pleasant, concerning the manner in which he was likely to be received by the Monarch . . . and he was, with the usual mental anxiety of those in such a situation, framing imaginary questions from the King, and over-toiling his spirit in devising answers to them" (Scott 1973, 134). In this passage, Nigel (Lord of Glenvarloch) is imagining what sort of reception he will get from King James I when he arrives at the Court. His embedded narrative is in a future-oriented, counterfactual mode and is trying to anticipate future events by containing within it another embedded narrative— that of the King. This view of the King's mind can therefore be called a *doubly embedded narrative*. Ryan's term for this phenomenon is *recursive embedding* (1985, 723).

"He tried to put his mind inside Rourke's caper" (Connelly 1993, 333). This sentence occurs in a thriller in which the detective finally realizes that Rourke, an FBI agent, is in fact the villain. The detective attempts to view the storyworld from a different aspect: not any more from an aspect that assumes that Rourke has been helping the murder investigation; but from an aspect that accepts that he is the murderer. All the previous events have to be reinterpreted by the detective and also, if possible, by the reader. The detective and the reader do this by putting their mind inside Rourke's caper, by trying to create a narrative of the storyworld from his aspectual viewpoint: Why did he commit the first murder? How did he conceal his involvement? Why did he kill again? And so on. It is a pivotal moment in the plot when the detective abandons his previous attempt to construct the old I-that-is-Rourke inside his own mind, and tries to reconstruct a new one. So, we have an embedded narrative, the detective's, that contains within it a view or an interpretation of another embedded narrative, Rourke's. However, as with previous insights relating to the workings of genre fiction, this point need not be limited to a particular genre. *All* fiction is read by means of doubly embedded narratives. *Emma* has the power that it has because it is propelled by Emma's doubly embedded narrative of Knightley. She wonders about what image Knightley has of her in his mind, and she cares desperately about what it is.

All this is also true of real minds. We have narratives of others that are more or less detailed, more or less accurate, more or less prone to change. Equally, people vary in the extent to which they attempt to control the narratives that others have of them, and, of course, they vary in the extent to which these attempts are successful. As I said in chapter 2, section 4, Schank and Abelson maintain that in a role theme, "a particular actor's goals are determined by his role. . . . Once a role theme is invoked, it sets up expectations about goals and actions" (1977, 132–33). The social role that we acquire as it is formed within the embedded narratives of others becomes part of our situated identity. Our own goals and actions are necessarily influenced by the expectations of others. Those people who, for example, dress flamboyantly and say they do not care what others think of them are the ones who, in reality, care most.

Incredibly, doubly embedded narratives even occur in the animal kingdom. In *Kinds of Minds*, Daniel Dennett explains the "thinking" behind a bird's decision to distract a predator from its chicks: "I'm a low nesting bird, whose chicks are not protectable against a predator who discovers them. This approaching predator can be *expected* soon to discover them . . . unless I distract it; it could be distracted by its *desire* to catch and eat me, but only if it *thought* there was a *reasonable* chance of its actually catching me (it's no dummy); it would contract just that *belief* if I *gave it evidence that* I couldn't fly anymore; I could do that by feigning a broken wing, etc" (1996, 122). As Dennett remarks, it defies credence "to suppose that any bird goes through anything like the soliloquy here. Yet that soliloquy undoubtedly expresses the rationale that has shaped the behavior, whether or not the bird can appreciate the rationale" (1996, 122). The rationale that Dennett describes is based on the bird's assumptions about and predictions of another creature's behavior. In whatever form that it takes, the bird's cognitive functioning is based on some kind of doubly embedded narrative.

With regard to fictional minds, Uri Margolin draws a clear and useful distinction between the original or "real" characters who exist in the storyworlds of third-person narratives and the "versions" of these characters who exist in the belief worlds of other characters. He describes this difference as between ontological and epistemic versions (1996a, 114–15). That is, the original is "real" within the ontology of the storyworld, while the versions exist only within the epistemic belief worlds of the other characters. It is perhaps worth dwelling on this distinction for a while from a situated identity perspective. Imagine that you are trying to establish the personality or mind of a character. If the narrator says that he is, say, mean, then that is ontologically clear. But what about the cases where the "real" character says that he is generous, but his versions are mean in the sense that all the other characters think that he is mean? If it is clear that the reader will find him mean also, then there is an interesting sense in which the ontologically real character is less real than the epistemological versions. What I wish to do is to query where "the mind" occurs because recursive embedding can often be more accurate than the original embedded narrative. So it can be true to say of character A's mind that he has an angry disposition if this characteristic is contained within the doubly embedded narratives of B, C, and D but angrily denied by A himself. As in real life, characters are continually attempting to reconstruct aspects of the minds of others by the process of third-person ascription, even in the absence of specific cues such as external action. This is amusingly illustrated when underreaction leads to the " . . . what? . . . WHAT? . . ." syndrome. (This is the situation that you often see in sitcoms when an uneasy character reacts more and more frenziedly to another character simply staring at them.)

An informative way to look at narratives is to examine the distance between a character's view of their own embedded narrative and the doubly embedded narratives of others relating to that character. Embedded narratives and the doubly embedded variety relate in interesting ways. For example, they may coincide or they may be divergent; if divergent, the doubly embedded narrative can be more accurate (Knightley's of Emma in *Emma*) or less accurate (Pip's of Miss Havisham as his benefactress in *Great Expectations*); the views of the reader might change on the relationship (as in the latter case almost certainly and the former case possibly). Sometimes doubly embedded narratives are rich and detailed (Dorothea's of Casaubon in *Middlemarch*) and sometimes barely existing (as in all the characters in *Vile Bodies*). The interest of many novels is to see how the various embedded and doubly embedded narratives interweave, merge, conflict, become reconciled, and so on. Rich and complex patterns result.

One way to divide intramental and intermental doubly embedded narratives is as follows: an individual thinking about another individual; an individual thinking about a group; a group thinking about an individual; and a group thinking about another group. Several of the examples of the four categories from *Vile Bodies* that are considered in the following discussion could just have easily been used in the context of the discussion of the intermental thinking in the previous section. The key to the fictional minds in *Vile Bodies* is that there is a good deal of intermental thinking but very little evidence of doubly embedded narratives. There is very little indication of the existence of one character in the mind of another. The following examples tend to be rather marginal and fleeting cases that are very negative in content. There is no evidence of a doubly embedded narrative that is sustained in any richness or depth over the whole of the novel. The lack of doubly embedded narratives demonstrates some very solipsistic states of mind: the combination of this and the amount of intermental thinking vividly conveys the sensation of being alone in a crowd. The lack of explicit and continued doubly embedded narratives contributes substantially to the callous and unfeeling quality of the novel. Following the discussion of a few examples from *Vile Bodies*, I will conclude this section with some much richer examples of doubly embedded narratives taken from three other novels.

Individual-individual. This is a good example of prototypical doubly embedded narrative:

> (62) Adam was quite pleased to lunch with Simon Balcairn, though he knew there must be some slightly sinister motive behind this sudden hospitality. (71)

It is one character speculating about the motives of another character's action in the context of that second character's whole mind. "Adam sat in the back of the car with Miles, who was clearly put out about his friend's lack of cordiality (138)". is another rare example. Adam's mental event is the awareness of Miles's mental event: discomfiture at a third party's unfriendly behavior and so, possibly, unfriendly state of mind. So, three individual embedded narratives enmesh.

> (63) It was about now that Adam remembered that he was engaged to be married. (28)

This is a doubly embedded narrative that, given that it is a man thinking about his fiancée, is of a disturbingly casual and attenuated variety.

One example turns out to be amusingly counterfactual.

> (64) It was fortunate, [Mr Benfleet] reflected, that none of the authors ever came across the senior partner, that benign old gentleman. . . . He often wondered in his uneasy moments what he would find to say when Rampole died. (27–28)

Mr. Benfleet is worrying because he has created a fictitious doubly embedded narrative of the benign Mr Rampole as a avaricious old tyrant in order to scare the authors into accepting unreasonable contractual terms. His concern is related to the conflict between this fictitious doubly embedded narrative and the real doubly embedded narrative that he has of the authors who, he anticipates, will be difficult to control when the fictitious one ends. Mr Benfleet's state of mind is reminiscent of Bakhtin's notion of the *word with a sideways glance*: the uneasy anticipation of the conflicting viewpoint of another.

In a scene between Lady Ursula and her mother (114), the two discuss her marriage prospects without any meeting of minds at all. The mother is simply not listening to her daughter's doubts and misgivings. There is, therefore, a conspicuous and significant absence of the kind of genuine and accurate doubly embedded narrative that the reader would expect in this sort of situation. The mother is completely solipsistic and is making no attempt to reconstruct within her own mind what her daughter's thoughts might be. That is the charitable explanation. The other is that she *has* done this and is ignoring the result. It is not clear which.

Individual-group. This character is thinking in typically negative terms about the group or set to which she belongs:

(65) One day she would surprise them all, thought Miss Mouse. (44)

In example 66, an individual is thinking about himself as part of a pair and making decisions about actions in the future. They are ironic because they are mistaken:

(66) When Nina and he were married, he thought, they would often come down there for the day after a really serious party. (61)

Group-individual. The examples of this sort of doubly embedded narrative tend to be rather negative. This one is obviously rather callous:

(67) the Younger Set . . . cheered up wonderfully when they heard about Miss Runcible's outrageous treatment at the hands of the Customs officers. (23)

The context to the next example, which is no better, is that Miss Runcible has been barred from the hotel because she is wearing trousers and is waiting outside in the cold:

(68) They spent a long time over luncheon because it was warm there, and they drank Kummel over the fire until Miss Runcible came in very angrily to fetch them out. (129)

This sentence involves intermental action but any doubly embedded narrative is conspicuously and typically absent. Put simply, and stripped of my newly minted narrative-theory jargon, they did not think about what it might be like for Miss Runcible to be hungry, lonely, and cold.

I would like to introduce here yet another new term—the *fully doubly embedded narrative*. This occurs when the reader never meets a character directly, and he or she exists for the reader only through the doubly embedded narratives of other characters. I have already mentioned Rebecca in Daphne du Maurier's novel *Rebecca*. Another is the painter character in Agatha Christie's whodunit *Five Little Pigs*. Emily in William Faulkner's "A Rose for Emily" is a famous example of a fully doubly embedded narrative. In fact, it is an intermental fully doubly embedded narrative because she is known only through the group embedded narrative of the townspeople. It is shared in that by and large the townspeople agree on the sort of mind that Emily had; the fully doubly embedded narratives in the other two cases are conflicted, in that the narrative action arises from the existence of very different views of the absent character.

Group-Group. Plenty of examples of this sort as they relate to sub-groups and group conflict were given earlier in section 3 on intermental thought.

Now let us consider some very different examples from other novels. First, the reader begins the initial, tentative, and hypothetical construction of Lydgate's embedded narrative in *Middlemarch* by making use of the doubly embedded narratives of other characters. The reader first hears of Lydgate indirectly when Lady Chettam and Mrs Cadwallader are discussing him. These are the main points: "Tell me about this new young surgeon, Mr Lydgate. I am told he is wonderfully clever: he certainly looks it—a fine brow indeed" (1977, 61). Mrs Cadwallader replies that "He is a gentleman. . . . He talks well" (1977, 61). Lady Chettam agrees that he is "really well connected. . . . One does not expect it in a practitioner of that kind" (1977, 62). Mrs Cadwallader then notices that Dorothea Brooke "is talking cottages and hospitals with him. . . . I believe he is a sort of philanthropist" (1977, 62). So, what do we find out about him in the twenty-one lines of text before we meet him? We learn that he is apparently young, clever, good-looking, a well-connected gentleman, someone who talks well, a sort of philanthropist, and innovative and successful. These words on the page will now be transformed by the reader into an already pre-existing imaginary individual with a past that is part of the *Middlemarch* storyworld. His embedded narrative started twenty-five odd years ago, and the reader is now engaged in reconstructing it.

This conversation is largely a consideration of Lydgate's mind. Some features are obviously related to his mental life: being clever, philanthropic, and successfully innovative. Others are slightly more indirect: "talking well" is a description of behavior that implies a series of mental attributes such as cleverness, confidence, awareness of others, and so on. Being a gentleman is yet more indirect but presumably has implications for the way the mind works. In addition to these explicit qualities, it is also part of the competence of the reader to construct, this time by indirect means, some aspects of Lydgate's mental life that are implicit in what we have been told. Let us say, for example, having these qualities makes it likely that he is not only self-confident and ambitious but also altruistic, imaginative, and idealistic. The reader is using material on Lydgate's social and publicly available mind that has been refracted through the conflicting world views of the two different embedded narratives of Mrs Cadwallader and Lady Chettam. His mind exists in their minds. Their minds are interacting with, conflicting with, and interrogating the constructions that they have formed of his mind. They disapprove of his being both a gentleman and a doctor and also of the fact that he is a doctor with ideas about the advancement of medicine. Although the characters do not explicitly speculate about the causal network behind Lydgate's behavior, there is an implicit puzzlement over the motives that a gentleman would have for wanting to become a doctor. Lydgate's own motivation becomes more explicit in the direct access to his mind later in the passage. Later events appear to show that the views of the two characters were fairly accurate in their discussions of Lydgate's mind. And, to use a familiar but significant phrase, there are some respects in which he may not "know his own mind." In the next chapter Lydgate is scornful about the possibility of losing his balance and falling in love, and we find out later that this is precisely what Lydgate *does* do.

A group-group doubly embedded narrative occurs in an apparently trivial incident in another of Evelyn Waugh's novels, *Men at Arms*. The protagonist, Guy Crouchback, has arrived in a new Army camp as part of a group of officers from the Barrack camp. At the dining table they see another group of officers from the Depot camp that they do not know. The two groups do not speak.

[Crouchback] was the first to go. Soon after him the Depot Batch rose from the table. One or two of them hesitated, wondering whether they ought not to speak to the newcomers, but by now all heads at the Barrack batch table were bent over their plates. The moment passed before it was recognized.

"Matey bastards, aren't they?" said Sarum-Smith. (1964, 89)

Later, the narrator reports that "There was no enmity between the two groups but there was little friendship. They continued as they had begun, eating at separate tables and inhabiting separate bedrooms" (1964, 93). It seems to me that the discourse conveys in a sensitive and careful manner a typical problem in social relations. A trivial incident, like two people not acknowledging each other in the corridor the first time they pass, achieves an importance completely out of proportion to its true significance because it can be so difficult to put it right on subsequent occasions. A coldness can soon arise for no other reason than the initial awkwardness. In these situations, embedded narratives are not just doubled, they are tripled, quadrupled, and so on, and so on. In fact, when it comes to social embarrassment, embedded narrative growth is probably exponential. "He'll think that I think that he thinks that I think . . ." As a child I read a *Reader's Digest* story in which a man goes to borrow a wig from a neighbor for some amateur theatricals. While he walks he thinks of all the reasons why his neighbor will not want to lend it, a few reasons why he will, yet more and even stronger reasons why he will not, and so on. When the man gets there and his neighbor opens the door, the man shouts, "Keep the damn wig, then! I never wanted it anyway!" The difference in the *Men at Arms* case is that the difficulty is being experienced by two groups. Although the passage is beautifully understated, anyone who is prone to this sort of problem will experience an instant and uncomfortable thrill of recognition on reading the words, "the moment passed." And this thrill will in no way be diminished by the fact that what is being described here is intermental and not intramental doubly embedded narratives.

I will conclude this chapter with an individual-individual doubly embedded narrative. I said in chapter 1 that the following passage was the kind of fictional mental functioning that I was interested in and that I very much hoped that when you read it again here more of its full significance would be revealed:

> Brunetti watched as Murino absorbed this information, then waited as the other man began to consider what his visible response should be. All of this took only seconds, but Brunetti had been observing the process for decades and was familiar with it. The people to whom he presented himself had a drawer of responses which they thought appropriate, and part of his job was to watch them as they sifted through them one at a time, seeking the right fit. Surprise? Fear? Innocence? Curiosity? He watched Murino flip through them, studied his face as he considered, then discarded various possibilities. He decided, apparently, on the last.
>
> "Yes? And what would you like to know, Commissario?" (Leon 1996, 199)

Because I hope that what I am now going to say is completely predictable, I will keep it brief. The passage presents the whole of Brunetti's mind in action, including states of mind such as dispositions and beliefs and also emotions. Both characters are employing purposive mental functioning. Murino's mind is public and social because Brunetti's third-person ascriptions of mental states to Murino are successful and accurate. The presentation of Brunetti's whole mind contains elements of characterization (for example, Brunetti's familiarity with the process). All the information on the two minds that is made available in this passage forms part of Brunetti's embedded narrative and also of Murino's. The storyworld is aspectual because we experience Murino from

Brunetti's aspectual point of view. The passage has an important teleological value in that it affects the end of the story. The two characters are engaged in competitive intermental thinking: each is trying to out-think the other. It is clear that Brunetti's embedded narrative contains within it an accurate doubly embedded narrative for Murino. Finally, Murino's identity is situated somewhat closer to Brunetti's view of him than to his own view of himself.

8

Further Applications

I see this book as being the first of a pair. This one constructs the theoretical framework within which the next one will illustrate more fully the whole of the social mind in action. The purpose of this chapter is to describe in outline the proposed content of the second book.

Chapter 1, section 4 referred to a number of issues that could not be considered within the limits of this study but that would benefit from further examination within the perspective that I have advocated. I will briefly discuss two particularly fruitful applications: the historical approach and the implications of some of the counterintuitive aspects of cognitive science. The whole of the social mind in action within fictional texts can be explored further in a number of different directions: for example, how fictional minds are constructed in the first-person novel; how fictional minds are constructed within fictional texts of different historical periods; how fictional minds are constructed within various genres of fiction; how real minds are constructed in historical narrative; how real/fictional minds are constructed in the *roman a clef*; and how fictional minds are constructed in plays and films. This program of study is clearly more than a lifetime's work. Each of these issues deserves separate full-length treatment. The priority that I will now consider in a little detail is the historicized approach toward the constructions of fictional minds within different historical periods.

A possible framework for the diachronic study of fictional minds might consist of the close textual analysis of passages from some examples of the following: the Bible (books from both the Old and New Testament); classical narratives; early modern narratives; eighteenth-century novels; nineteenth-century "classic realist" novels; late-nineteenth-century "reflector" novels; twentieth-century modernist novels; twentieth-century formally conservative novels; and twentieth-century postmodernist novels. The purpose of the study would be to begin to suggest some answers to the following two questions: What are the features of the fictional-mind constructions of a particular historical period that are characteristic of that period and different from other periods? What are the similarities in fictional-mind constructions that obtain across some, most, or all periods? The two questions are equally important. I stress this because it has been the fashion for some time in literary theory to look primarily for the differences between various phenomena. However, cognitive science has shown that it can be equally informative to look also for basic underlying similarities.

This historicized course of study might proceed along the following lines:

(a) It would begin with the study of a wide range of pre-novel and early novel texts in order to see what remained constant and what changed in the presentation of characters' whole minds over a long period of time. The analysis would attempt to show how readers of these narratives build up a sense of characters' minds throughout their full length. It would set out in detail all the evidence that is made available to the reader on characters' embedded narratives. The analysis would then attempt to demonstrate how the plots of these narratives comprise the aggregate of their embedded narratives.

(b) The study would then examine the debate on the formation of the early English novel that is referred to later. This is the point at which the extended use of the direct-access device gave rise to the self-conscious examination of its epistemological and ethical implications.

(c) It would then analyze a small number of classic texts such as *Emma*, *Middlemarch*, and *The Ambassadors* in order to put into practice the methodology described in stage a. The importance of this part of the study is that it would show how narratives work once the full range of naturalized devices is in place and before they become self-consciously problematized.

(d) Finally, the study would be extended to the modernist and postmodernist novel, in order to analyze their highly self-conscious reactions against the norms for mind presentations that were established in the nineteenth century. For example, it may be worth pursuing the notion that postmodernist texts playfully disrupt the causal flow of consciousness, motives, and action that was established as part of the nineteenth-century norm; however, this study would attempt to find out not only what changes were brought about by the modernist and postmodernist programs but also what remained constant in whole mind presentations.

As an example of the sort of historical research that I envisage, I will talk briefly about stage b. The following quotes seem to form the possible basis for a historicized view of the study of the minds presented in the early English novel:

We be men and nat aungels, wherfore we knowe nothinge but by outwarde significations. (Sir Thomas Elyot, quoted in McKeon 1987, 132)

[A series of letters offers] the only natural Opportunity . . . of representing with any Grace those lively and delicate Impressions which *Things present* are known to make upon the Minds of those affected by them. (Samuel Richardson, quoted in McKeon 1987, 414)

It would be an ill office in us to pay a visit to the inmost recesses of his mind, as some scandalous people search into the most secret affairs of their friends, and often pry into their closets and cupboards, only to discover their poverty and meanness to the world. (Henry Fielding, quoted in Watt 1957, 273)

As to the present situation of her mind I shall adhere to the rule of Horace, by not attempting to describe it, from despair of success. (Henry Fielding, quoted in Watt 1957, 273)

It is our province to relate facts, and we shall leave causes to persons of much higher genius. (Henry Fielding, quoted in Watt 1957, 273)

It is not enough that your Designs, nay that your Actions are intrinsically good, you must take Care they shall appear so. If your Inside be never so beautiful, you must preserve a fair Outside too. (Fielding 1995, 93)

Whether the insatiable Curiosity of this good Woman had carried her on to that business, or whether she did it to confirm herself in the good Graces of Mrs *Blifil* . . . I will not determine. (Henry Fielding, quoted in Doody 1996, 147)

She follows the Maxim of Clarissa, of declaring all she thinks to all the people she sees, without refflecting [*sic*] that in this Mortal state of Imperfection Fig leaves are as necessary for our Minds as our Bodies, as tis as indecent to shew all we think as all we have. (Lady Mary Wortley Montague of Harriet Byron, quoted in McKeon 1987, 414)

His was but a knowledge of the outside of a clockwork machine, while yours was that of all the finer springs and movements of the inside. (Samuel Johnson to Sarah Fielding of her brother Henry Fielding, quoted in Spender 1986, 185)

A man must dive into the recesses of the human heart. (Samuel Johnson, quoted in McKeon 1987, 416)

It is a mercy our thoughts are conceald from each other. O if at our social table we could see what passes in each bosom around we would seek dens and caverns to shun human society. (Sir Walter Scott, quoted in Robertson 1994, 165)

I do not mean that Nigel literally said aloud with his bodily organs the words which follow in inverted commas . . . but that I myself choose to present to my dearest reader the picture of my hero's mind, his reflections and resolutions, in the form of a speech, rather than that of a narrative. In other words, I have put his thoughts into language. [It is] the most natural and perhaps the only way of communicating to the spectator what is supposed to be passing in the bosom of [the character]. There are no such soliloquies in nature it is true. . . . In narrative, no doubt, the writer has the alternative of telling that his personages thought so and so, inferred thus and thus, and arrived at such and such a conclusion; but the soliloquy is a more concise and spirited mode of communicating the same information. (Scott 1973, 294–95)

These remarks show that a debate on the presentation of fictional minds existed during and after the formation of the English novel. In the terms used by Michael McKeon in his erudite and deeply impressive study, *The Origins of the English Novel 1600–1740* (1987), the views show a close interest in questions of truth (1987, 20). They raise epistemological concerns about how we can know the contents of other minds and, once they are known, how they can be presented in narrative. They also reveal ethical doubts about whether such information should be presented in this way. The quotes show clear evidence of strong feeling. The inside view of the mind by the narrator is regarded as a potentially powerful and threatening force. It is considered to be strange, unfamiliar, and requiring justification. Later, in the nineteenth century, the device became easier to accept, more familiar, and not requiring justification. It became a convention. The Richardson quote is particularly interesting in its use of the word "natural." On this account, direct access to fictional minds is unnatural. How did it become naturalized?

The debate about how fictional minds can be presented, and also whether or not their contents should be revealed at all, illustrates very clearly McKeon's notion of the fusion of ideology and epistemology in the construction of narrative (1987, 20). However, it is important to establish precisely where Henry Fielding's evident moral outrage is directed: Is he saying that the direct presentation of minds should not be attempted because it is trivial or because it is not possible, or both? One result of Fielding's epistemological and ethical doubts is the large number of explicit paralipses (omissions of information by the narrator) relating to the presentation of the mind in *Tom Jones*. Here are some more examples to add to the ones given earlier: "Whether she really felt any Injury . . . I will not say" (1995, 396); "Whether she had forgiven him or no, I will not determine" (1995, 66); and more generally, "I am not possessed of any Touchstone, which can distinguish the true from the false" (1995, 43); and using the narratorial "we," "we never chuse to assign Motives to the Actions of Men, when there is any Possibility of our being mistaken" (1995, 169). The epistemological skepticism and the ethical doubts are combined in the last remark: the former in the possibility of being mistaken, the latter in the resulting moral obligation not to assign motives. These quotes are not isolated examples. I have identified nearly one hundred paralipses related specifically to fictional minds in *Tom Jones*. However, more analysis is required before it can be said with confidence that they relate to an acknowledgement by the narrator of the uncertain nature of his knowledge about characters' minds as opposed, say, to the author's elaborate sense of irony.

Any study of how the naturalization of the device of direct access to characters' minds developed between the beginning of the early English novel and the assured and mature use of the device by Jane Austen, Elizabeth Gaskell, and George Eliot might focus on the Gothic novel. For example, in Horace Walpole's *The Castle of Otranto* during Isabella's flight from Manfred, the reader is given extended direct access to her mental state and the current of her immediate thoughts, even including some free indirect discourse (1982, 22–28). In view of the date of publication (1764), the question arises as to whether this presentation of her mind was a new development in the narrative fiction of the period. After all, the novel was published only fifteen years after *Tom Jones* (1749). It is necessary to establish whether, given Gothic's obvious interest in states of mind such as fear, anxiety, uncertainty, and curiosity, the Gothic novel played an important part in developing the presentation of the mind in narrative fiction. This might be a rigidly Anglocentric perspective, and so account would need to be taken of parallel, and perhaps earlier, developments in the French novel.

I will conclude this section with a brief note on a specific theoretical issue. Fiction embodies what—in the fields of cognitive psychology, the philosophy of mind, and other cognitive sciences—is known as *folk psychology*. This label is intended to cover our standard, everyday, unthinking, "commonsense" assumptions about how our minds and the minds of others work. Fictional narrators employ folk psychology, and it would be unreasonable to expect novelists to do otherwise. However, some of the real-mind discourses that I have used question some of the basic components of folk psychology. This is a recurring tension and one that is not easy to resolve. It is possible at this stage only to refer to it and to make it explicit. The consciousness debate is concerned not only with folk-psychology notions of how we think but also with more counterintuitive versions of the process. An extreme example of this sort of theorizing is Dennett's argument in *Consciousness Explained* that there is no "Cartesian theatre" in which a unified and single flow of consciousness takes place—what we experience as consciousness is merely an amalgam of the various "multiple drafts" that are produced across all of the different regions of the whole brain. As soon as we become accustomed to this sensation, we experience it as a continuity of consciousness. Further thought needs to be given to whether or not there is a place for such obviously non-folk-psychological ideas in an analysis of fictional minds. For example, it might be that fictional-mind constructions in both the modernist and postmodernist novel are, as Dennett himself suggests, interestingly consistent with his ideas.

Another counterintuitive cognitive science theory that has implications for a study of fictional minds concerns what is termed the *fundamental attribution error* (FAE). I said in chapter 2 that the rich and complex relationship between dispositions and specific contexts, events, and so on is at the heart of the value of novel reading. We ask ourselves continually, Given the sort of disposition that this particular character has, how will he or she react in this specific situation? However, the FAE theory casts doubt on our accuracy in weighing up the relative importance of disposition and context when attempting to predict characters' reactions. The FAE is "the tendency of observers to overestimate how much another's behavior is determined by the person's stable traits" (Morris, Ames, and Knowles 1999, 46). That is, we tend to overestimate the importance of a person's character in finding an explanation for the way in which they behave in a particular situation and underestimate the importance of the situation that they are in. Put crudely, the implication of the FAE is that different sorts of people in the same situation tend to behave in the same way; and the same sorts of people in different situations tend to behave in different ways. It is interesting to note, given that the novel is characteristic of Western culture, that "findings that the FAE is stronger in Western, individualistic societies than in collectivist societies such as China seem to reflect different lay theories about the autonomy of individuals relative to social groups" (Morris, Ames, and Knowles 1999, 47). The FAE is an unsettling finding for literary criticism and narrative theory, both of which tend to be based on the assumption that characters behave in the way that they do because of the personalities that they have. It is not often while reading a novel that we say, "Well, anyone would have done what she did!" We are more likely to say, "Well, that's typical of her to do that!" In any event, what are the implications of the FAE? Does the whole practice of novel reading reinforce the error? Is that a bad thing? Obviously I do not have answers to these questions, but perhaps they are worth mentioning at this point in order to acknowledge that the relationship between the cognitive sciences and narrative theory might not all be plain sailing.

Conclusion

In one sense, as R. D. Laing says, we are invisible to each other. In another sense, the activities of our minds are perfectly visible to others in our actions. The reader's experience of the minds of characters in novels does not depend solely on the strange device of the narrator giving direct access to the inner workings of fictional consciousnesses. Just as in real life the individual constructs the minds of others from their behavior, so the reader infers the workings of fictional minds and sees these minds in action from observation of characters' behavior and actions. Novels contain a wide variety of material or evidence on which readers base their conjectures, hypotheses, and predictions about fictional minds. The importance of the new perspectives suggested in this book is that in various ways fictional minds are seen not as private, passive flows of consciousness, but as engaged, social processes of mental action. The concept of embedded narratives is a key mediational tool with which to analyze this aspect of fictional minds. In particular, I have argued that one of the most important of the frames used by readers to understand texts is the continuing-consciousness frame. I have focused on three neglected subframes: thought and action, intermental thought, and doubly embedded narratives. I have also attempted to show that analysis of a number of sub-subframes can reveal how much information on fictional minds is available to the reader even within a behaviorist narrative such as *Vile Bodies*. I conclude by suggesting that what is now required is the application of this approach to a wide range of other texts. It is possible that these devices are significant constituents of all narrative discourses, but further work on this point is required. When the social mind exists for those who would explain it, narrative theory will understand better how characters do and undergo things in the storyworld and how mental processes take place in their natural habitat of the houseyard, the marketplace, and the town square because these are the places in which the fictional mind extends beyond the fictional skin.

Sometimes you read a book that contains arguments that are ingenious. You think I am not sure that I followed it all, but I am sure that it must be right. In any event, I certainly cannot think of any objections to it. The person who wrote it must be brilliant because it was quite difficult to follow in several places.

I would never have thought of it myself. My one concern is that it seemed a little contingent, a little arbitrary. What I mean is that I cannot rid myself of the feeling that a completely different line of argument could have been presented that would have seemed just as plausible.

But at other times you read a book that is very different. Its argument is so overwhelmingly convincing that you think I kind-of knew that already! Or at least, it feels now as though on some level or other I always knew it, even though I had never articulated it to myself. In any event, having read it, it seems so obvious now. It is very odd that, as it now seems so obvious, no one as far as I know has ever said it before. The person who wrote it was very lucky to be in the right place at the right time. The second type of book tends to have a more profound impact than the first. These books often become part of the way that the people who read them think about the subject of the study. People who read them see things a little bit differently. I would like this to be one of those books.

Bibliography

Fiction

Ambler, Eric. 1984. *Epitaph for a Spy*. London: Dent. (Orig. pub. 1938.)

Austen, Jane. 1996. *Emma*. Edited by Ronald Blythe. Harmondsworth, England: Penguin. (Orig. pub. 1816.)

Behn, Aphra. 1994. "The History of a Nun." In *Oroonoko and Other Writings*, edited by Paul Salzman. Oxford: Oxford University Press. (Orig. pub. 1689.)

Conan Doyle, Arthur. 1981. *The Penguin Complete Sherlock Holmes*. Harmondsworth, England: Penguin.

Connelly, Michael. 1993. *Black Echo*. Boston: St Martin's.

Dick, Philip K. 1999. *Do Androids Dream of Electric Sheep?* London: Millennium. (Orig. pub. 1969.)

Dickens, Charles. 1965. *Great Expectations*. Edited by Angus Calder. Harmondsworth, England: Penguin. (Orig. pub. 1861.)

———. 1971. *Bleak House*. Edited by Norman Page. Harmondsworth, England: Penguin. (Orig. pub. 1853.)

———. 1995. *Hard Times*. Edited by Kate Flint. Harmondsworth, England: Penguin. (Orig. pub. 1854.)

Eliot, George. 1977. *Middlemarch*. Edited by Bert G. Hornback. New York: Norton. (Orig. pub. 1872.)

———. 1996. *Adam Bede*. Edited by Valentine Cunningham. Oxford: Oxford University Press. (Orig. pub. 1859.)

Fielding, Henry. 1995. *Tom Jones*. 2d ed. Edited by Sheridan Baker. New York: Norton. (Orig. pub. 1749.)

Flaubert, Gustave. 1950. *Madame Bovary*. Translated by Alan Russell. Harmondsworth, England: Penguin. (Orig. pub. 1857.)

Highsmith, Patricia. 1968. *Strangers on a Train*. London: Pan. (Orig. pub. 1949.)

Joyce, James. 1986. *Ulysses*. Corrected edition. Edited by Hans Walter Gabler. Harmondsworth, England: Penguin. (Orig. pub. 1922.)

Leon, Donna. 1996. *Acqua Alta*. London: Macmillan.

———. 1997. *The Death of Faith*. London: Macmillan.

———. 2001. *A Sea of Troubles*. London: Heinemann.

Lewis, Matthew. 1998. *The Monk*. Edited by Christopher Maclachlan. Harmondsworth, England: Penguin. (Orig. pub. 1796.)

Lodge, David. 2001. *Thinks . . . .* London: Secker and Warburg.

Pears, Iain. 2000. *Giotto's Hand*. London: HarperCollins.

Proust, Marcel. 1996. *Swann's Way*. Translated by C. K. Scott Moncreiff and Terence Kilmartin. Revised by D. J. Enright. London: Vintage. (Orig. pub. 1922.)

Pynchon, Thomas. 1996. *The Crying of Lot 49*. London: Vintage. (Orig. pub. 1966.)

Scott, Sir Walter. 1973. *The Fortunes of Nigel*. St. Albans, England: Panther. (Orig. pub. 1822.)

———. 1975. *Old Mortality*. Edited by Angus Calder. Harmondsworth, England: Penguin. (Orig. pub. 1816.)

———. 1995. *Rob Roy*. Edited by John Sutherland. Harmondsworth, England: Penguin. (Orig. pub. 1817.)

Thackeray, William Makepeace. 1994. *Vanity Fair*. Edited by Peter L. Shillingsburg. New York: Norton. (Orig. pub. 1848.)

Thompson, Jim. 2002. *The Getaway*. London: Orion. (Orig. pub. 1958.)

Walpole, Horace. 1982. *The Castle of Otranto*. Edited by W. S. Lewis. Oxford: Oxford University Press. (Orig. pub. 1764.)

Waugh, Evelyn. 1964. *Men at Arms*. Harmondsworth, England: Penguin. (Orig. pub. 1952.)

———. 1996. *Vile Bodies*. Harmondsworth, England: Penguin. (Orig. pub. 1930).

Wharton, Edith. 1979. *The House of Mirth*. Harmondsworth, England: Penguin. (Orig. pub. 1903.)

White, Edmund. 2001. *The Married Man*. London: Vintage.

Theoretical Sources

Aczel, Richard. 1998. "Hearing Voices in Narrative Texts." *New Literary History* 29: 467–500.

Au, Terry. 1999. "Language and Thought." In *The MIT Encyclopedia of the Cognitive Sciences*, edited by Robert A. Wilson and Frank C. Keil. Cambridge: MIT Press.

Auerbach, Erich. 1953. *Mimesis: The Representation of Reality in Western Literature*. Translated by Willard R. Trask. Princeton: Princeton University Press.

Bakhtin, Mikhail. 1981. *The Dialogic Imagination*. Translated by Caryl Emerson and Michael Holquist. Austin: University of Texas Press.

————. 1984. *Problems of Dostoevsky's Poetics*. Translated by Caryl Emerson. Manchester: Manchester University Press.

Bal, Mieke. 1997. *Narratology: Introduction to the Theory of Narrative*. 2d ed. Toronto: University of Toronto Press.

Baldick, Chris. 1996. *Criticism and Literary Theory 1890 to the Present*. London: Longman.

Banfield, Ann. 1982. *Unspeakable Sentences: Narration and Representation in the Language of Fiction*. Boston: Routledge.

Barnden, John A. 1995. "Simulative Reasoning, Common-Sense Psychology, and Artificial Intelligence." In *Mental Simulation: Evaluations and Applications*, edited by Martin Davies and Tony Stone. Oxford: Blackwell.

Barthes, Roland. 1990. *S/Z*. Translated by Richard Miller. Oxford: Blackwell.

Bateson, Gregory. 1972. *Steps to an Ecology of Mind: A Revolutionary Approach to Man's Understanding of Himself*. New York: Ballantine.

Bickerton, Derek. 1967. "Modes of Interior Monologue: A Formal Definition." *Modern Language Quarterly* 28: 229–39.

Blackburn, Simon. 1994. *The Oxford Dictionary of Philosophy*. Oxford: Oxford University Press.

Bolton, Derek. 1995. "Self-Knowledge, Error and Disorder." In *Mental Simulation: Evaluations and Applications*, edited by Martin Davies and Tony Stone. Oxford: Blackwell.

Bonheim, Helmut. 1982. *The Narrative Modes: Techniques of the Short Story*. Cambridge, England: Brewer.

Booth, Wayne C. 1987. *The Rhetoric of Fiction*. 2d ed. Harmondsworth, England: Penguin.

Bremond, Claude. 1973. *Logique du Récit*. Paris: Seuil.

Brewer, William F. 1999. "Schemata." In *The MIT Encyclopedia of the Cognitive Sciences*, edited by Robert A. Wilson and Frank C. Keil. Cambridge: MIT Press.

Brinton, Laurel. 1980. "Represented Perception: A Study in Narrative Style." *Poetics* 9: 363–81.

Brothers, Leslie. 1999. "Emotion and the Human Brain." In *The MIT Encyclopedia of the Cognitive Sciences*, edited by Robert A. Wilson and Frank C. Keil. Cambridge: MIT Press.

Chatman, Seymour. 1978. *Story and Discourse: Narrative Structure in Fiction and Film*. Ithaca NY: Cornell University Press.

Chomsky, Noam. 1965. *Aspects of the Theory of Syntax*. Cambridge: MIT Press.

Clark, Andy, and David J. Chalmers. 1998. "The Extended Mind." *Analysis* 58: 7–19.

Cohn, Dorrit. 1978. *Transparent Minds: Narrative Modes for Presenting Consciousness in Fiction*. Princeton: Princeton University Press.

———. 1999. *The Distinction of Fiction*. Baltimore MD: Johns Hopkins University Press.

Coward, Rosalind, and John Ellis. 1977. *Language and Materialism: Developments in Semiology and the Theory of the Subject*. London: Routledge.

Culler, Jonathan. 1975. *Structuralist Poetics: Structuralism, Linguistics, and the Study of Literature*. London: Routledge.

———. 1980. "Fabula and Sjuzhet in the Analysis of Narrative: Some American Discussions." *Poetics Today* 1 (3): 27–37.

Damasio, Antonio. 2000. *The Feeling of What Happens: Body, Emotion and the Making of Consciousness*. London: Heinemann.

Davies, Martin. 1999. "Consciousness." In *The MIT Encyclopedia of the Cognitive Sciences*, edited by Robert A. Wilson and Frank C. Keil. Cambridge: MIT Press.

Davies, Martin, and Tony Stone. 1995. "Introduction." In *Mental Simulation: Evaluations and Applications*, edited by Martin Davies and Tony Stone. Oxford: Blackwell.

Dennett, Daniel C. 1991. *Consciousness Explained*. Harmondsworth, England: Penguin.

———. 1996. *Kinds of Minds: Towards an Understanding of Consciousness*. London: Weidenfeld and Nicholson.

Descartes, René. 1998. *Meditations and Other Metaphysical Writings*. Translated by Desmond M. Clarke. Harmondsworth, England: Penguin.

Dillon, George L., and Frederick Kirchhoff. 1976. "On the Form and Function of Free Indirect Style." *PTL* 1 (3): 431–40.

Doležel, Lubomír. 1988. "Mimesis and Possible Worlds." *Poetics Today* 9 (3): 475–96.

———. 1995. "Fictional Worlds: Density, Gaps, and Inference." *Style* 29 (2): 201–14.

———. 1998. *Heterocosmica—Fiction and Possible Worlds*. Baltimore MD: Johns Hopkins University Press.

Doody, Margaret Anne. 1996. *The True Story of the Novel*. London: Harper-Collins.

Dry, Helen. 1977. "Syntax and Point of View in Jane Austen's *Emma.*" *Studies in Romanticism* 16 (1): 87–99.

Duncan, Susan. 1999. "Language and Communication." In *The MIT Encyclopedia of the Cognitive Sciences*, edited by Robert A. Wilson and Frank C. Keil. Cambridge: MIT Press.

Eagleton, Terry. 1983. *Literary Theory: An Introduction.* Oxford: Blackwell.

Eco, Umberto. 1981. *The Role of the Reader: Explorations in the Semiotics of Texts.* London: Hutchinson.

Ehrlich, Susan. 1990. *Point of View: A Linguistic Analysis of Literary Style.* London: Routledge.

Ellis, Andrew, and Geoffrey Beattie. 1986. *The Psychology of Language and Communication.* Hove and London: Erlbaum.

Elster, Jon. 1999. *Alchemies of the Mind: Rationality and the Emotions.* Cambridge: Cambridge University Press.

Emmott, Catherine. 1997. *Narrative Comprehension: A Discourse Perspective.* Oxford: Clarendon.

Fauconnier, Gilles. 1997. *Mappings in Thought and Language.* Cambridge: Cambridge University Press.

Flavin, Louise. 1987. "*Mansfield Park*: Free Indirect Discourse and the Psychological Novel." *Studies in the Novel* 19: 137–59.

Fludernik, Monika. 1993. *The Fictions of Language and the Languages of Fiction: The Linguistic Representation of Speech and Consciousness.* London: Routledge.

———. 1996. *Towards a "Natural" Narratology.* London: Routledge.

Forster, E. M. 2000. *Aspects of the Novel.* Harmondsworth, England: Penguin.

Freeman, Norman H. 1995. "Theories of the Mind in Collision: Plausibility and Authority." In *Mental Simulation: Evaluations and Applications*, edited by Martin Davies and Tony Stone. Oxford: Blackwell.

Frege, Gottlob. 1970. "On Sense and Reference." In *Translations from the Philosophical Writings of Gottlob Frege*, edited by P. Geach and M. Black. Oxford: Blackwell.

Friedman, Melvin. 1955. *Stream of Consciousness: A Study in Literary Method.* New Haven CT: Yale University Press.

Geertz, Clifford. 1993. *The Interpretation of Cultures: Selected Essays.* London: Fontana.

Genette, Gerard. 1980. *Narrative Discourse: An Essay in Method.* Translated by Jane E. Lewin. Ithaca NY: Cornell University Press.

————. 1988. *Narrative Discourse Revisited.* Translated by Jane E. Lewin. Ithaca NY: Cornell University Press.

Gerrig, Richard J. 1993. *Experiencing Narrative Worlds: On the Psychological Activities of Reading.* New Haven CT Yale University Press.

Ginsburg, Ruth, and Shlomith Rimmon-Kenan. 1999. "Is There a Life after Death? Theorizing Authors and Reading *Jazz.*" In *Narratologies: New Perspectives on Narrative Analysis,* edited by David Herman. Columbus: Ohio State University Press.

Goldman, Alvin J. 1995. "Empathy, Mind, and Morals." In *Mental Simulation: Evaluations and Applications,* edited by Martin Davies and Tony Stone. Oxford: Blackwell.

Gopnik, Alison. 1999. "Theory of Mind." In *The MIT Encyclopedia of the Cognitive Sciences,* edited by Robert A. Wilson and Frank C. Keil. Cambridge: MIT Press.

Gordon, Robert M. 1999. "Simulation vs. Theory-Theory." In *The MIT Encyclopedia of the Cognitive Sciences,* edited by Robert A. Wilson and Frank C. Keil. Cambridge: MIT Press.

Greimas, A. J. 1983. *Structural Semantics: An Attempt at a Method.* Lincoln: University of Nebraska Press.

Habermas, Jürgen. 1984. *The Theory of Communicative Action.* Vol. 1. Translated by Thomas McCarthy. Boston: Beacon.

Heal, Jane. 1995. "How to Think About Thinking." In *Mental Simulation: Evaluations and Applications,* edited by Martin Davies and Tony Stone. Oxford: Blackwell.

Hegel, Georg Wilhelm Friedrich. 1931. *The Phenomenology of Mind.* 2d ed. Translated by J. B. Baillie. London: Allen and Unwin.

Herman, David. 1997. "Scripts, Sequences, and Stories: Elements of a Postclassical Narratology." PMLA 112 (5): 1046–59.

————. 1999a. "Introduction: Narratologies." In *Narratologies: New Perspectives on Narrative Analysis,* edited by David Herman. Columbus: Ohio State University Press.

————. 1999b. "Towards a Socionarratology: New Ways of Analyzing Natural-Language Narratives." In *Narratologies: New Perspectives on Narrative Analysis,* edited by David Herman. Columbus: Ohio State University Press.

————. 2002. *Story Logic: Problems and Possibilities of Narrative.* Lincoln: University of Nebraska Press.

————, ed. 2003a. *Narrative Theory and the Cognitive Sciences.* Stanford CA: CSLI Publications.

————. 2003b. "Stories as a Tool for Thinking." In *Narrative Theory and the Cognitive Sciences*, edited by David Herman. Stanford CA: CSLI Publications.

Hernadi, Paul. 1972. "Dual Perspective: Free Indirect Discourse and Related Techniques." *Comparative Literature* 24: 32–43.

Hirschfeld, Lawrence A. 1999. "Naïve Sociology." In *The MIT Encyclopedia of the Cognitive Sciences*, edited by Robert A. Wilson and Frank C. Keil. Cambridge: MIT Press.

Holyoak, Keith J. 1999. "Psychology." In *The MIT Encyclopedia of the Cognitive Sciences*, edited by Robert A. Wilson and Frank C. Keil. Cambridge: MIT Press.

Hutchins, Edwin. 1995. *Cognition in the Wild*. Cambridge: MIT Press.

————. 1999. "Cognitive Artifacts." 1999. In *The MIT Encyclopedia of the Cognitive Sciences*, edited by Robert A. Wilson and Frank C. Keil. Cambridge: MIT Press.

Ingarden, Roman. 1973. *The Literary Work of Art: An Investigation on the Borderlines of Ontology, Logic, and Theory of Literature*. Translated by George C. Grabowicz. Evanston IL: Northwestern University Press.

Iser, Wolfgang. 1978. *The Act of Reading*. London: Routledge.

Jackendoff, Ray. 1983. *Semantics and Cognition*. Cambridge: MIT Press.

Jahn, Manfred. 1983. "Narration as Non-communication: On Ann Banfield's *Unspeakable Sentences*." Available from *http://www.uni-koeln.de/~ame02/jahn83.htm*.

————. 1992. "Contextualizing Represented Speech and Thought." *Journal of Pragmatics* 17: 347–67.

————. 1997. "Frames, Preferences, and the Reading of Third Person Narratives: Towards a Cognitive Narratology." *Poetics Today* 18 (4): 441–68.

————. 1999a. "'Speak, friend, and enter': Garden Paths, Artificial Intelligence, and Cognitive Narratology." In *Narratologies: New Perspectives on Narrative Analysis*, edited by David Herman. Columbus: Ohio State University Press.

————. 1999b. "Stanley Fish and the Constructivist Basis of Postclassical Narratology." Available from *http://www.uni-koeln.de/~ame02/jahn99xa.htm*.

————. 1999c. "More Aspects of Focalization: Refinements and Applications." Available from *http://www.uni-koeln.de/~ame02/jahn99b.htm*.

James, William. 1981. *The Principles of Psychology*. Vol. 1. Cambridge: Harvard University Press.

Johnson-Laird, Philip N. 1999. "Mental Models." In *The MIT Encyclopedia of the Cognitive Sciences*, edited by Robert A. Wilson and Frank C. Keil. Cambridge: MIT Press.

Kosslyn, Stephen M., and Carolyn S. Rabin. 1999. "Imagery." In *The MIT Encyclopedia of the Cognitive Sciences*, edited by Robert A. Wilson and Frank C. Keil. Cambridge: MIT Press.

Kripke, Saul. 1980. *Naming and Necessity*. Oxford: Blackwell.

Laing, R. D. 1967. *The Politics of Experience and the Bird of Paradise*. Harmondsworth, England: Penguin.

Leech, Geoffrey, and Michael Short. 1981. *Style in Fiction: A Linguistic Introduction to English Fictional Prose*. London: Longman.

Lewis, David. 1973. *Counterfactuals*. Cambridge: Harvard University Press.

Lodge, David. 1990. *After Bakhtin: Essays on Fiction and Criticism*. London: Routledge.

———. 2002. *Consciousness and the Novel: Connected Essays*. London: Secker and Warburg.

Lubbock, Percy. 1921. *The Craft of Fiction*. London: Jonathan Cape.

Luria, Alexander. 1982. *Language and Cognition*. New York: Wiley.

Maloney, J. Christopher. 1999. "Functionalism." In *The MIT Encyclopedia of the Cognitive Sciences*, edited by Robert A. Wilson and Frank C. Keil. Cambridge: MIT Press.

Margolin, Uri. 1986. "The Doer and the Deed: Action as a Basis for Characterization in Narrative." *Poetics Today* 7(2): 205–25.

———. 1987. "Introducing and Sustaining Characters in Literary Narrative: A Set of Conditions." *Style* 21 (1): 107–24.

———. 1989. "Structuralist Approaches to Character in Narrative: The State of the Art." *Semiotica* 75(1–2): 1–24.

———. 1990. "Individuals in Narrative Worlds: An Ontological Perspective." *Poetics Today* 11 (4): 843–71.

———. 1995a. "Changing Individuals in Narrative: Science, Philosophy, Literature." *Semiotica* 107 (1–2): 5–31.

———. 1995b. "Characters in Literary Narrative: Representation and Signification." *Semiotica* 106 (3–4): 373–92.

———. 1996a. "Characters and their Versions." In *Fiction Updated: Theories of Fictionality, Narratology, and Poetics*, edited by Calin-Andrei Mihailescu and Walid Hamarneh. Toronto: Toronto University Press.

———. 1996b. "Telling Our Story: On 'We' Literary Narratives." *Language and Literature* 5 (2): 115–33.

———. 2000. "Telling in the Plural: From Grammar to Ideology." *Poetics Today* 21 (3): 591–618.

———. 2003. "Cognitive Science, the Thinking Mind, and Literary Narrative."

In *Narrative Theory and the Cognitive Sciences*, edited by David Herman. Stanford CA: CSLI Publications.

McCrone, John. 1999. *Going Inside: A Tour Round a Single Moment of Consciousness*. London: Faber.

McHale, Brian. 1978. "Free Indirect Discourse: A Survey of Recent Accounts." PTL 3: 249–87.

―――. 1981. "Islands in the Stream of Consciousness: Dorrit Cohn's *Transparent Minds*." *Poetics Today* 2 (2): 183–91.

―――. 1983. "Unspeakable Sentences, Unnatural Acts: Linguistics and Poetics Revisited." *Poetics Today* 4 (1): 17–45.

McKeon, Michael. 1987. *The Origins of the English Novel, 1600 to 1740*. Baltimore MD: Johns Hopkins University Press.

―――, ed. 2000. *Theory of the Novel: A Historical Approach*. Baltimore MD: Johns Hopkins University Press.

Morris, Michael W., Daniel Ames, and Eric Knowles. 1999. "Attribution Theory." In *The MIT Encyclopedia of the Cognitive Sciences*, edited by Robert A. Wilson and Frank C. Keil. Cambridge: MIT Press.

Nagel, Thomas. 1974. "What Is It Like to Be a Bat?" *The Philosophical Review* 83 (4): 435–50.

Nebel, Bernhard. 1999. "Frame-Based Systems." In *The MIT Encyclopedia of the Cognitive Sciences*, edited by Robert A. Wilson and Frank C. Keil. Cambridge: MIT Press.

Neumann, Anne Waldron. 1986. "Characterization and Comment in *Pride and Prejudice*: Free Indirect Discourse and 'Double Voiced' Verbs of Speaking, Thinking, and Feeling." *Style* 20 (3): 364–94.

Oatley, Keith. 1999. "Emotions." In *The MIT Encyclopedia of the Cognitive Sciences*, edited by Robert A. Wilson and Frank C. Keil. Cambridge: MIT Press.

Onega, Susana, and José Angel Garcia Landa, eds. 1996. *Narratology: An Introduction*. London: Longman.

O'Neill, Patrick. 1994. *The Fictions of Discourse: Reading Narrative Theory*. Toronto: University of Toronto Press.

O'Shaughnessy, Brian. 1997. "Trying (as the Mental 'Pineal Gland')." In *The Philosophy of Action*, edited by Alfred R. Mele. Oxford: Oxford University Press.

Parkin, Alan. 2000. *Essential Cognitive Psychology*. Hove: Psychology Press.

Pascal, Roy. 1977. *The Dual Voice: Free Indirect Speech and Its Functioning in the Nineteenth Century European Novel*. Manchester: Manchester University Press.

Pavel, Thomas G. 1986. *Fictional Worlds.* Cambridge: Harvard University Press.

Perry, Menakhem. 1979. "Literary Dynamics: How the Order of a Text Creates its Meanings." *Poetics Today* 1 (1–2): 35–64, 311–61.

Pinker, Steven. 1994. *The Language Instinct: The New Science of Language and Mind.* Harmondsworth, England: Penguin.

———. 1997. *How the Mind Works.* Harmondsworth, England: Penguin.

Poulet, Georges. 1955. "The Circle and the Centre: Reality and *Madame Bovary.*" *Western Review* 19: 245–60.

———. 1969. "Phenomenology of Reading." *New Literary History* 1 (1): 53–68.

Priest, Stephen. 1991. *Theories of the Mind.* Harmondsworth, England: Penguin.

Prince, Gerald. 1982. *Narratology: The Form and Functioning of Narrative.* Berlin: Mouton.

———. 1987. *A Dictionary of Narratology.* London: Scolar.

———. 1996. "Narratology, Narratological Criticism, and Gender." In *Fiction Updated: Theories of Fictionality, Narratology, and Poetics,* edited by Calin-Andrei Mihailescu and Walid Hamarneh. Toronto: Toronto University Press.

Propp, Vladimir. 1968. *Morphology of the Folktale.* Translated by Laurence Scott. Austin: University of Texas Press.

Ramirez, Juan D. 1992. "The Functional Differentiation of Social and Private Speech: A Dialogic Approach." In *Private Speech: From Social Interaction to Self-Regulation,* edited by Rafael Diaz and Laura Berk. Hove and London: Erlbaum.

Reed, Edward S. 1996. *Encountering the World: Towards an Ecological Psychology.* Oxford: Oxford University Press.

Ricoeur, Paul. 1984. *Time and Narrative.* Vol. 1. Translated by Kathleen McLaughlin and David Pellauer. Chicago: University of Chicago Press.

Rimmon-Kenan, Shlomith. 1983. *Narrative Fiction: Contemporary Poetics.* London: Routledge.

Robertson, Fiona. 1994. *Legitimate Histories: Scott, Gothic, and the Authorities of Fiction.* Oxford: Clarendon.

Ron, Moshe. 1981. "Free Indirect Discourse, Mimetic Language Games and the Subject of Fiction." *Poetics Today* 2 (2): 17–39.

Ronen, Ruth. 1988. "Completing the Incompleteness of Fictional Entities." *Poetics Today* 9 (3): 497–514.

———. 1994. *Possible Worlds in Literary Theory.* Cambridge: Cambridge University Press.

Rosenthal, David M. 1999. "Introspection." In *The MIT Encyclopedia of the Cog-*

nitive Sciences, edited by Robert A. Wilson and Frank C. Keil. Cambridge: MIT Press.

Russell, Bertrand. 1940. *An Enquiry into Meaning and Truth.* London: Allen and Unwin.

Ryan, Marie-Laure. 1985. "The Modal Structure of Narrative Universes." *Poetics Today* 6 (4): 717–55.

———. 1986. "Embedded Narratives and Tellability." *Style* 20: 319–40.

———. 1991. *Possible Worlds, Artificial Intelligence, and Narrative Theory.* Bloomington: Indiana University Press.

———. 1997. "Postmodernism and the Doctrine of Panfictionality." *Narrative* 5 (2): 165–87.

Ryle, Gilbert. 1963. *The Concept of Mind.* Harmondsworth, England: Peregrine.

Schank, Roger C., and Robert P. Abelson. 1977. *Scripts, Plans, Goals, and Understanding: An Inquiry into Human Knowledge Structures.* Hillsdale NJ: Erlbaum.

Searle, John R. 1992. *The Rediscovery of the Mind.* Cambridge: MIT Press.

Seifert, Colleen M. 1999. "Situated Cognition and Learning." In *The MIT Encyclopedia of the Cognitive Sciences,* edited by Robert A. Wilson and Frank C. Keil. Cambridge: MIT Press.

Short, Michael, Elena Semino, and Jonathan Culpeper. 1996. "Using a Corpus for Stylistics Research: Speech and Thought Presentation." In *Using Corpora in Language Research,* edited by Jenny Thomas and Michael Short. London: Longman.

Skinner, B. F. 1964. "Behaviorism at Fifty." In *Behaviorism and Phenomenology: Contrasting Bases for Modern Psychology,* edited by T. W. Wann. Chicago: University of Chicago Press.

Smith, Brian Cantwell. 1999. "Situatedness/Embeddedness." In *The MIT Encyclopedia of the Cognitive Sciences,* edited by Robert A. Wilson and Frank C. Keil. Cambridge: MIT Press.

Sparshott, F. E. 1967. "Truth in Fiction." *Journal of Aesthetics and Art Criticism* 26: 3–7.

Spender, Dale. 1986. *Mothers of the Novel: 100 Good Women Writers Before Jane Austen.* London: Pandora.

Sperber, Dan, and Lawrence Hirschfeld. 1999. "Culture, Cognition, and Evolution." In *The MIT Encyclopedia of the Cognitive Sciences,* edited by Robert A. Wilson and Frank C. Keil. Cambridge: MIT Press.

Stanzel, Franz. 1984. *A Theory of Narrative*. Translated by Charlotte Goedsche. Cambridge: Cambridge University Press.

Sterelny, Kim. 1999. "Language of Thought." In *The MIT Encyclopedia of the Cognitive Sciences*, edited by Robert A. Wilson and Frank C. Keil. Cambridge: MIT Press.

Sternberg, Meir. 1982. "Proteus in Quotation-Land: Mimesis and the Forms of Reported Discourse." *Poetics Today* 3 (2): 107–56.

———. 2001. "How Narrativity Makes a Difference." *Narrative* 9 (2): 115–22.

Strawson, Galen. 1997. "The Self." *Journal of Consciousness Studies*. 4 (5–6): 405–28.

Strawson, P. F. 1959. *Individuals: An Essay in Descriptive Metaphysics*. London: Methuen.

Todorov, Tzvetan. 1977. *Poetics of Prose*. Ithaca NY Cornell University Press.

Trevarthen, Colwyn. 1999. "Intersubjectivity." In *The MIT Encyclopedia of the Cognitive Sciences*, edited by Robert A. Wilson and Frank C. Keil. Cambridge: MIT Press.

Turner, Mark. 1991. *Reading Minds: The Study of English in the Age of Cognitive Science*. Princeton: Princeton University Press.

———. 1996. *The Literary Mind*. Oxford: Oxford University Press.

van Dijk, Teun A. 1976. "Philosophy of Action and Theory of Narrative." *Poetics* 5: 287–338.

van Gulick, Robert. 1999. "Self-Knowledge." In *The MIT Encyclopedia of the Cognitive Sciences*, edited by Robert A. Wilson and Frank C. Keil. Cambridge: MIT Press.

Volosinov, Valentin. 1973. *Marxism and the Philosophy of Language*. Translated by Ladislav Matejka and I. R. Titunik. London: Seminar.

Vygotsky, Lev. 1986. *Thought and Language*. Translated by Alex Kozulin. Cambridge: MIT Press.

Watt, Ian. 1957. *The Rise of the Novel*. London: Hogarth.

Weinberg, Henry H. 1984. "Centers of Consciousness Reconsidered." *Poetics Today* 5 (4): 767–73.

Werth, Paul. 1999. *Text Worlds: Representing Conceptual Space in Discourse*. London: Longman.

Wertsch, James V. 1991. *Voices of the Mind: A Sociocultural Approach to Mediated Action*. Cambridge: Harvard University Press.

———. 1999. "Vygotsky, Lev Semenovich." In *The MIT Encyclopedia of the Cognitive Sciences*, edited by Robert A. Wilson and Frank C. Keil. Cambridge: MIT Press.

White, Geoffrey. 1999. "Ethnopsychology." In *The MIT Encyclopedia of the Cognitive Sciences*, edited by Robert A. Wilson and Frank C. Keil. Cambridge: MIT Press.

White, Hayden. 1978. *Tropics of Discourse: Essays in Cultural Criticism*. Baltimore MD: Johns Hopkins University Press.

———. 1987. *The Content of the Form: Narrative Discourse and Historical Representation*. Baltimore MD: Johns Hopkins University Press.

White, Stephen L. 1999. "Self." In *The MIT Encyclopedia of the Cognitive Sciences*, edited by Robert A. Wilson and Frank C. Keil. Cambridge: MIT Press.

Wilson, Robert A. 1999a. "Individualism." In *The MIT Encyclopedia of the Cognitive Sciences*, edited by Robert A. Wilson and Frank C. Keil, Cambridge: MIT Press.

———. 1999b. "Philosophy." In *The MIT Encyclopedia of the Cognitive Sciences*, edited by Robert A. Wilson and Frank C. Keil, Cambridge: MIT Press.

Wilson, Robert A., and Frank C. Keil. eds. 1999. *The MIT Encyclopedia of the Cognitive Sciences*. Cambridge: MIT Press.

Wittgenstein, Ludwig. 1958. *Philosophical Investigations*. Oxford: Blackwell.

———. 1974. *Tractatus Logico-Philosophicus*. Translated by D. F. Pears and B. F. McGuinness. London: Routledge.

Index

Numbers in italics refer to definitions of terms or to particularly important examples of their use.

Austen, Jane, 59–60, 199, 215, 244; *Emma*, 1–2, 4, 18, 35, 60, 112–16, 119–20, 131, 141, 145, 158, 170–75, 183–84, 190–92, 198–99, 203, 215, 231, 233, 241; *Pride and Prejudice*, 97, 158–59
authentic novel, 153
author, 16, 21, 67, 75, 244; implied, *16–17*, 45, 228
autism, 138, 199; and Asperger's syndrome, 138

Bakhtin, Mikhail, 15, 84, 141, 147–48, 152–57, 163, 174, 187, 221, 225, 227, 234
Baldick, Chris, 22
Bal, Mieke, 17, 30, 36–37, 48–49, 51, 63–64, 179–80
Balzac, Honoré de: *Eugenie Grandet*, 160
Banfield, Ann, 26–27, 63, 65, 72, 105–6, 123, 132
Barnden, John A., 110
Barthes, Roland, 37, 39
Bateson, Gregory, 11, 157
Beattie, Geoffrey, 93
behavior. *See* action
behaviorism, 10, 108, 124, 139–40, *206*
behaviorist narrative, 41, 48, 140, 206–7, 246
Behn, Aphra, 25, 58; "The History of a Nun," 165–67
beliefs, 46, 113, 116, 133, 143; and action, 19, 118–20, 178; and characters' epistemic worlds, 91, 194–96, 232–33; and embedded narratives, 183, 188, 192; and mental action, 106–7, 109, 177; and social mind, 153, 155, 161–62, 219, 224; and speech categories, 72–73, 207; and states of mind, 13, 19, 38, 53, 58, 67, 81–82, 173, 238
Benedict, Ruth, 117
Bible, 22, 240
Bickerton, Derek, 60, 63, 66–67, 78

Bildungsroman, 197
Blackburn, Simon, 97
Boccaccio, Giovanni: *The Decameron*, 210
body: and action, 118–19, 122, 223; and ascription, 128, 131–32, 140; and sensations, 99, 104; and social mind, 134, 242
Bolton, Derek, 146
Bonheim, Helmut, 65, 74
Booth, Wayne C., 17, 33, 68, 210, 216
brain, 4, 93–96, 117, 147, 179; and cognitive science, 44–45, 88–90, 108, 135; physical composition of, 105, 111, 119, 160, 245
Bremond, Claude, 28
Brewer, William F., 46
Brinton, Laurel, 63
Brothers, Leslie, 115
Byron, Harriet, 242

Camus, Albert: *L'Etranger*, 117
canonical novels, 23, 25, 188, 240–41
Cartesianism, 97, *127*, 139–40, 144, 245. *See also* Descartes, René
causation, 164, 176, 205, 207, *216–18*, 222–24, 241; and action, 81–83, 118, 122, *172–73*, 185, 211, 237; knowledge of, 101, 126, 140, 144; and mental events and states, 19, 43, 52, 58, 116; and narrative, 30–31, 111, 180, 201
Cervantes, Miguel de: *Don Quixote*, 204
Chalmers, David J., 96, 104, 120, 157, 161–62, 164–65, 222
Chandler, Raymond, 140
characterization, 36–44, 156, 174–75, 217–18, 238; and action, 123–24, 137; and mind, 19, 58, 73–74, 81–82, 108; and narrative, 180–81, 185, 210, 232–33; and role of reader, 2, 12, 112–13, 176, 207
Chatman, Seymour, 63, 75, 78, 83–85

CPSIA information can be obtained
at www.ICGtesting.com
Printed in the USA
LVOW07s1119261117
557337LV00008B/308/P